To Alan Fordham
from
James Moore

Gurdjieff and Mansfield

Gurdjieff
and Mansfield

James Moore

ROUTLEDGE & KEGAN PAUL
LONDON, BOSTON AND HENLEY

First published in 1980
by Routledge & Kegan Paul Ltd
39 Store Street, London WC1E 7DD,
9 Park Street, Boston, Mass. 02108, USA and
Broadway House, Newtown Road,
Henley-on-Thames, Oxon RG9 1EN
Set in 10 on 12 Bembo by
Rowland Phototypesetting Ltd, Bury St Edmunds, Suffolk
and printed in Great Britain by
St Edmundsbury Press, Bury St Edmunds, Suffolk
© James Moore 1980
No part of this book may be reproduced in
any form without permission from the
publisher, except for the quotation of brief
passages in criticism

British Library Cataloguing in Publication Data

Moore, James
Gurdjieff and Mansfield.
1. Gurdjieff, George
2. Mansfield, Katherine – Friends and associates
3. Philosophers – Russia – Biography
4. Novelists, New Zealand – Biography
I. Title
197'.2   B4249.G84   80-40132

ISBN 0 7100 0488 5

In memory of Bill Dixon

Contents

	Preface	xi
	Acknowledgments	xv
1	Beauty and the Beast	1
2	Katherine Mansfield	7
3	George Ivanovitch Gurdjieff	19
4	Ida Constance Baker	35
5	Piotr Demianovich Ouspensky	48
6	John Middleton Murry	65
7	Alfred Richard Orage	79
8	The Caucasus	94
9	The Alps	112
10	Cosmic Anatomy	125
11	The Initiation of the Priestess	143
12	The Harrowing of John Middleton Murry	161
13	Beelzebub	179
14	Cultural Bon Ton	194
15	Rites of Passage	209
	Abbreviations	225
	References	227
	Select Bibliography	249
	Index	253

Illustrations

Between pages 78 and 79

1 Programme design for Gurdjieff's Institute 1923
  (*by courtesy of The Gurdjieff Society*)

2 George Ivanovitch Gurdjieff
  (*by courtesy of Keystone Press*)

3 Katherine Mansfield
  (*by courtesy of the Alexander Turnbull Library*)

4 John Middleton Murry
  (*by courtesy of Peter Day*)

5 Ida Constance Baker
  (*by courtesy of Peter Day*)

6 Piotr Demianovich Ouspensky★

7 (a) Beatrice Hastings
  (*drawing by Modigliani*)

  (b) Alfred Richard Orage
  (*by courtesy of Mrs C. S. Nott*)

8 (a) Gurdjieff in old age
  (*by courtesy of Photos Andrieux*)

  (b) Middleton Murry in old age
  (*by courtesy of the Radio Times Hulton Picture Library*)

★ Every effort has been made to trace the copyright holder of this illustration. In future editions we shall be pleased to acknowledge appropriately anyone able to authenticate his claim.

Preface

Immersing myself for many years in the lives of Katherine Mansfield and George Ivanovitch Gurdjieff, I received the extraordinary impression of two powerful literary rivers, arising in the 1920s from the same spring, and running parallel for fifty years without confluence. The thing was peculiar even in its symmetry: Gurdjieffian apologists spared merely a line or two for Mansfield, and in Mansfield biography Gurdjieff was dismissed in a grudging footnote. My interest in both individuals fully aroused, I felt at some Khartoum, where the Blue and White Niles of Mansfield and Gurdjieff studies finally met and threatened to sweep me away. Perhaps if I could keep my head above water, there was a book to be written.

The only synthesis publicly available was a kind of 'Beauty and the Beast' cartoon, and this I somehow could not swallow. All my reading of Mansfield spoke to me of her intelligence and strength of character. And when I listened to the music of Gurdjieff, I sensed, rightly or wrongly, a deep compassion. Three long interviews stand out from all the rest. The first, undertaken on behalf of the *Guardian*, brought me together with Peter Brook in the basement of his Kensington flat. We sipped lemon tea while he talked about his coming film on Gurdjieff, *Meetings with Remarkable Men*. The second took me up to Hampstead, where Frank Lea, friend and biographer of John Middleton Murry, lay in a tiny room. Alone and in more or less constant pain, cut off from everything he valued, Lea received me with gallant hospitality and good humour. For my part I gave him all the attention and consideration I could summon. As the sun went down, we drank together what must have been his last bottle of Pernod. Within literally a few days, he had ceased to exist. But no meeting was more crucial than that with Mrs C. S. Nott. As Rose Mary Lillard, she had been present at the Prieuré from the day Katherine Mansfield arrived until the night she died. Mrs Nott's integrity and impartiality were shining and she was able to transmit, from that now distant time, vivid and trustworthy impressions. After a full life, Mrs Nott herself died on 11 October 1979 in her eighty-second year, while this book was being edited. So the bridges to the past fall away behind us.

One thing stood out immediately I began to write: to focus narrowly on Fontainebleau would be to miss an entire dimension. By what lines of convergence had Mansfield, Gurdjieff, Orage, LM, Ouspensky and John Middleton Murry come to stand at their general rendezvous? What excursions, what predispositions, what fate or accident drew them together? From these inescapable questions sprang my six preliminary biographical sketches. And when the lines had crossed over and begun to diverge, how did Murry and Gurdjieff prosecute their lives? For me that held unusual interest.

One cannot go all the way with Livy, who would have made Pompey win the battle of Pharsalia if the turn of the sentence required it, but neither has one much respect for the specialist who (as Marshall McLuhan glacially expresses it) 'never makes small mistakes while moving towards the grand fallacy'. Within the decent bounds of biographical licence, I offer here my truth. I am not such a duffer as to suppose I possess the *real* truth about these extraordinary human beings. We are acquainted with source documents, but much has been lost; some people wrote nothing at all and other people wrote fibs. In any case, source documents are at best 'the scum and the lees of bygone men'. Knowing myself so slenderly, it would be crazy to suggest I know Mansfield and Gurdjieff from a few paper remnants.

Through my researches, I happened to meet and form a friendship with Bill Dixon, to whom this book is dedicated. A member of The Gurdjieff Society, Dr Dixon was practising to take part in the Movements for Peter Brook's film. Unfortunately, just a week before those extraordinary sequences were shot at Pinewood, he died suddenly, aged only forty, leaving a wife and six children. I personally never met anyone who had a more life-giving sense of humour or a more robust independence of mind. May his memory keep me indifferent alike to any praise or blame that this small book attracts.

James Moore
London 1979

> I have a continuing interest in the book's theme and will be pleased to hear from readers competent to augment or qualify my biographical material. Write to James Moore c/o Routledge & Kegan Paul.

Acknowledgments

The two prime centres for studies of Mansfield and Gurdjieff are, respectively, the Alexander Turnbull Library at Wellington, New Zealand and The Gurdjieff Society in London. Both institutions were magnanimously generous to me.

My key indebtedness to Mrs Nott, I have acknowledged in the preface. Her contribution was matched by the unstinting help of Professor Antony Alpers of Queen's University, Kingston, Ontario, the foremost academic authority on Katherine Mansfield. If my general picture of Gurdjieff is less fantastic than some which have appeared, it is due solely to help received from Madame H. H. Lannes and Monsieur Henri Tracol, two of his senior pupils. Lord Pentland and Michel de Salzmann interrupted busy schedules to make inquiries on my behalf.

Arthur Koestler, J. B. Priestley, Professor Wallace Martin, the world authority on A. R. Orage, Professor R. T. Sussex of James Cook University and Rutherford D. Rogers, curator of the P. D. Ouspensky Memorial Collection at Yale University Library, were all responsive to queries. Particularly generous in their help were Janet Horncy of Turnbull and my young friend Catherine Harrison, author of the bibliography 'G. I. Gurdjieff: the man, his work, and its influence', who gave such attention to my book's index.

My access to books was facilitated by the British Museum, the New Zealand High Commission and the Royal Asiatic Society; by John Cowell and Maria Faulkner of Westminster Library and above all by Sir Malby S. Crofton Bt, in his capacity as Leader of the Council of the Royal Borough of Kensington and Chelsea; and by the Borough Librarians who bore my intrusions so patiently. The editor Peter Day, an intimate friend of LM's, most kindly provided photographs, memories and copyright permissions. Mrs Dorothy Maffett, with quixotic generosity, gave me her rare typescript copy of the unpublished memoirs of Ethel Merston, and Miss Rina Hands kindly provided me with fugitive access to the brief unpublished memoir of Dr Mary Bell. Mr J. I. Somers, whose knowledge of Ushe Narzunoff is unrivalled, disclosed some very rare papers. Other material and help was kindly volunteered by Basil Tilley, Adam Nott, Michael Currer-Briggs, Eric Boagey, Dr Jon Thompson, Mrs N. Tingey OBE, John Haggarty the playwright, George Baker, Geoffrey Watkins of Watkins Bookshop and by Mme Christiane Mortelier of Victoria University NZ. Jennifer Koralek and Jeremy Finlay helped with photos. Jennifer Bruce Lockhart was good enough to convey certain delicate messages for me with expletives deleted. The manuscript was immaculately typed by my friend and neighbour Mary Young; a daunting task which she shouldered cheerfully and intelligently.

Finally I should confess that my book would never have been accomplished but for the implacable encouragement of my old friends Frances Toner and Jeffrey Somers, who confronted my dangerous problems with a courage which bordered on recklessness. They share now in my unenviable responsibility.

ACKNOWLEDGMENTS

Copyright

The preponderant majority of quotations in this book are either out of copyright or are, I am best advised, brief enough individually and in aggregate to permit publication without explicit permission, under the normal convention of 'fair dealing'. I none the less wish to express my sincerely felt gratitude to all these authors dead and alive for their material. Here it is perhaps also proper that I acknowledge the interest of Mrs Clarence Nagro in her grandfather's book *In Search of the Miraculous*, which is copyright in the United States by Harcourt Brace Jovanovich. Also that I pay my dutiful respects to the late Madame Olga de Hartmann for a modest use of material from her copyright *Our Life with Mr Gurdjieff* by Thomas de Hartmann. Madame de Hartmann's death in September 1979 severs forever our link with Gurdjieff of the Moscow days.

For explicit permission to quote extensively from copyright material my thanks are due: to Triangle Editions (New York) and to my own publisher Routledge & Kegan Paul for all the works of G. I. Gurdjieff; to the Society of Authors (as literary representatives of the respective estates of Katherine Mansfield and John Middleton Murry) for *Katherine Mansfield's Letters to John Middleton Murry 1913–1922* and *Between Two Worlds* by John Middleton Murry; to Peter Day (as literary representative of the estate of Ida Constance Baker) for *Katherine Mansfield: The Memories of LM*.

Chapter 1

Beauty and the Beast

Everyone who was anyone was in Paris that wonderful spring of 1923.

Ezra Pound contrived an opera from Villon's poetry and gave it in the old Salle Pleyel. Gertrude Stein was snapping up André Massons. James Joyce moved diligently from one musical event to the next. In Diaghilev's loge at the Ballets Russes, Picasso sat like a king, admiring his new theatre curtain – two running women of Thurberesque enormity. Stravinsky presented his *Noces,* with Poulenc, Auric, Meyer and Milhaud playing the four pianos. Cocteau arrived at the première of his *Les Mariés de la Tour Eiffel* wearing high hair and woollen mittens. Man Ray was pushing back the frontiers of photography with his studies of combs and pins. Ernest Hemingway began the education of his first baby by training it to catch flies, breeding on the Left Bank. Breton broke Tzara's arm at the Théâtre Michel and Fernand Léger launched his cubist cinema, *Ballet Mécanique.* And the sun shone and shone.[1]

What a pity that the writer Katherine Mansfield could not enjoy this perfect spring. She was young, she was beautiful, she was gifted, and now suddenly she was dead.

It was the greater pity because Katherine Mansfield herself was perfect. 'KM was perfect,' wrote her husband John Middleton Murry. She was 'A princess manifest, a child withouten stain.' His view, based on the privileged insights of marriage, was widely and repeatedly echoed. The *Bookman,* with less data at its disposal, felt nevertheless able to assert that Katherine was 'among the saintliest of women'. *La Vie Spirituelle* compared her with St Thérèse of Lisieux, the Little Flower of Jesus.

The eight volumes of Katherine's writings issued posthumously between 1923 and 1930 had a reception which can be described as warm. 'It seemed to me the most exquisite prose I had ever read – extraordinarily alive, extraordinarily poetic and exquisitely feminine. It was the prose of a woman who was, as it were, all sensibility – of a soul that was all tremulous awareness.' In particular Katherine's *Journal* and *Letters* stirred readers to hyperbolic enthusiasm. 'Eggwegs', 'bregglechik', 'bigglechiks', 'basticks', 'cream*b*', she wrote, and to the critics it seemed they heard again 'the *Mimes* of Herondas or the letters of Alciphron'.

A whole nursery of young men imagined in Katherine a safe and unresisting playmate: 'the doll-like seriousness of face and doll-like eyes, combined to make a picture which was not merely enchanting. It was for me terribly disturbing. I was going to fall in love with her – and I was going to fall hard and deep.'

Consummation was of course out of the question. 'Could one have . . . so ethereally delicate a consciousness, a consciousness so easily wounded and *live*?' That was the difficulty. One could not. Katherine lay buried in the cemetery of Avon, and even there she was not safe from a disquieting imagination. When she was re-interred in 1929,[2] Monsieur Boutemps, the sexton, reported that she was as fresh as a daisy. 'Death had preserved her in the state that it had carried her off six years earlier.' So vital was her appearance that the good Madame Boutemps exclaimed, 'raise the lid so that Katherine may breathe.'

For years trophy-hunters quested for *appartement* 52 on the sixth floor of the Select Hôtel and hungrily clawed the wallpaper from its walls.[3] Alone in this room in October 1922, high above the city, Katherine had made 'the soul's desperate choice': she would enter Gurdjieff's Institute for the Harmonious Development of Man in the Château du Prieuré des Basses-Loges at Fontainebleau-Avon.

Paris had been 'improved' beyond recognition, but at Fontainebleau you can still walk thoughtfully through the forest, along the Katherine Mansfield path, over the Katherine Mansfield crossroads, past the Katherine Mansfield rock and down at last to the Prieuré, where a plaque, almost gratuitously, celebrates her name. Here on the night of 9 January 1923 she passed from this world.

Who was Gurdjieff and what, essentially, was the Mansfield–Gurdjieff relationship? A hundred journals, from *Elle* to the *New Zealand Railways Magazine,* paint basically the same chiaroscuro picture: Katherine Mansfield, precious, enchanting, holy, fragile; half genius, half saint, half leprechaun; and in blackest contrast George Ivanovitch Gurdjieff, the man who did her wrong. Sanctimonious biographers deplore 'his violent temper, greed for money, personal lust, Byzantine extravagance and spectacular megalomania, which scarcely reflected the Wisdom of the East.' Supercilious journalists write him off as '50 per cent charlatan, 47 per cent con-man, and 3 per cent choreographer.' In numerous accounts Gurdjieff is defined with stark simplicity as 'the man who killed Katherine Mansfield'. The schoolboy crudity of the draughtsmanship should not lead us to reject out of hand the underlying characterisation. A vision which has generally satisfied the European intelligentsia for half a century warrants a cooler appraisal.

But first a recapitulation. If, during Katherine's brief stay, the world had seen the Gurdjieff Institute as a slightly dubious refuge, 'one particularly weird among the asylum-clinics or nursing homes for pathological cases which were being opened all over Europe', then after her death it was condemned as a sinister *maison de fous.* D. H. Lawrence himself trumpeted out the judgment of the literary establishment: 'I have heard enough about that place at Fontainebleau where Katherine Mansfield died, to know it is a rotten, false, self-conscious place of people playing a sickly stunt.'

A strange milieu certainly for a sick woman. Here at the Gurdjieff Institute she 'submitted herself to the most farcical therapeutics imaginable, such as dancing round the pig-sties. Katherine Mansfield, a writer of near genius, allowed herself to take part in this grotesque charade. She was glad to wash her emaciated but still beautiful face in these charlatanesque waters.' It was wrong, it was regrettable, it was downright incomprehensible.

But if the picture pains us, how much more painful was Katherine's own experience. Gurdjieff's regime was based on 'the rigors of suffering, hardship, torture, even with whips . . . long hours of meditation'. And what a fearsome figure. 'His shaved Tartar's skull, sprung from one of Gogol's novels, contains . . . a chaos of forces which cannot even be guessed.' From such a teacher you can scarcely expect an education or a therapy in line with modern progressive ideas. 'It was as if he were a slave-master or wild-animal trainer, with an invisible bull-whip swishing inaudibly through the air.' Katherine's fragility, her exquisite femininity, her world-stature as a writer, offered scant protection here. 'No one could escape Gurdjieff's lash. "You all dirt" he would shout at them.'

But the indictment is not finished. The question is not merely whether Gurdjieff was an authoritarian, who confined Katherine in a 'small, chill, fireless room', but whether he wronged her in more exotic ways. 'Gurdjieff kept in his penitentiary colony one room, furnished with rich Eastern rugs and divans, in which . . . they celebrated rites more voluptuous.' This general if veiled allusion to the *droit de seigneur* was focused in the observation of a New York society lady. 'I understand that Mr Gurdjieff lives at Fontainebleau with Katherine Mansfield and that they call themselves "The Forest Lovers".' How on earth did it happen? How could this pure girl, 'among the saintliest of women', lend herself to such practices? We are indebted to a French journal for the required explanation.

> Then Gurdjieff seemed to concentrate upon his powers of spell-binding. His eyes, from which emanated an insidious intoxication, passed slowly over the foreheads of his pupils . . . everyone fell into a cataleptic state. The sleepers, among whom figured Katherine Mansfield, seemed to savour the voluptuousness of their state of prostration.

But the shame afterwards. The unfortunate feeling of having let oneself down. 'What depths of mental anguish, rivalling in a sense, analogically at least, the tortures of the Saints of God in the dark night of the spirit are revealed in her *Letters* at this time.'

The adverse judgment upon Gurdjieff is sustained, broadcast and, above all, it is absolutist. If Katherine is a Christlike figure who 'assumed the hair shirt in a clinic which was also her Garden of Gethsemane', then Gurdjieff is the Antichrist himself. 'In order to situate Gurdjieff and his movement, the one and only question the seeker has to resolve is whether or not God is omnipotent. If the answer is in the affirmative, then Gurdjieff and his hosts are doomed.' Indeed an article in the *New Adelphi,* edited by Murry, vaguely parallels Gurdjieff with the mythical king of the world who, through a smoking gate in remote Mongolia, issues from his subterranean kingdom of Agharti. Nor need we travel so far afield. In European literature the theme of the wronged woman and the predatory Satanic male has been worked out in wide variation and metamorphosis: Catherine Earnshaw and Heathcliff; Trilby O'Ferrall and Svengali; Clarissa Harlowe and Lovelace. The stereotype Gurdjieff has all Heathcliff's elemental force and Svengali's power of influence, while the identikit Katherine has Trilby's innocence with Clarissa's high intelligence and moral elevation. No one can deny the potency of the myth, and no one can erase those passages which place Gurdjieff and Katherine squarely within it. But perhaps the time has come to ask if they are rightly situated there. It would be important to know because their statures are reciprocally in question. If Gurdjieff savaged an innocent woman, he was blameworthy: if Katherine confided her final months to a charlatan, she was at best 'the *simpleton,* who like Parsifal climbed all the rocky steps of the road of salvation and was caught by Gurdjieff'. But simpletons are not perfect.

Katherine's apologists have been quick to recognise this problem, and have worked without sparing themselves to explain it away. To begin with, they emphasise that there was a term on Katherine's infatuation. We are given an account of her final hour, in which she concedes that her husband, the hard-headed Murry, has been right all along. 'I think you were justified when you called Gurdjieff a mountebank,' she sighs. The disenchantment may have come a little late but the great thing is that it has come at all. There it stands, specially written into the record in a fictional biography. Even more audacious is the defence of Professor Gordon, merely that, before auditing Katherine's account, the entire Gurdjieff entry should be struck from the balance sheet. 'The final scenes of faith-healing under the guidance of a crazy Russian . . . can hardly be the basis of a fair judgement either of her real quality or of her view of life.'

You may think such triple-entry book-keeping ethical, or you may not. The real question is, is it actually necessary? We have, theoretically at least, another hypothesis available. If Gurdjieff were not so crazy. If Katherine showed a rare and precocious discernment in recognising his quality and placing herself under his influence. If . . .

But reputations are not to be salvaged in this speculative way. Only the facts themselves may shed some light, when – drawing in the supporting actors, Murry, Orage, Ouspensky and LM – we retrace the extraordinary lives of Gurdjieff and Katherine to their convergence.

Notes

1. My scenario relies substantially on Margaret Anderson's account in *My Thirty Years' War: An Autobiography* (Alfred A. Knopf, London 1930).
2. Katherine Mansfield was first buried in Avon cemetery on 12 January 1923 and Murry caused her grave to be covered shortly afterwards with a stone slab inscribed:

    Katherine Mansfield
    wife of
    John Middleton Murry

    It is an unexpected denotation of the author of 'Prelude' and somehow conjures up Katherine's spirited protestation to Edwin Muir: 'I'm *not* Mrs Murry, I'm Katherine Mansfield.' Unfortunately Murry did not pay the necessary burial fees. Certainly he had passed through traumatic circumstances and thus, it is said, he forgot. Nevertheless it was a glaring omission and one he could simply have rectified when he returned to the Prieuré in the second week of April 1923. He did not. Accordingly the cemetery authorities deemed Mrs Murry to have had a 7th class funeral and in due course reinterred her in a *fosse commune*. (8th class funerals were reserved for paupers.) Katherine's father Sir Harold Beauchamp was first alerted to this state of affairs in 1929. He did not judge it worthwhile even troubling Murry with the matter. Instead he arranged for his son-in-law Captain Charles M. Renshaw to go to Avon. Duly commissioned, M. Boutemps the sexton did his work and for a third and final time Katherine Mansfield was committed to the ground. She now lay near Mme Ostrowska, Gurdjieff's wife and the chief dancer in The Initiation of the Priestess. In 1949 Gurdjieff himself was buried there.
3. For a riveting account of Gallic enthusiasms, read Christiane Mortelier's 'The Genesis and Development of the Katherine Mansfield Legend in France', an article based on a paper delivered at the 12th AULLA Congress in Perth, Australia, February 1969.

Chapter 2

Katherine Mansfield

To write about Katherine Mansfield is rather like walking into a minefield. Nowhere is the *furor academicus* more baleful; nowhere are loyalties more fierce, sensibilities more frayed. One well-intentioned account drew a particularly glacial comment from an intimate of hers. He said, 'The only true statement in it was that she was born in New Zealand.' It would be naive to suppose this man was much concerned by cracks in surface arrangements – genealogy, postal-address codes and railway timetables. Katherine Mansfield poses her biographers a far more challenging problem – the matter of interpretation. In the final analysis, who was Katherine and what was the meaning of her brief life?

Kathleen Mansfield Beauchamp[1] was born on a geological fault line in the small, wooden, 'earthquake-proof' house at no. 11 Tinakori Road, Wellington, New Zealand, at eight o'clock on the morning of Sunday 14 October 1888. At this early point in her chronicle certitude is left behind. There exists a cracked and faded photograph of Kathleen at about the age of seven. Significantly enough she is already in fancy dress, as the wife of General Tom Thumb. The picture is altogether charming but strangely enigmatic. What was the inner climate of the little actress? Experts rush forward with bland reassurance. 'It was an altogether happy childhood.' Are they really so sure? Less debatable is the domestic context. Kathleen grew up by the seaside in an extended, close-knit, patriarchal, affluent, respectable, colonial family, where servants polished the silver and the Chinese greengrocer called deferentially at the kitchen door. From this unlikely and prosaic background was to spring a rather unusual woman.

Avant-garde is not a description one can truthfully apply to the magazine of Wellington Girls' High School, but in 1898, with the publication of 'Enna Blake', it scored a genuine first. 'This story,' pondered the editor, 'written by one of the girls who have lately entered the school, shows promise of great merit.' No one remembers the name of the perceptive editor today, but the contributor 'Kathleen Beauchamp, aged nine years,' they cannot seem to forget.

By the time the little authoress was ten, two charismatic masculine figures were imprinted in her imagination and affective life. The first was her father Hal Beauchamp, a patriarchal figure with a strong life-aim. Beauchamp's shy domestic reserve offset an awesome business drive, which had already won him a directorship of the Bank of New Zealand and would carry him on to a knighthood. The second figure was an adored only-brother, six years Kathleen's junior. This was Leslie Heron Beauchamp, destined to signify so much to Kathleen in his life and his death.

As birthday followed birthday, Harold Beauchamp began to feel a twinge of concern. No one would question that Wellington had everything to offer – dances, picnics, swimming, garden-parties – but was everything quite enough? He resolved that his talented and blossoming daughter must enjoy the benefits of a liberal education, and in 1903 sent her to London to board at Queen's College in Harley Street. Clearly this was a solid establishment. It had been founded in 1848 with the aid of the Governesses' Benevolent Institution and 'represented the first great effort of Victorian England to meet with due decorum the new demand for the adequate education of women.' The Lady Resident, Miss Camilla Croudace, was a woman of distinction, who wore a little lace cap and had once been pursued by a wolf in the Crimea. Kathleen, on her first day in this arch-auspicious milieu, encountered the girl Ida Baker, and began that very close relationship with her which was to last all her life, and earn her two full pages in Dr Jeannette Foster's egregious work, *Sex Variant Women in Literature: A Historical and Quantitative Survey.*

Biographical references to this period are discreet. 'In spite of her intensive life at Queen's with a variety of literary and erotic awakenings and passionate friendships, chiefly with Ida Baker, Katherine didn't abandon the 'cello.' Nor for that matter did she fail to experiment with many modes of behaviour and to widen her horizons by reading Ibsen, Maupassant, Pater, Verlaine and, her especial discovery, Oscar Wilde. Without going into troublesome details, we may simply say that by the time the seventeen-year-old Kathleen was brought back to New Zealand in 1906, she had enjoyed a liberal education within a much wider curriculum than that envisaged by Harold Beauchamp. In fact the transition from Kathleen to Katherine had been accomplished.

The girl's deep response to music and her formidable persistence with the violoncello are not to be laughed at. They are genuine indexes to her character. Another undeniable index is the powerful and omnivorous sexuality so conspicuous in her life and absent from her writings. She carried home not only special memories of Ida Baker but of 'Caesar', alias Arnold Trowell, a pale-faced, red-headed New Zealand musical prodigy. Entering her journal on the SS *Corinthic,* Katherine recorded, 'It is not one man or woman that is music and violins – it is the whole octave of sex.' This adoption of the word octave has, incidentally, a Gurdjieffian ring, which is anachronistic but far from unique in Katherine's journal from that time. In 1908, the girl who was to end her life in Gurdjieff's Institute for the Harmonious Development of Man wrote this passage: 'To weave the intricate tapestry of one's own life, it is well to take a thread from many harmonious skeins – and to realise that there must be harmony.'

Meanwhile, back in New Zealand, all was discord. Her family failed to understand her. Even Leslie was exasperatingly away at boarding school. Wellington was 'Philistia' itself, no place for a woman of letters. She snatched a wild affair with sweet Edie Bendall ('Last night I spent in her arms. . . . I cannot lie in my bed and not feel the magic of her body'). But happiness eluded her. Filling her notebooks from cover to cover with sketches, poems and vignettes, Katherine 'was completely self-centred, she was ruthless.' Her life aim had crystallised: at all costs she would be a writer. It was now that Hal Beauchamp withdrew her from the social round of Wellington and packed her off on a long wagon trip into the remote volcanic regions of Rotorua and Urewera country. It is usually said that this was a simple diversionary tactic. But perhaps we should credit the father with more wit: a sense of his daughter's need for something real in place of precocious sophistication; for honest fatigue and vital impressions of the natural world. Certainly memories of her land became for her a rich and unforgettable legacy. Yet the big question remained: where finally was she to establish herself? In Katherine's mind there was only one answer. London was *'la seule chose'*. Seeing this fixed determination, Harold Beauchamp and his wife let go lightly, and their daughter left New Zealand, never to return. Lady Ward, the prime minister's wife, threw a farewell party but Wellington newspapers, with their unerring sense of priorities, splashed the visit of an Anglo-Welsh rugby team and gave Katherine Mansfield exactly thirteen words. 'Miss K. Beauchamp sailed on the *Papanui* to continue her literary studies abroad.' The exile and her cello were passed through British customs on 24 August 1908 and Ida Baker met the boat-train. Katherine was nineteen, 'a girl come back to make her living in London without health or money or influential friends, with no assets but talent and pride.'

Truth told, Katherine had other assets, not counting the £100 per annum allowance from her father. Consider the red, red lips. The nut-brown hair with the schoolboy fringe. The 'round oval face like ivory.' And then her master-feature, 'the beautiful eyes, dark, sombre and questioning.' With great verve and less judgment the enchanting teenager thrust herself into London life. What was it Oscar Wilde had said – 'Push everything as far as it will go'? In the space of one year she had got herself pregnant by Garnet, 'Caesar's' twin brother; falsified her age at Paddington registry office and gone through her 'inconsequential, almost surrealistic first marriage' to George Bowden; run away to Glasgow to join the chorus of the Moody Manners Opera Company; taken to the regular use of veronal; and suffered a regrettable miscarriage in the anonymity of Wörishofen, a Bavarian resort famous for the hydropathic cure of the godly Pastor Kneipp. The one thing she had not done was publish any stories.

Back in London the runaway wife showed her manuscripts to the rueful George Bowden. Yes, he suggested, there was someone it might be worth sending them to – Orage, editor of the *New Age*. Characteristically Katherine did not send her material: she took it to Orage the very same day. Even to track down the editor's office was not so simple. The address, 38 Cursitor Street, was downright unhelpful and any less-determined author of Bavarian sketches might well have been balked. Not in this case. As if she had done it all before, Katherine threaded her way along Took's Court and in through the obscure back door set in a whitewashed wall. To the rhythmic beat of the presses, she climbed two flights of narrow stone stairs, coolly outfaced the formidable secretary, Miss Alice Marks, and, papers in hand, was shown into the editorial presence. The encounter had a significance which stretched forward into time. Before her stood Alfred Richard Orage, the man who, for better or worse, would one day introduce her to Gurdjieff.

Whatever else may be said of Orage, he knew literary talent when he saw it. The very next issue of the *New Age* featured Katherine's 'The Child-Who-Was-Tired', a sensitive re-creation of a Tchekov piece. Miss Mansfield had staked everything in leaving New Zealand 'to be a writer'. She had broken every rule in the book in rushing to see Orage. Suddenly, miraculously, she was vindicated. It was a very sweet moment. And Orage wanted more. In succeeding months he published those acidic Bavarian stories, which a year later, in 1911, made up her first book, *In a German Pension*. Characteristically Orage went further than publishing Katherine; he nicknamed her 'the Marmozet' and befriended her without reservation. She had pitifully few visitors when, shortly afterwards, she was convalescing from peritonitis, but one of them was Orage. At weekends he invited her down to his cottage at Seaford, with his editorial assistant and mistress Beatrice Hastings. Katherine, actually moved into Orage and Beatrice's flat at 39 Abingdon Mansions. He interested her in the mime form of Theocritus, which became for her a potent influence. It was through Orage's introduction that Katherine soon found an attractive Thames-side flat at Cheyne Walk.

Established here, Katherine composed for her several admirers a *fin de siècle* stage set. 'She had made the place look quite beautiful – a couple of candles stuck in a skull . . . a lamp on the floor shining through yellow chrysanthemums, and herself accurately in the centre, in a patterned pink kimono.' It is alleged of Katherine during this foggy autumn of Roger Fry's Post-Impressionist Exhibition that 'she took risks with her health which her Grandmother would have gently but firmly forbidden.' Katherine's own journal, referring to Walter Rippman, who formerly taught her German irregular verbs at Queen's College, is rather more explicit.

When the bells were striking five the Man came to see me. He gathered me up in his arms and carried me to the Black Bed. Very brown and strong was he. . . . It grew dark, I crouched against him like a wild cat. Quite impersonally I admired my silver stockings bound beneath the knee with spiked ribbons, my yellow suède shoes fringed with white fur. How vicious I looked! We made love to each other like two wild beasts.

This was all very well, but before long Katherine was saying she was pregnant again. Against her medical background the possibility seems remote, but the faithful Ida Baker, who was now obliged to visit Rhodesia, left £60 to cover expenses. 'I was gone for about five months and when I returned in the autumn I found no baby and a closed bank account.' Literature, it seems, was to have first claim on Katherine's attention. No doubt in due course it would bring its own rich rewards, but the immediate perspective seemed bleak indeed.

It was here that fate played a strange trick. Among the phalanx of struggling beginners whom Orage had ushered into print was a young undergraduate of 'Himalayan earnestness' – a Mr John Middleton Murry. His first published work, a critical essay on Bergson and Plato, is perhaps too little known. Very soon Murry had broken away from Orage to edit his own *avant-garde* magazine *Rhythm* ('suburban slosh' the *New Age* called it, unkindly), under the daunting slogan 'Before art can be human again it must learn to be brutal.' Katherine, never missing a trick, immediately sent him 'The Woman at the Store', a study of murder in the New Zealand backblocks, which he had the sense to publish. And when Murry chanced on a review copy of Katherine's *In a German Pension* in its bright orange dustcover, his interest was compounded, for the stories 'seemed to express with a power I envied, my own revulsion from life'. Within weeks an introduction was facilitated, and it took place at 84 Hamilton Terrace, the self-same street in which Katherine had met her first husband.

Katherine managed this initial meeting with superb effrontery. Wearing a simple dove-grey evening frock with a single flower, she arrived in a taxi, late, and offered, instead of an explanation, her considered opinion that the German translation of Artzibashev's *Sanine* was in every sense more conscientious than the French. Murry, already struggling with his red plum soup was dumbfounded. At subsequent meetings Katherine was more forthcoming. 'Why not take a room in my flat? . . . We could move the piano. . . . Would seven-and-six be too much?' It was not too much. Ida Baker shifted the piano and the gentleman moved in to 69 Clovelly Mansions on 11 April 1912.

At this period John Middleton Murry was very much the Oxford man, and for a little while he succeeded in maintaining certain minimum standards: the formal handshake at bedtime, and so on.

'Goodnight Murry.'

'Goodnight Mansfield.'

This shilly-shallying exasperated and puzzled Katherine. 'Why don't you make me your mistress?' she asked.

Seated on the floor, Murry slowly raised both legs in the air and waved them about. Before art could become human again it must learn to be brutal. 'I feel it would spoil – everything,' he explained mildly.

'So do I,' she replied.

But Katherine's annoyance was short-lived. Murry's scruples were strong, no doubt, but not so strong as nature and proximity. Before too long the editor of *Rhythm* slept in the arms of his contributor.

What was the basis of this unlikely conjunction? Some have seen in it a kind of Benthamite utilitarianism. 'Murry was the editor of a promising review; Katherine had written a book that was being talked about. Murry had no home, except his parents' house; Katherine had a flat. Murry had no money to count on; Katherine had two pounds a week.' This is admirable as far as it goes, but there was also something darker: an obscure psychological complicity between consenting adults. 'I got the impression of an angry tigress keeping watch and ward over a stray cat which had wandered into the jungle and wanted, half-heartedly, to get back to the world of pavements and free milk.'

To follow Katherine and Murry through all the vicissitudes of their early relationship is impossible here. They were a man and a woman; at times they were happy, at times they were sad. Already in 1911 Katherine was tubercular, a fact completely unknown to either of them; she was no longer capable of conceiving children; she was married already and for years could not get her divorce. Ida Baker was never far away, an indispensable character in 'the story of a triangular love affair'. Between Katherine and Murry an absolute trust was never achieved. They used different banks, and lent and repaid monies to each other on a formal basis. By fits and starts they rose to the heights of their professions, she as an author, he as a literary critic. Slowly her health declined. They were forever changing address – thirteen times in the space of two years. Often they lived quite separately and sometimes the Channel lay between them. It seems difficult to contest the verdict that – psychologically, sexually, professionally and spiritually – they were not on the same scale. Relatively speaking Katherine had indeed chosen Tom Thumb.

1915 is a vintage Mansfield year, but a bitter one. On the strength of a few *billets* from the Parisian *chansonnier* and novelist Francis Carco, *'Je vous aime chaque jour davantage'* etc., Katherine was toying with the notion of changing her man. She was twenty-six, disappointed in her work and wholly disillusioned with Murry. In Europe the periodic process of reciprocal destruction was in full spate.

In February, Katherine's brother Leslie arrived in London from New Zealand to join the South Lancs in the authentic contemporary spirit: 'Well dears most people think that by the time my training etc. is over there will be no more men off to the front. If there are it will be summer time and more of a picnic than anything else, so DON'T WORRY!' Katherine was exultant at seeing him; bought and wore the badge of his regiment; rushed to show him to Orage; drew from him also perhaps – the question is contentious – the money to visit Corporal Carco, now on the western front. Thus there was added to the Mansfield canon, the episode of 'the exalted girl who, in the thick of the First World War, defied all reasonable considerations and trekked her totally insane way from London into the battlefield of Gray.' At the station Corporal Francis, terribly pale, saluted and sang, 'Follow me, but not as though you were doing so.' Katherine was using Genêt Fleuri, a bitter-sweet floral perfume with muguet and heliotrope. It was perhaps the archetypal brief encounter. What with everything else going on, 'The act of love seemed somehow quite incidental' and the musical corporal was left with gratifying if hazy memories of *'la jeune australienne'*, which stood him in good stead for the rest of his life. After three days at Gray a disenchanted Katherine set out again for London and her 'weary truce' with Murry, while Carco returned to less exhausting duties as postman to a bakery unit.

Worse, much worse, was to follow. Leslie qualified as a bombing officer, received his commission and went to France. On 7 October 1915 at Ploegsteert Wood he was demonstrating the proper way to throw grenades with a catapult, when one exploded in his hand. He is buried a little north of Armentières. 'Lift my head, Katie, I can't breathe,' he said, just before he died.

Leslie was twenty years old. He was her only brother. Those who have suddenly, wastefully, brutally, lost their nearest and dearest, can enter Katherine's feelings. Others cannot.

I believe in immortality because he is not here, and I long to join him. First my darling, I've got things to do for both of us, and then I will come as quickly as I can. Dearest heart I know you are there, and I live with you, and I will write for you.

With her feelings she knew he was there. It was certainly not the moment to query if her feelings were trustworthy. She could not retire in good order into the prepared positions of a religious credo. She had none. Thoughts about God – these indeed she had had. Long ago there was the childlike vision.

O God, I want to sit on your knees
On the all-too-big throne of Heaven,
And fall asleep with my hands tangled in your grey beard.

Later there was even the hint of some intriguing metaphysical speculation: 'do you think there was more than one creator who designed the universe?' Yet now it was all as light as thistledown; it had not the weight of her feelings.

Katherine Mansfield had more than a creed, more than ready-made answers: she had an authentic question. It began at the nearest point – with herself. She really wished to understand her complex nature and her place in the grand scheme. She hungered for a quality of truth not obtainable at Woolworth's. The devil on her left shoulder was certainly as convincing as the angel on her right. She felt and suffered from the denying force present in herself, in her writing and in every phenomenon, the 'snail under the leaf', and she reached upward for some kind of reconciliation.

There was no one to share her search, and no one of spiritual authority to guide it. Her friend D. H. Lawrence offered her the fanciful utopia of 'Rananim'; Aleister Crowley offered her drugs.[2] To Murry least of all could she turn.

Katherine: I always wanted 'to get down to myself' when I was seventeen. From twenty to twenty-four, certain moments of music, a tree waving outside, seemed to take me to myself. I realised by their contrast with me at other moments that there was a self to get to.

J. M. M. Isn't that a lie?

She was alone.
And being alone, she struggled forward searching in her own way. She longed to contact her original mind:

> 'Sorry. There's no reply,' tinkles out a little voice.
> 'Will you ring them again – Exchange? A good long ring. There must be somebody there.'
> 'I can't get any answer.'

No doubt she exaggerates her capacity for self-observation but it is unquestionable that she worked away at it, as a route to self-knowledge. 'She once said that even in moments of the most intense living there was always part of herself which stood aside, looking on, noting all.' Even at fourteen she knew with unshakeable conviction that the insights of real importance lay within her. 'To find Truth, Katherine said, she would go down into herself, deep down, like sinking to the bottom of a dark well. Waiting at the bottom Truth would come to her.' There, in the deepest layer of herself to which she could dive, was something inviolable; free from perturbation by death – even her brother's, even her own.

> In the profoundest Ocean
> There is a rainbow shell,
> It is always there, shining most stilly
> Under the greatest storm waves.

Late in 1917 Murry became indisposed and went to rest at Garsington, country house of the literary hostess Lady Ottoline Morrell. With marvellous irony Katherine feared he might have consumption: 'One of his lungs is slightly affected', she wrote worriedly. On a freezing November night she went down to see him. Travelling from Wheatley Station in an open dogcart, she contracted pleurisy, and by December the tuberculosis she had incubated so many years could no longer be disguised. In January 1918, alone and with a 'flat-iron burning in her chest', she made a nightmare journey past Fontainebleau to Bandol on the Côte. By

February she was writing to Murry to report the first bright arterial haemorrhage: 'this is *not* serious, does *not* keep me in bed, is absolutely easily curable, but I have been spitting a bit of blood.' Katherine's decree in the case *Bowden* v. *Bowden* would soon become absolute, and she was sustained by the thought of marrying Murry. It was perhaps a case of hope too long deferred. When Katherine finally fought her way back to Kensington after a racking three-week delay in Paris at the height of the Big Bertha artillery bombardment and Zeppelin night attacks, when she went through the colourless registry office formalities, it all somehow seemed hardly worth the trouble. Murry put his handkerchief quickly to his lips and turned away when she coughed. Three weeks later they were apart again and reproaching each other by post. 'You never once held me in your arms and called me your wife.'

There is a very haunting description of Katherine at about this time. 'Her rings slid up and down her fingers as she made tea. Against the purple wall she was like a china figure, a deliberate decoration, with her neat black head, white hands and white face.'

In 1918 tuberculosis was not so much a diagnosis as a prognosis: it was a death sentence. We can plot its incidental meaning for Katherine: the severance of ordinary human contact, 'I must not borrow a handkerchief . . . or drink out of loving cups, or eat the little bear's porridge with his spoon'; the doomed and hectic flight from one resort to another, Bandol, San Remo, Ospedaletti, Menton, Baugy, Montana, Randogne, Sierre; the humiliating invalidism, '*This* is reality – bed, medicine bottle, medicine glass marked with tea and tablespoons, guaicol tablets, balimanate of zinc'; the heightened intensity lent to the writer's struggle and the woman's search. All this we can plot. What a healthy man cannot enter into, what he cannot peripherally touch, is the realisation of an individual who must 'constantly sense and be cognisant of the inevitability of his own death.'

Notes

1   In the autumn of 1903 Kathleen Mansfield Beauchamp, aged fifteen, took as her nom de plume her grandmother's name, Katherine Mansfield. About 29 July 1910, aged twenty-one, while staying with Orage and Beatrice Hastings at 39 Abingdon Mansions, Kensington, she actually began going under this style. In the present biography she is

re-baptised around the age of seventeen; academic purists may carp but I hope general readers will benefit. As for my honoured heroine, who in fact drew from a Joycean quiver of pseudonymous Christian names (Katherine, Kath, Kass, Kassie, Katie, K.T., Katya, Katerina, Yékaterina, etc.), she – I am sure – will excuse a little nomenclatural licence.

2 Katherine's attendance at one of Crowley's hashish parties is mentioned both by LM and Anne Estelle Rice. The brief contact probably took place in the house of Gwendoline Otter before she met Orage. While Katherine's spirit rose up 'pink and paradisiacal' her hands arranged matches in patterns on the floor; as the effect of the drug diminished, she thought she saw 'hundreds of parcels on shelves identically marked "Jesus Wept" '. This isolated escapade must be treated with proper reservation: Katherine never fell under Crowley's baleful personal influence, indeed she summed him up as 'a pretentious and very dirty fellow'; nor is there the slightest connection between Crowley and Gurdjieff. Beatrice Hastings, in her vituperative book *The Old 'New Age': Orage – and Others,* amazingly asserts that Crowley was Orage's best friend. However, in *The Great Beast,* John Symonds's definitive biography of Crowley, Orage is not even cited.

Chapter 3

George Ivanovitch Gurdjieff

Gurdjieff was born in four different countries on three different dates and his name was not Gurdjieff.

Alexandropol on the Shiraki Steppe has the distinction of being the subject's birthplace. Whether this town was proper to Armenia or Georgia, the Ottoman sultanate or Tsarist Russia, was a vexed question, provoking people to infuriated offensive abuse. Once the place was named Gumru, then Alexandropol; and today, with superb irony, it is called Leninakan. Earthquakes are frequent. Gurdjieff's birthday can be stated with almost clinical precision; the date 28 December 1877 is set down in black and white in his Nansen passport. Unfortunately, to the sorrow of all who prize consistency, inferential dating strongly suggests 1872; and, further to confuse the issue, Gurdjieff himself confessed that the year of years was actually 1866. Once, in New York, immigration officials were consternated to read documentation showing that George Ivanovitch Gurdjieff was born in the remote future. 'No mistake,' said Gurdjieff, 'You go arrange.'

His father Greek, his mother Armenian and his tutors Russian, the boy's patronym Georgiades evolved first into Gurdjian and finally Gurdjieff. It was all a reflection of a madly changing world. On the night of 17 November 1877 Gazi Mukhtar Pasha was defeated by the Armenian general Count Loris Melikov and Tsarist forces entered the city of Kars. 100,000 Turks fled west before the Russians into high Anatolia. Kars and its environs became a vacuum and into it, pell-mell, rushed fiercely independent groups of Armenians, Greeks, Assyrians, Kurds, Tartars, Molokans, Romanies, Yezidis – and the family Gurdjieff. The enormous cattle herds of Gurdjieff's father had been wiped out by plague and now he earned a precarious living as a carpenter. Certainly there was little money to spare; when Gurdjieff and his brother Dmitri were rivals in love, it was not the same girl they were contesting, it was the only pair of shoes. For no one in Kars were conditions easy. The houses were little better than mud huts. The fortress city crouched in the mountains, struck by winter blizzards, pounded by an implacable summer sun. Dust and flies in summer, snow in winter, and in spring a sea of inglorious mud. To the south-east, through the trees, out of the foothills where gold and arsenic were mined, rose the volcanic massif of Ararat.

The young Gurdjieff sang in the choir, fought and adventured with his schoolfellows, went hunting for wild duck on Lake Alagheuz, and acquired the knack of making and mending almost anything mechanical. The wider world which met his gaze was almost inconceivably different from our own. The middle-eastern province of a ramshackle empire, whose supreme autocrat ruled from his Winter Palace in remote St Petersburg. A world where the patriarch, craftsman, nomad, poet and wise man still had a real place. A world of villages, *quartiers* and encampments, where each group had its own language, music, dancing, ritual, laws and hierarchy. A world where religion was a living force, bewilderingly fragmented. A world which begged a question.

And yet the general ambience is not sufficient to explain Gurdjieff's orientation and search. Peter Brook puts it this way: 'Immediately interesting questions arise. What selected the boy out of all his contemporaries and set him off in this direction? What forces were engaged in the struggle of the young man?' Certainly he came under special and extraordinary influences. There was that dying admonition of his grandmother, 'Eldest of my grandsons! Listen and always remember my strict injunction to you. In life never live as others do. . . . Either do nothing – just go to school – or do something nobody else does.' It was advice the little boy took very gravely. If others slid downhill head-first he would slide down backside-first; if they threw their ball in the air, he would bounce his, somersault, and catch it with the thumb and middle finger of his left hand. A year or so later, Father Borsh, dean of Kars Military Cathedral, plucked Gurdjieff from the Russian municipal school and personally assumed responsibility for his formal education. The dean himself taught him mathematics; Sokolov, a physician, taught him anatomy and physiology; graduate candidates for the priesthood taught him their particular specialisations. For the poor carpenter's son in an obscure provincial backwater, this was indeed exceptional treatment.

And yet in itself this is not explanation enough. Surely what was critical was that Gurdjieff was peculiarly exposed to 'supernatural' phenomena. He witnessed a paralytic dancing, after the man's painful pilgrimage to a saint's tomb had won a cure. He stood in torrential rain after an archimandrite had prayed to a holy icon, for an end to a ruinous drought. He experienced the uncanny accuracy of the fortune-teller Eoung-Ashokh Mardiross. He observed a dying consumptive miraculously cured by Mariam Ana, the Tartar Virgin Mary. He saw a young Yezidi boy trapped, as if by walls of glass, in nothing more tangible than a circle drawn round him in the sand. Likely or unlikely, these incidents from Gurdjieff's memoirs are a 'dramatic imperative': the hinge on which his whole life turns.

Sheer astonishment was his first reaction; then he was seized by a craving for a natural explanation, in practical operative terms. Hoping to find it, he plunged headlong into Western science. Soon, he reports, 'there was not a single book on neuropathology and psychology in the library of Kars military hospital that I had not read and read very attentively,' and yet he emerged none the wiser. Still less was he satisfied with the half-baked explanations of the Kars intelligentsia. 'That is simply hysteria,' explained Dr Ivanov, when asked about the Yezidi boy. On which Gurdjieff comments acidly, 'I already well understood that hysteria is hysteria, but I wished to know something more.'

It was Gurdjieff's remarkable father who provided the first clue. Besides being a carpenter, John Georgiades was an *ashokh*[1] or bardic poet. His recitations from the epic of Gilgamesh, king of Uruk, and the Flood before the Flood, implanted in his son the idea of search, of mystery, of allegorical meaning and the prodigious span of history. And one thing more. As Gurdjieff sat curled in the woodshavings of his father's workshop, and listened to his faultless chanting, a strange idea began to dawn in him. If the epic of Gilgamesh could survive so long in oral transmissions, was it not possible – just possible – that some truer explanation of the miraculous was also passing by word of mouth, from teacher to pupil, from the remote past into the remote future. It was a working hypothesis on which he staked his life. It was to draw him into the remotest fastnesses of Asia; expose him three times to near-fatal gunshot wounds; and engage his formidable energies for twenty years.

It has vanished, that world of Gurdjieff's youth, never to return. In his time there was a real thread to unravel: shamanists, yogis, holy men, fakirs, *staretz,* Turkoman Babas; Hesychasm at Mount Athos; remote theocratic societies in Tibet and Abyssinia; 107 orders of dervishes; religious solitaries and brotherhoods. Strangely in contrast was the cocksure European technology, infiltrating east along precarious railway tracks. It was an age too of heroic archeology and heroic exploration. Even Americans were digging in Babylon. In five great expeditions through Asia, the Russian Prjevalsky emulated the wanderings of Marco Polo. Tsarist imperialists and the British Raj competed for a domain of influence in Afghanistan, Chitral, Kashmir and Tibet. The Khyber pass was a strategic lynchpin. Behind snowy ramparts, the forbidden city of Lhasa called insistently to aspirants in esotericism and political chicanery.

Consider. Was not Gurdjieff rather well equipped to make his journey into the interior? He was young, robust and energetic. He spoke Armenian, Greek, fluent Turkish and passable Russian. He had natural contacts with the Greek and Armenian churches and societies. He was audacious and ingenious in disguise. He had an inborn aptitude for 'eliciting from people their most sacred aims and intentions . . . and of discussing and exchanging views with innumerable people who, in comparison with others, are real authorities.' Above all, he had an aim which almost rattled within him, an irrepressible striving to understand the significance of human life.

Gurdjieff gives an account of the long search in his strange book *Meetings with Remarkable Men.* In Egypt near the pyramids he encountered Prince Yuri Lubovedsky, an older man qualified by direct experience to guide him. Together they came to play leading roles in The Seekers of Truth, an informal group of some twenty men and one woman, 'the inimitable and fearless Mme. Vitvitskaia'. Travelling in twos and threes, or converging for major expeditions, The Seekers found their way to remote religious communities and archeological sites. They met many remarkable men, collected traditional music and sacred dances, and discovered fragments of an unknown teaching. 'There were all kinds of specialists among us. Everyone studied on the lines of his particular subject. Afterwards, when we forgathered, we put together everything we had found.'

And where, meanwhile, did the money come from? Vividly the book conveys the impression of a man living on his native wit. Nothing was too small or too large to engage Gurdjieff's attention. He serviced typewriters and sewing machines; he cured drug-addicts and psychosomatic patients by hypnotism; he dealt shrewdly in carpets, antiques and Chinese cloisonné; he sold pickled herrings and oil wells; he started restaurants, built them up and disposed of them; he remodelled corsets; he even clipped and painted sparrows and off-loaded them as 'American canaries'.

Meetings with Remarkable Men is not exactly history. Its very characters, like Vitvitskaia and Lubovedsky, may be composites or symbols. Comb it with rabbinical nicety and yet you can extract no clear-cut itinerary, no geographic co-ordinates, no unequivocal dating. And this is hardly surprising, for Gurdjieff chose that his words should bear a double, even a triple meaning. Certainly they handle the outer world, but they define simultaneously the inner terrain of man's psyche, and Gurdjieff cannot be charged with imprecision here. In his description of Yangihissar, with its unique climatic polarisation; in his evocation of the river Amu Darya; in his quite extraordinary chronicle of The Seekers of Truth crossing the Gobi desert – Gurdjieff encrypts a persuasive geography of the psychological interior and the route he followed to penetrate it.

Academics will not be very happy with this as a record of the period 1891 to 1911. Not that there seems real need to challenge the general picture of five great expeditions: to Egypt, Crete and the Holy Land; to Abyssinia and the Sudan; to Persia and Transoxiana; to Siberia; and finally to Afghanistan, the Pamirs and India. Still less is there any doubt about Gurdjieff's essential pre-occupation – it was the search for hidden knowledge. Very well. But did the young man take no wife? Had he no professional *métier*? Could he really survive twenty years by 'selling American canaries'? And how did he travel so freely in oriental Russia? What were the peculiar conditions of his life which gave him 'the possibility of gaining access to the so-called "holy-of-holies" of nearly all hermetic organisations such as religious, philosophical, occult, political and mystic societies, congregations, parties, unions etc.' Asia is large;

twenty years is a long time. Someone, someday, confronts a Herculean task: the quest for the historical Gurdjieff.

Already the glyph of Gurdjieff's search is not vacuum-sealed from the world of history books. They are linked by some tenuous filaments. Take the Stalin connection.[2] In old age it was one of Gurdjieff's stories that he had been with Stalin at the theological seminary of Tiflis. It seems highly improbable that the empty formalism of that grim institution would have held Gurdjieff's attention very long, but Stalin, under his real name Joseph Vissarionovich Djugashvili, was unquestionably there from October 1894 until his expulsion on 27 May 1899. Stalin left the seminary a committed revolutionary, and Trotsky, no less, reports that he was soon operating under the cover name, *inter alia,* of 'Nizheradze'. Immediately a fascinating link is made. When Gurdjieff wrote *Meetings with Remarkable Men* there was one chapter too sensitive for publication; the story-line concerned some betrayal of trust. The title of this suppressed chapter was – 'Prince Nijeradze'.

Cover names? Yes, the historian will certainly have to grapple with the problem of aliases. Gurdjieff could adopt an identity like someone else choosing a necktie. And with very good reason, if he played the role of a political agent – perhaps a double agent – in Central Asia. Hardly a new hypothesis this; it has long circulated among intelligence circles, Russian *émigré* circles and even among Gurdjieff's pupils. It would explain so much: his freedom of movement, his exemption from conscription, his entrée to clandestine organisations.

But if names are unreliable, then on what may one depend? Only on an intelligent matching process. On one side all scholastically unimpeachable facts, biographical, historical, geographical; on the other Gurdjieff himself as pictured in his writings, music and dances, and even in extra-canonical traditions. Essentially we are looking for a Caucasian born between 1872 and 1877, of a specific height and build and appearance. A man with a piquant sense of humour. An explorer deeply interested in sacred dances, who visited hidden monasteries and convents. Someone connected with remarkable men in Russia and with the highest spiritual authorities in Tibet; an innovator who taught that man's perceptive apparatuses resemble 'clean wax phonograph discs'. More circumstantially, no doubt, we are looking for someone on whom the New Delhi authorities maintained an intelligence dossier; someone who attached importance explicitly to the Younghusband expedition to Lhasa in 1904, and implicitly to the extraordinary Buryat Mongol, Aghwan Dordjieff, tutor to the thirteenth Dalai Lama. We are looking for an author who mentions an 'objectively maleficent official presentation to the Czar'; an astonishing transit of the Gobi desert; pilgrims measuring their length on the earth as they struggle to a shrine. Now suppose we can actually find such a man and that he disappears from history virtually at the moment Gurdjieff materialises in Tashkent. Well . . .

Armed with our Gurdjieff identikit, is it not tempting – dangerously tempting – to try to make an arrest? Suspect number one is surely Narzunoff. Born in 1874, Ushe Narzunoff is an established figure in biographies, geographical papers and intelligence reports. In 1898 he studied sacred dancing in monasteries bordering the Gobi, including the unmapped convent of Youndoun-beisssin-kure. In January 1900, as Dordjieff's emissary, he visited Paris.[3] His purchases here included a phonograph and wax cylinders. In March 1900 he went by sea to India and was detained for questioning by the Darjeeling police. During this time he expressed great anxiety that a powerful and unknown man, Koukanssen, had made off with the scientific instruments he was taking to the Dalai Lama. It later turned out that Koukanssen was Narzunoff's own agent, Thomas Cook & Son, who safely delivered the consignment to Lhasa. Narzunoff was twenty-six years old, 5 ft 10 in. in height, well-built and broad, with a shaven head, down-turned moustache and medium complexion. His passport was issued in Stavropol in the Caucasus. Narzunoff was travelling at Dordjieff's expense but in his pocket was a letter from the Russian Prince Uktomsky, describing him as a *zaissan* or Kalmuk noble, proceeding to Tibet on pilgrimage and in the interests of science. Deported to Odessa, Narzunoff was met by Dordjieff himself. They went together first to Livadia, where Dordjieff was received by Tsar Nicholas II, and on to distant Urga in Mongolia. On 5 January 1901, Dordjieff, Narzunoff and six chosen companions left Urga to make a noteworthy 84-day trek across the Gobi and the mountains to Lhasa. Narzunoff was received by both the Dalai and Panchen Lamas. Photography was forbidden in Tibet, but Narzunoff risked taking a shot of pilgrims measuring their length round the perimeter of Lhasa. Some years later he produced photos of his Tibetan wife and two sons Daidan and Dorje. The last picture of Narzunoff himself was taken in 1908, after which he disappeared entirely.

The Narzunoff–Gurdjieff equation is beguiling – very beguiling. But in the end nothing robust is established. Some of the photographs of Narzunoff could well depict a youthful Gurdjieff; others transparently could not. Almost, one is left with the impression of two different Narzunoffs. Time and scholarship may furnish a witty answer to this riddle. Meanwhile it is safer perhaps to return to Gurdjieff's own story.[4]

Slowly, painfully, he accumulated a formidable battery of ideas, powers and techniques, and then, at about the age of thirty-five, a long-deferred revolution occurred in his life: he exchanged the role of pupil for that of teacher. Gurdjieff's first essay in this direction seems to have been rather ambivalent. In 1910 the Chinese invaded Tibet, the Dalai Lama fled to India and Gurdjieff went to Tashkent in Uzbekistan. Here he accepted, from among the Russian garrison society, dilettante pupils in 'occultism'. In fact he was more preoccupied with observing the 'various manifestations in the waking state . . . of these trained and freely moving "Guinea Pigs", allotted to me by Destiny for my experiments,' and with creating a definite amount of capital by substantial business transactions. In a period of feverish activity he amassed a million roubles and two invaluable collections, one of Chinese cloisonné, the other of oriental carpets. 'Finally . . . I liquidated all my affairs; and . . . near the end of the year 1913, I went to Moscow to begin to actualise in practice what I had taken upon myself as a sacred trust.'

We are now fast approaching the copper-bottomed, attested Gurdjieff chronicle, but one final speculation cries out for inclusion. In the winter of 1913 Paul Dukes, a young music student at the St Petersburg *conservatoire* was taken by a friend to meet a remarkable man. 'Call him Prince Ozay,' he said. 'But his name doesn't matter.' Well, perhaps it does matter – perhaps it was Gurdjieff. Intriguing too that the name Ozay so strikingly resembles Ushe.

Dukes entered a drab back-street tenement near the Nicolas station, down a corridor, through a door knocked in the wall – and into another world. His host, thickset, dark and bearded, sat cross-legged in a patterned silk dressing-gown on a low divan. Sumptuous oriental carpets hung on the walls. Invited to the divan, Dukes removed his shoes and discovered with acute embarrassment a hole in his sock. 'You believe in ventilation!' said Prince Ozay.

'Good thing – nothing like fresh air!' Abruptly he turned the conversation to esoteric Christianity and the Lord's Prayer. This, explained Ozay, was in fact designed as a devotional breathing exercise, to be chanted on a single even breath. 'A low, rich, musical bass note about G_2 below middle C, began to sound in the room, pure and dry amid the muffled hangings.' Ozay's entire torso was vibrating, and it communicated to Dukes something 'like a mild electric current'.

Prince Ozay now developed an extraordinary theme. Prayer had 'something to do with digestion and even with the quality and circulation of the blood.' The attention must be equally divided among three elements: the breath, the sound and the words. Christ himself had taught his disciples to pray like this, secretly and individually. 'It is closely concerned with how a man breathes and no two persons breathe exactly alike.' The aim was not to petition or extol but to attune with the Logos: 'What you might call the World's tonic note.' Miraculously it was possible to echo this note 'because every octave is a replica at a different level of every other octave, as everybody knows.' When Dukes tired he was quickly brought a tray with *zakuski* and drinks. 'Try my own concoction,' said Ozay, 'much better than whisky.'

Everything about this incident shrieks out 'Gurdjieff' but there is one impediment: Prince Ozay spoke in passable English. If it was indeed Gurdjieff, he did not maintain the Ozay fiction very long. Here in Moscow in 1913 he suddenly emerges from the shadows, in his own name and his own right; an enigmatic figure without antecedents. Finally he crosses the frontier between legend and independent corroborative witness; between 'The Tiger' of Turkestan' and 'Monsieur Gurdjieff'. Before this point he is a riddle out of Asia: now he is being swept into the bloody vortex of European history.

There is a rich irony in Gurdjieff's statement that 'the most suitable place would be Russia, which at that time was peaceful, rich and quiet.' He was incapable of making such a naive analysis. The extravagant celebrations of 1913 marking the three-hundredth anniversary of Romanov rule were to prove the last flicker of a dying flame. Trotsky put it this way: 'As a lamp before it goes out flares up with a bright although smoky light, so the nobility before disappearing gives out an oppositional flash which performs a mighty service for its mortal enemy.'

The Russian empire, comprising one sixth of the terrestrial land mass, was the greatest contiguous area ever submitted to a single government in the history of mankind. It stretched from the Arctic to the Himalayas, from the Baltic to Alaska. Its governance would have challenged the strongest and wisest being, and the Tsar was scarcely that. Now in the nineteenth year of his reign, Nicholas II, Autocrat of all the Russias, was a dapper, watery-eyed enigma, with narrow shoulders and a suicidal belief in the divine right of kings. His German-born Tsarina, the neurotic Alexandra Feodorovna, was cordially disliked as a foreign interloper. Her only son, Alexei the Tsarevich, heir to the throne, had haemophilia. 'By that time all vital decisions were taken, not even in the Tsar's study, but in the Empress's "mauve boudoir", under the ominous portrait of Marie Antoinette, and at the instance of Rasputin.' Once beyond the palace walls, conditions were not rosy. There was hunger. When Gurdjieff arrived in 1913 nearly three-quarters of a million workers were out on strike; a year later there were twice that number. The *okhrana* or Tsarist secret police – the detested 'Pharaohs' – kept watch and took names. The Fortress of Peter and Paul, the Russian Bastille, was full to overflowing. Despite this, the tide of assassinations and *jacqueries* rose steadily; revolutionaries were briskly robbing banks and mail trains to finance the cause. In the wings Lenin and Trotsky were waiting.

A certain elasticity of imagination is required to associate Gurdjieff with the imperial court; its 'Inscrutable, exquisitely polite cadet sentries. Long-forgotten, sulky, arrogantly obsequious *ancien-régime* functionaries' faces. Glossy, brilliant officers slithering over the dubious parquet.' And yet it was from this milieu that Gurdjieff chose Countess Ostrowska, seemingly a lady-in-waiting to the Tsarina, and took her for his 'uniquely and sincerely beloved wife.' Questions abound. Was she indeed a countess? Or had she the more adventurous background of the quasi-fictional Vitvitskaia? When and where was the marriage ceremony? Or was there one at all, if Gurdjieff had a wife in Tibet? Perhaps all that can be said, all that need be said, is that this Polish-born lady was a natural aristocrat, talented and beautiful, who remained at Gurdjieff's side for the rest of her short life.

By now Gurdjieff was constellating round him in Moscow two confidential groups of serious and intelligent pupils, who could work together. Their teacher was an imposing figure. His dark, widely spaced eyes had extraordinary penetration; beneath the fierce moustache, his smile was compassionate but ironic. Above the temples, between the occiput and the frontal region, his head was unusually high. The deep relaxation of all his movements induced a feeling of well-being in those near him. The *mise-en-scène* which he contrived, served a definite purpose. 'His small apartment on the Bolshaia Dmitrovka, all the floors of which were covered in the Eastern style with carpets and the ceiling hung with silk shawls, astonished . . . by its special atmosphere.' Revered by his pupils and in full possession of his powers, he might have hoped to achieve a great deal. Fortunately or unfortunately, however, on 28 June 1914 events precipitated in Sarajevo which frustrated Gurdjieff's efforts to establish in Russia both his family life and his Institute.

On 1 August Germany declared war on Russia, and Tsar Nicholas found himself swept upward on an atavistic wave of national fervour. He threw his soldiers, pitifully armed, into the furnace. Four million died in five months. Nicholas himself spared no personal efforts. He renamed St Petersburg, Petrograd. He banned the public speaking of German and the public sale of vodka. He went to military headquarters at Mogilev and played dominoes. He instructed that his next jewelled Easter egg from the house of Fabergé should be mounted on shrapnel.

The epoch's surrealistic undertones are as palpably evident in Gurdjieff's recruiting methods as in the Tsar's crisis measures. In November, at the height of the war, a notice appeared in the newspaper *Golos Moskvi* referring to the scenario of an oriental ballet, *The Struggle of the Magicians,* written by a certain Hindu. This 'Hindu' transpired to be none other than Gurdjieff. Yet in his teaching from this period there was nothing oriental, Hindu or surrealistic. In meeting after meeting, Gurdjieff unfolded an astonishingly clear and cohesive body of data. It is quite outside the scope of this book to delineate Gurdjieff's hierarchy of ideas, to suggest its provenance or to evaluate it. Like every other system it is completely rejected by many people accounted intelligent. But who can question that Gurdjieff's presentation was an incredible *tour de force*? Who can measure the voltage of that intellect and not receive a certain shock? By the summer of 1916 his work was intensifying, and its centre of gravity had shifted from Moscow to Petrograd. By working under Gurdjieff's direction and pooling their insights, his group members were offered a chance of relative freedom. 'You do not realize your own situation. You are in prison. All you can wish for, if you are a sensible man, is to escape. But how escape? It is necessary to tunnel under a wall. One man can do nothing. But let us suppose there are ten or twenty men – if they work in turn and if one covers another they can complete the tunnel and escape.' Already he had recruited first-rank pupils whose specialisation lay in the direction of his ideas: Ouspensky was a writer, Stjoernval a physician, Zaharoff a mathematician. One piece of the jigsaw remained to be found: Gurdjieff needed a musician.

On 16 December 1916 in Petrograd, in an episode of almost unbelievable *grand guignol,* Grigory Efimovitch Rasputin was treacherously murdered by members of the imperial house. Gurdjieff was also occupied in Petrograd at this time, because it was just then he found the musician he could work with.

Thomas Alexandrovitch de Hartmann had already a good deal to show for his life and was searching for something of deeper significance. Worldly success had come early. At twenty-one he had seen his four-act ballet *The Pink Flower* performed at the Imperial Opera, with the Tsar himself in the audience, and Fokine, Karsavina Nijinsky and Pavlova in the cast. Now aged thirty, he was serving as a Guards officer in the comfortable ambience of Tsarskoye Selo, the Russian Windsor, fifteen miles south of Petrograd. Hartmann knew that his friend Andrei Zaharoff had found a teacher of real weight and he desperately wanted an introduction. Gurdjieff engineered their first meeting in a highly inappropriate eating-house, and arrived wearing detachable cuffs which were none too clean. De Hartmann comments fastidiously, 'To say the least, it was a café for an extremely mixed crowd, which walked the Nevsky day and night; and if anyone were to find out I had been there, I would have had to leave my regiment.' Gurdjieff himself summed up the café less obliquely. 'There are usually more whores here,' he said conversationally. Fortunately de Hartmann kept his balance in this specially contrived situation. He persisted in his aim and, with his young wife Olga, was admitted to the groups, where he 'learned more of the theory of music from Georgiy Ivanovich than in any of the schools.'

In early February 1917 a strange event occurred. As the Petrograd group saw him off at the Nikolaevsky station, Gurdjieff underwent a sort of transfiguration.

He was different! In the window we saw another man, not the one who had gone into the train. He had changed during those few seconds. It is very difficult to describe what the difference was, but on the platform he had been an ordinary man like anyone else, and from the carriage a man of quite a different order was looking at us, with a quite exceptional importance and dignity in every look and movement, as though he had suddenly become a ruling prince or a statesman of some unknown kingdom to which he was travelling and to which we were seeing him off.

It was true. Gurdjieff was leaving Petrograd for the last time, and the ground was falling away behind him. It happened that a well-known journalist shared his compartment; a few days later he published in a newspaper the first description of Gurdjieff by someone outside his circle:

My fellow traveller kept to himself also; he was a Persian or Tartar, a silent man in a valuable astrakhan cap; he had a French novel under his arm. He was drinking tea, carefully placing the glass to cool on the small window-sill table; he occasionally looked with the utmost contempt at the bustle and noise of those extraordinary, gesticulating people. And they on their part glanced at him, so it seemed to me, with great attention, if not with respectful awe.

'They worry themselves a great deal,' he said, his face motionless and sallow, in which the black eyes, polite as in the Oriental, were faintly smiling.

He was silent and then continued:

'Yes, in Russia at present there is a great deal of business out of which a clever man could make a lot of money.' And after another silence he explained:

'After all it is the war. Everyone wants to be a millionaire.'

'Don't you make profits too?'

He smiled particularly quietly and said with gravity:

'We always make a profit. It does not refer to us. War or no war it is all the same to us. We always make a profit.'

But time was running out. In the nine days between 23 February and 3 March 1917, all the archducal chickens came home to roost. Tsarist rule, begun in 1547 when Ivan the Terrible was crowned in the Ouspensky cathedral in Moscow, ended with ignominious abdication in a railway siding at Pskov. Citizen Nicholas Romanov was returned under guard to Tsarskoye Selo, where his unfortunate children had caught the measles. On Easter Monday 3 April Lenin arrived in Petrograd, 'transported in a Sealed Train like a plague bacillus'. Gurdjieff's Russia, 'peaceful, rich and quiet', was now bankrupt, in flames and gripped by mass psychosis. Gurdjieff himself was quietly at home in Alexandropol. He had left Moscow for the Caucasus one week before the revolution broke out.

Using Ouspensky, Gurdjieff now contacted his Moscow and Petrograd groups, calling them to new work with him. They forgathered in a small country villa in Panteleimon Street in Essentuki on the northern foothills of the Caucasus. Through the chaos of that imploding Tsarist society just thirteen pupils had managed to break out. Contrasted with the 25,000,000 men who would die in the approaching civil war, this nucleus was a statistical nullity. Yet upon it rested Gurdjieff's hopes for the future. He immediately launched into a six-week experiment of unprecedented intensity. 'It would be difficult even in six years to find room for everything that was connected with this time, to such an extent was it filled.' For periods they fasted, and 'the feeling of days which were endlessly long, of complete emptiness, of a kind of futility of existence, was new.' At other times they ate sumptuously. 'G. superintended the kitchen, and often prepared dinner himself. He proved to be a wonderful cook and knew hundreds of remarkable eastern dishes. Every day we had dinner in the style of some eastern country; we ate Tibetan, Persian, and other dishes.' At nights they had only four or five hours' sleep. The day was given up to special excursions, to searching exercises in posture, relaxation and sensation, and to the study of ideas. 'In general, during the short period of our stay at Essentuki, G. unfolded to us the plan of the whole work. We saw the beginnings of all the methods, the beginnings of all the ideas, their links, their connections and direction.'

After six weeks Gurdjieff seized on a pretext to disperse the company. The short Essentuki summer was drawing to a close. On 21 October 1917 the Bolshevik coup brought Lenin to power and closed forever any thought of returning to Moscow and Petrograd. In February 1918 Gurdjieff sent a letter to his groups there, again urging them to break out to the Caucasus. Forty came. 'We began rhythmic exercises to music, dervish dances, different kinds of mental exercises, the study of different ways of breathing, and so on.' Meanwhile to forestall investigation by the Piatigorsk Bolshevik government, it was expedient for the colony to assume some *persona* with socialist overtones. 'Think out something like *Sodroojestvo* and "earned by work" or "international" at the same time,' said G. 'In any case they will not understand. But it is necessary for them to be able to give us some sort of name.' But by now Bolshevism was not enough. Essentuki had a Gilbertian cast of administrations and armies to contend with: there were various local factions, to say nothing of the Greens – bandit deserters from both the Reds and the Whites. As Gurdjieff puts it laconically, 'Sometimes on getting up in the morning we would not know under which government we were that day and only on going out into the street would discover what politics had to be professed.' The roads were choked with refugees. One rainy morning, two odd-looking conveyances pulled up at Gurdjieff's door and shadowy forms emerged;

> I gradually began to realize that these were people, or more exactly skeletons of people, with only their burning eyes alive, clad in rags and tatters, their bare feet covered with wounds and sores. . . . These people turned out to be relatives of mine, among them my own sister with her six little children.

At dawn on 15 May 1918 a Turkish army had crossed the ravine of the river Arpa-tchai into Armenia and fallen suddenly on Alexandropol. Here Gurdjieff's father, eighty-five years old, had died from his wounds, protecting his house while his family escaped. All his life Gurdjieff had revered his father, and his grief now had real weight. Emotionally and materially he was under extreme pressure. His money had long since been swallowed up in the revolution, but on all sides were people who looked to him for their daily bread. By August the situation had reached crisis point. His pupils of military age now faced conscription by contending factions – with the hideous likelihood they would end up killing each other. Essentuki was circled about by rival armies, and already at night in the streets there was shooting. The end seemed close. By all ordinary standards Gurdjieff and his movement were finished.

He resolved that something must be done.

Notes

1. This tradition, like so many, trembles on the verge of extinction, but Sayakbai Karalayev, a Kirghiz *ashokh*, has committed to magnetic tape a poem of over a million lines describing the destinies of central Asia from the beginning of time. It is simply one of several epics he knows.
2. The characters and beliefs of Gurdjieff and Stalin are at polar opposition. Their putative connection remains the subject of fanciful speculation, most of which does not bear critical examination. There is for example the suggestion that Stalin, while studying at the Tiflis Seminary, lodged with the Gurdjieff family and left them owing a considerable sum of money; but in fact the strictly regimented Seminary permitted no pupils to live outside its walls. Unaccountably however it does seem that in May 1935, Gurdjieff actively explored the possibility of going to live in Stalinist Russia, and was promptly offered admission by the Soviet authorities, but only on conditions he would not accept. In 1967 Stalin's only daughter Svetlana Iosifovna Alliluyeva defected to America. On 7 April 1970 she married the chief architect of the Taliesin Association of Architects, (William) Wesley Peters, widower of Olgivanna Lloyd Wright's first daughter Svetlana.
3. The idea that Gurdjieff and Dordjieff were one and the same man has been strongly canvassed in some quarters. That this is quite impossible is instantly seen from their photographs; a judgment authoritatively endorsed by Madame Alexandra David-Neel in 'Gurdjieff et Dordjieff', *Les Nouvelles Litteraires* (Paris, 22 April 1954). That Dordjieff was one of those remarkable men from whom Gurdjieff learnt, is a possibility less easy to dismiss.
4. Responsibility for first advancing and developing the interesting Narzunoff–Gurdjieff hypothesis belongs incontrovertibly to James Webb, distinguished author of *The Occult Establishment* (Library Press/Open Court, La Salle, Illinois, 1976). I, however, am relying directly on extensive material provided me from British and Russian sources by Jeffrey Somers FRAS, whose study of Ushe Narzunoff is of long standing. An entire bibliography would be required to list all fragments touching directly or indirectly on Narzunoff. Probably the most important published source remains Alistair Lamb's *Britain and Chinese Central Asia* (Routledge & Kegan Paul, 1960), which repays close study.

Chapter 4

Ida Constance Baker

To say the least it was a coincidence. In 1903, on the first day that Kathleen Beauchamp presented herself at Queen's College, a monitor was plucked at random to show her to her room overlooking the mews. Twenty years later this same monitor dropped a little bunch of marigolds onto Katherine Mansfield's coffin at Avon. She stood dry-eyed although she had good cause to weep: in the time between she had been Katherine's confidante, friend, financier, nurse, laundress, cook and bottle-washer, doormat, sexual partner and, not infrequently, the bane of her existence. The name of this *bonne à tout faire* was Miss Baker.

Born in unremarkable Stuston in Suffolk on 19 January 1888, Miss Baker was christened Ida Constance. Two months later the infant child was in Rangoon at the height of noon, where her father the peppery Colonel Oswald Baker was out in the midday sun. There she remained for seven imperial years, until the family returned to London and an impeccable address in Welbeck Street.

From 1897 onward two oddly contrasting figures might be seen each morning, progressing with embarrassing slowness down Wimpole Street. These were the Baker girls on their way to Queen's College School. May Baker, although crippled by polio, was sharp as a sparrow, but the tall Ida, who took size nine in brogues, wilted like a solicitous question mark. At college she was not unsuccessful. She was a competent violinist; her intimate familiarity with the Domesday Book won her golden opinions from Professor Cramb;

in time she was even made a monitor. Yet when all was said and done it was a thousand pities that Ida Baker could not engage her energies more unreservedly. There were no two ways about it; the girl was as uncommitted as dry litmus paper. In the spring of 1903 her mother, the long-suffering Mrs Baker, passed from her troublesome alliance to a better world, and in the autumn the colonel's daughter, more abstracted than ever, became a boarder at Queen's College. Fifteen years old, gauche, rapt, her eyes puzzled, her shock of flaxen hair falling down to her waist, Ida Constance Baker resembled nothing so much as Sleeping Beauty waiting for her prince to come. It was just at this point that Miss Beauchamp arrived from Wellington and, by a preternatural foresight, was confided to the monitor's care. 'Katherine looked at me steadily with calm, deeply dark eyes.'

It was Kathleen who seized the initiative. 'Let's be friends,' she began. Soon the two girls could be seen whispering together in the little alleys and short cuts near Queen Anne Street. 'Let me tie your veil,' Ida proposed humbly. But Kathleen required rather more than the tying of veils. Then Ida swore the blindest oaths of fealty: if Kathleen actually killed someone with a hat pin, she would on no account criticise. But Kathleen required rather more than oaths; she had special tastes. Ida was 'good conduct girl' for her class, but she was also besotted with love. Where did it begin, this act of splendid commitment, this 'thing' between consenting adolescents in private? Was it by the remotest chance in the elegant and deserted college waiting room under the painting of Queen Victoria? We cannot guess. 'Her body was obedient but how slowly and gravely it obeyed, as though protesting against the urge of her brave spirit.'

Nothing could better illustrate Kathleen's ascendancy than Ida's transformation into LM. 'As they sat on either side of their name-carved wooden desk Kathleen passed to Ida a slip with huge leaping letters – inches high: KATHERINE MANSFIELD. "My grandmother's name," she added, "and my *nom-de-plume*."' A nom de plume seemed a brave idea to Ida Baker. As a student violinist she would take a professional style herself, 'Katherine Moore', the maiden name of her dear mother who had faded so discreetly away. But what was this! The idea of two Katherines did not sit well with Miss Mansfield. It was confusing; egalitarian even. 'Lesley Moore' sounded much better; it bred a piquant ambiguity between her special friend and her extra-special brother. Ida was in no position to argue; she was 'a kind of walking shadow. Whatever Kathleen said or did was absolutely right.' In short, Ida Baker surrendered even her identity; she became Lesley Moore, quickly curtailed to LM, a colourless abbreviation crouching in the margins of literature.

The girls had been quick to agree the symbolic analogue of their relationship. Ida was the tall green column: Katherine the exotic bird who rested upon it between flights. Perhaps Ida was as insensible as a column: certainly the exotic bird was too frenetic to stay long on any one perch. There were for example the counter-attractions of the Maori girl Maata Mahupuka.

> Do other people of my own age feel as I do I wonder so absolutely powerful *licentious*. So almost physically ill – I alone in this silent clock filled room have become powerfully – I want Maata I want her – and I have had her – terribly – this is unclean I know but true. What an extraordinary thing – I feel savagely crude.

Quite how LM consoled herself when Katherine was occupied with Maata, or more orthodoxly with 'Caesar' Trowell, is not certain. She had her violin. And sometimes the college itself provided uplifting excursions to see the deserving poor. 'I gathered two strange pieces of information there,' recalls LM dreamily, 'that old women spent their time cutting wood into tiny bits to be used as raspberry seeds in the factory jam, and that the workers drank large quantities of vinegar.' Of such is the Kingdom of Heaven.

By now the guidelines were laid down for a lifetime's relationship. It was strangely complicit. Katherine would never receive Ida into her inner citadel, but Ida was attracted by repudiation. Katherine used Ida, but Ida dominated by the absolutism of her subservience. Their lives would declare with exclamation marks their reciprocal dependency. And there was sorcery in it. From Ida Baker, the dreamy vessel of Queen's College, Katherine conjured LM, a protective demon, which passed from her control. Already at seventeen Katherine had a consuming sense of her own destiny. She was a field marshal with an army of exactly one obedient private. 'You are the only person in the world who really believes in me,' she told LM.

In the two desolate years when Katherine languished back in Wellington, LM hugged this sentence like a secret talisman. Life with father was not exactly easy; he was so unpredictable and unfortunately he had 'ruined his digestion on curries'. It was the letters from Wellington which saved her – those precious tokens that Katherine had not forgotten her. Nor had she: 'The ghost of L.M. ran through my heart, her hair flying, very pale, with dark startled eyes.' And then – what bliss – Katherine returned. On 24 August 1908 the taxi drew up before the Baker apartment in Montagu Mansions. When Katherine met the colonel, Greek met Greek. A few days later, to Ida's sorrow and the colonel's relief, Katherine removed to Beauchamp Lodge, a gaunt, sepulchral, vaguely bohemian hostel for music students, fronting a canal behind Paddington Station.

Money was her first problem. Fifteen shillings a week was not a lot for shoes, concerts, cigarettes, afternoon teas, cello lessons, Arabian shawls and violets. Katherine could, and bravely did, pick up the odd guinea performing at parties. 'Ah'm a sinner, Ah'm an unlucky man,' she crooned. But what was a guinea? She sold her beloved cello for three pounds. But what was three pounds? LM rushed in with her widow's mite. 'I had then very little money myself, about twelve pounds a year till I reached twenty-one . . . it was some help, and spending it was always a fine adventure.'

Distraction – that was Katherine's heaviest cross at Beauchamp Lodge. Always someone barging in for tea or rending the air with scale exercises. Why, in an atmosphere like this, Tchekov himself could not have created. But Carlton Hill: Ah, Carlton Hill! There was peace and quiet there all right, and what is more, she had an invitation to go, and what is more, her very good friends the Trowell boys lived there. So Katherine went to live *chez* Trowell at 52 Carlton Hill. In vain did Caesar Trowell shake his carroty locks and bang out inverted Neapolitan sixths on the piano. His hour was gone. Katherine's volatile affections had shifted to his brother 'gentle, sweet-tempered, quiet Garnet.' She slept with him; she ran away with him; she might well have married him. Unhappily, as LM noted with mixed feelings,' she really could not bear to see the way that Garnet ate his egg.' It was all too much. A chastened Katherine returned to Beauchamp Lodge.

There is no restorative quite like a spate of passionate love-letters, and Katherine served them up to her friends with cocoa and irony. The signatory was not Garnet: it was one George Charles Bowden, 'pink and white, spick and span', whom she had met under the roof of the superbly-named Dr Caleb Saleeby. A singing teacher and tenor performer at second-rate concerts, Bowden's infatuation with a girl eleven years his junior was to earn him a lot of grief and win him a microscopic place in history.

LM was dispatched to inspect the gentleman, and went to his flat in Paddington. It was night when she left, and a barrel-organ was playing 'Mabel dear, listen here, I'm afraid to go home in the dark.' It gave her quite a turn. Bowden himself Ida found to be a good grey goose; Katherine, pregnant by Garnet, endorsed this judgment to the unqualified extent of accepting Bowden's lightning proposal of marriage. But in what spirit? On 2 March 1909 LM was obliged to witness the ceremony and found the bride 'dressed completely in black, with a dreadful shiny black straw hat on her head.' Paddington registry office seemed equally funereal. Katherine, falsely claiming to be twenty-two, entered in the space for father's profession the words, 'General Merchant'. Thus, accompanied only by her lesbian champion, the daughter of the chairman of the Bank of New Zealand, the future author of 'Prelude', friend of Lawrence and pupil of Gurdjieff, was married to a virtual stranger.

The union was not blessed by issue; indeed it was not even consummated. In twenty-four hours Katherine fled to the refuge of a little Swiss hairdresser in George Street, and then on to join Garnet in Glasgow. Yet here fresh disappointments awaited her. Perhaps Garnet objected to some small detail, like the fact that she had married someone else. The horrified Ida was soon receiving desperate letters, written under the influence of veronal, in which all the words were double. By May, Mrs Beauchamp had swept in from New Zealand to rescue and admonish her errant daughter. The fact that Katherine was four and a half months pregnant incredibly escaped Mrs Beauchamp's notice, but her failed marriage and her Sapphic tendencies did not. How might it be that a child of hers could find herself in such an unthinkable situation? Some bad influence was to be suspected. Ida Baker! Yes that was it. Katherine's relationship with Ida Baker lay at the root of the matter. Katherine should be taken instantly to Bad Wörishofen, where Pfarrer Kneipp in his day had performed such wonders with his watering-can; lesbianism would surely give way before a sensible regime of healthy exercise and cold baths. They knew about these things there. As for Ida, she could go absolutely anywhere – to the Canary Isles – just so long as it was oceans away. A discreet word was spoken to Colonel Baker, and a week later the postal services were doing brisk business between Bavaria and the Canary Isles. Mrs Beauchamp sailed back to Wellington on the *Tongariro* and cut Katherine out of her will.

When LM returned to London, it was to meet a new and strange demand from her still banished mistress. Katherine had lost her child. It was unfortunate, but would LM please send her another. Ida's character was hardening, tempered in the furnace of an unsatisfied desire. She unearthed an eight-year-old boy named Charlie Walter. 'Arrangements were easier in those days; we got a ticket, tied a label on him, and sent him across to her.' Unfortunately LM had picked a complete dud. 'He had spindly legs and a distended stomach; he had no appetite at all for simple wholesome food, and pined for the rubbish to which he was accustomed.' This unfortunate specimen was quickly shipped back across the Channel to graze in its natural habitat. If her caprice was heartless, Katherine paid for it with her life; surely she received the tuberculosis bacillus in 1910, and from Charlie Walter.

For LM, the spring of 1910 was a time of intoxicating meetings and goodbyes, dizzy triumphs and appalling dangers. Parting was such sweet sorrow when Colonel Baker left to farm in Rhodesia. Ida's loss was the Matabeles' gain – or perhaps it was the other way round. To cap it all, Katherine returned and immediately made her big breakthrough in the *New Age*. Here were riches for LM. Yesterday a nobody: today the confidante and special friend of a famous authoress. She alone had believed: now the whole world would be converted. But fate had unpleasant surprises in its armoury, and in March Ida received an alarming distress call. Katherine had been rushed into a second-rate nursing home and operated on for peritonitis. Worse and worse, 'the surgeon was displaying an unprofessional interest in her body.' This was fighting talk to LM. Immediately she summoned a 'growler', a horse-drawn four-wheeler, and, charging to Katherine's rescue, installed her by the seaside at Rottingdean. Orage came, and Beatrice Hastings. Poor George Bowden came, and LM was instructed to get rid of him. She evolved a plan to ditch him at the parish church and suggested he should go in alone, as she had no hat. 'Bowden snatched off his bowler and clapped it on my head, expecting me to enter into his pleasantry. He did not come any more.'

Katherine herself had rather more success in giving LM the slip. The summer sun brought recovery and the frenetic Cheyne Walk period, when young men crowded to her. The result was a kind of Judgment of Paris in reverse. 'Sometimes Ida Baker was required to engage an unwanted visitor in disheartening conversation – a task at which neither Penelope nor Scheherezade could have surpassed her.' But on other occasions Katherine pronounced a different verdict on the happy suitor, and in unmistakable terms.

> I lit a candle – the world faded away. I acted. He tore my clothes from my shoulders. I laughed – bent forward – graceful and lithe – blew out the candle and stood naked to the waist in the moon-lit room. 'My beautiful, my wonder!' He knelt before me, his arms round my body. I crushed him against me – shook back my hair and laughed at the moon. I felt mad with passion – I wanted to kill. . . . By and by he left me.

God knows how LM coped with this emotionally. She couldn't match the young men, but perhaps she could outlast them. This was a girl who could take a lot of punishment; she was very, very durable.

In April 1911 Colonel Baker required Ida to report to him in Rhodesia. Before leaving she gave Katherine £60 to cope with the expected arrival of a baby, and Katherine gave her a bunch of carnations. For five months the girls continued their relationship at arm's length. Ida had much to describe: the demeanour of her father and the trumpeting of the wild African elephant. Miss Mansfield too had plenty of material: abortion, bronchitis, pleurisy, fever and zoological observations of her own.

> Katherine described how, while she lay there alone, she experienced the strange power of levitation and found herself floating up to the ceiling. When the fever was high she would watch the little red elephants on the edge of her Indian cotton bedspread waving their trunks and processing solemnly round and round their limited pathway.

Autumn had come before the two correspondents met again and LM heard the dear voice of Katherine, 'Have you brought any money with you?' It was so good to feel wanted; to be first in friendship and in counsel. But time was running out; already John Middleton Murry, the supplanter, was hovering in the wings. When Murry moved in, on 11 April 1912, it was not a happy day for Ida Constance Baker. 'I did not know anything of Murry's plan and was happily looking forward to that week-end, as I was free to spend the whole of it with Katherine. Alas, on my arrival I had to help

Katherine fill his cupboard with good things to eat. Ida's own diet – physical and emotional – was now to become more spartan. Sent away, she joined a friend in founding the Parma Rooms, an ill-conceived business venture. It sounded grand in the *Rhythm* advert: 'Lesley Moore and Rebecca Rinsberry. Specialists: Scientific Hair-brushing and Face-Treatment. Hours 10 to 7.' But it was hardly a money-spinner. Hunger quickly reduced the colonel's daughter to making gruel from the oatmeal in the face-packs. So from 1912 to May 1913, LM juggled with three lives: long laborious days at the Parma Rooms; sober evenings with her sister at Luxborough House; and a desperate attempt not to lose touch with Katherine.

In the nature of things there was no love lost between LM and Murry. Take the business of her African walking stick: it unaccountably flew out of Murry's hand to be lost evermore in the marshes. He didn't stop to look for it. He did not apologise. 'It had been a personal extravagance of mine,' Ida recalls aggrievedly, 'and its polished smoothness was very precious to me.'

But really, what did LM want with walking sticks? More and more she seemed to have taken a vow of chastity, poverty and obedience. In May 1913 she gave Katherine her furniture and moved into a six-shilling-a-week room above a pub. 'It was bare and poor and unpainted but I hope tolerably clean. I know I had a broom somewhere.' Here she bedded down on a mattress on the floor, but occasionally her sleeping arrangements speak more plainly of her obsession. She would travel to Baron's Court and spend the night on the stone staircase outside Katherine and Murry's door, not daring to disturb them, not able to face the darkness alone.

In December 1913 Katherine and Murry solved this problem for her by decamping to Paris, taking LM's furniture and a pair of rude figures carved by Indian convicts for their memorable governor, Colonel Baker. At the beginning of 1914 Ida was again peremptorily called to her father in Rhodesia, but just as she was in the final ecstasy of preparation to sail, a frantic letter came from Katherine in Paris. Murry had lost his job, his nerve, all the furniture and, who could doubt it, two rude Indian figures. Would LM send money *immediately*! LM raised £5. No, the post office could not insure the money. Better tear the pound notes in half and send one lot in one envelope, one in another. 'Rather anxiously – since it seemed a dreadful thing to do: tear up English money,' LM complied.

Katherine, receiving the envelopes by different deliveries, first supposed that LM had gone mad; and it was indeed astonishing that she had not. Ida Baker sailed for Rhodesia on 27 March 1914. 'Have I ruined her happy life,' pondered Katherine, who did not come to see her off:

> am I to blame? When I see her pale, and so tired that she shuffles her feet when she walks . . . when I see the buttons hanging off her coats, and her skirt torn – why do I call myself to account for all this – and feel that I am responsible for her. She gave me the gift of herself. 'Take me, Katie, I am yours. I will serve you and watch in your ways, Katie. . . .' I ought to have proved my own worthiness of a disciple – but I did not.'

LM's Rhodesian exile – from spring 1914 to autumn 1916 – cut her off from central events in Katherine's life: from the Lawrence–Murry thing; the impact of the war; the *opéra bouffe* episode with Carco; and specially the death of Leslie. But here the letters spoke all too plainly. Was it not clear to the meanest intelligence that Leslie had been nearest and dearest to Katherine: to *her* Katherine? It was tragic he was gone, of course. Tragic. She would write a letter of condolence. Vaguely she sensed the ambivalence of her reaction and suffered from it. 'In turning over the memories of that time of Katherine's bereavement, I feel again and again my sins against the Almighty Spirit of Love.' Marooned with her irascible father among great plantations of eucalyptus trees, Ida reproached herself, and counted the days till her return.

When finally it came, the voyage back to England was not altogether a pleasure cruise; Colonel Oswald Baker had decided to step aboard. But in London, as Katherine met the boat-train, father and daughter were briskly separated and assigned to their rightful spheres. The colonel was donated to the Strand Palace Hotel, where for months he dragged his way round the weary stairs and corridors, like some great wasp which has felt the first sharp frost of winter. He struggled to get his bearings and could not. He proposed marriage to a lady and was refused. He had lost an empire and had not found a role. Baffled, the colonel trekked back to the uplands of Rhodesia, where his own dark fate awaited him. To Ida a more plebeian part was given: she was fed into the grand national effort to defeat the Kaiser. In the circumstances, cosmetic skin and hair treatment no longer seemed quite apropos, so LM was pushed through a six-week course in metal-work, and put to hard labour as a tool-setter in Mr Gwynne's aeroplane factory. The colonel's daughter rose in her lonely Hampstead rooms at half past five and clocked on in Chiswick at seven o'clock every morning. There is a nice entry in Virginia Woolf's diary, when her dinner with Katherine is strangely interrupted by a 'munition worker called Leslie Moor . . . another of these females on the border land of propriety, & naturally inhabiting the underworld.'

But patriotism was not enough; LM wanted her Katherine. From the factory gates she would plod her weary way through the twilight to see her, and, Ah, how fine it was – or would have been but for Murry. Sometimes she said goodnight to the literary couple too late to get home to Hampstead, and ended by sleeping with the down-and-outs in the crypt of St Martin-in-the-Fields. Then in the spring of 1917 LM's big moment arrived: Mansfield and Murry split up.

In her story 'Psychology' Katherine draws the picture of a woman pursued by 'an elderly virgin, a pathetic creature who simply idolized her (heaven knows why) and had this habit of turning up and ringing the bell and then saying, when she opened the door: "My dear, send me away!" ' Was it out of pity, then, that Katherine summoned LM to live with her in Old Church Street, Chelsea, or for memory's sake, or simply to placate her own 'night fears'? In any case, the best arrangement would be if LM did not appear in the evenings until nine o'clock. And another thing – if anyone called, it might be best if LM went to the cubicle behind the curtain and lay quite silently on her bed. Here Ida had some reservations, but not of course on her own account: 'though Katherine and I were content, it might have been inhibiting for the visitor to know that an unseen third person was present.'

In October 1917 Katherine rushed off to Garsington to nurse Murry through his cold, but she was quickly back, exhausted and in pain. 'It's nothing,' she assured LM, 'just a touch of pleurisy. I've had it before, it will go.' Now would LM please get off to the factory and not fuss; the 'daily' was coming regularly, and would see to everything. But the daily was not coming; it was not pleurisy; and it did not go away. 'So,' LM repeats in mantric self-indictment, 'I again failed her in her hour of need.'

Dr Ainger said Katherine must go south or risk 'galloping consumption'. LM certainly hankered to go to the Riviera with her Katie, but there was a war on; it was out of all question. She fussed and fretted and packed for her. 'I seem to remember a large fur muff owned by one or other of us. Then Murry and I anxiously saw her on to the boat train, swaying a little with weakness as she walked.' It was 8 January 1918. Katherine was twenty-nine and she had exactly five years to live. Soon came the hammer blows: Katie was no better; she was distinctly worse; she was downright ill. LM was beside herself. 'I decided instantly that I must go to her.' Murry warned her, 'No, don't go, she will be furious!' But LM had decided. The passport and permit office refused to give her the necessary documents. But LM had decided. She wept, she clamoured, she gave and asked no quarter. The journey south was a nightmare. When finally Ida staggered up to the Hôtel Beau Rivage in Bandol with a bag of squashed *rhum babas*, Katherine met her in the courtyard. 'What *have* you come for?'

Miss Mansfield at this moment in her work had no patience to accommodate LM. She was polishing her story *'Je ne Parle pas Français'*, that bitter-sweet indictment of Carco which threw Murry into such an ecstasy. (STHRY RECEIVID MAFNIFIIENT MURLY.) LM was a considerable, a very considerable, distraction.

> Meal times and walk times are quite enough to exasperate me and lash me into fury beyond measure. 'Katie mine, who is Wordsworth? Must I like him? It's no good looking cross because I love you, my angel, from the little tip of that cross eyebrow to the *all* of you. When am I going to brush your hair again?' I shut my teeth and say 'Never!' but I really *do* feel that if she could she'd EAT me. . . . It is impossible to describe to you my curious hatred and antagonism to her – gross, trivial, dead to all that is alive for me, ignorant and *false*.

Then perhaps there was some move she could make to get Ida off her back. Why yes – she would take her for a long walk and convince her she was perfectly well. So she took her long walk, and the next day the blood spurted from her mouth. Now suddenly the weathervane turned, and every impulse pointed Katherine north: to London, to Murry, to a physician she could trust. She had papers saying she must convalesce in France: very well, all she needed now were papers saying she must convalesce in England. It was simple. So LM sent for the doctor, 'and a dreadful little man came, who drank and was quite useless.' But at least 'Doctor Poached Eyes' could still hold pen to paper. Katherine steeled herself, and charmed the necessary certificate from him. Now it was LM's part: hours she spent, painfully gnawing her way through the bureaucratic net which bound her mighty friend, and at last it fell away. In the confusion of success, LM left her suitcase behind on the platform at Bandol.

Next in store was a three-week siege in Paris; a time of tense silences, punctuated by regular volleys from Big Bertha. Only on the cross-Channel steamer could the two women at last relax and play two-handed patience; unbelievingly they put a red on the black and wanted a seven and looked at each other with a wild surmise.

Katherine weighed 7 stone 7, but the great thing was that LM had got her back.

Curiously, though Katherine's marriage to Murry on 3 May 1918 was an emotional non-event all round, her tuberculosis quickly raised her to an exalted state: 'you see I am ever so gay – with long beams coming from my fingers and sparks flying from my toes as I walk.' And this despite LM's lugubrious sick-bed consolations: 'But Katie you might be paralysed or pock-marked or an ampute.' The situation was indeed serious, and Katherine needed LM's fanatical care. In July she asked her to come and live *à trois* with her and Murry at The Elephant, No. 2 Portland Villas, in Hampstead. 'For the sake of all that has been I ask that of you.' Ida demurred: 'I was . . . making some headway with my machinists. To go would mean losing all this.' It hardly sounded convincing even to herself, and when she left, the factory people clubbed together to give her a gold watch.

This instrument was to come in very handy at The Elephant. By nine o'clock Ida must sweep the carpets, polish the furniture and light Katherine's fire. Katherine should be brought her lunch tray at precisely one o'clock. As to diet, the doctor had prescribed steak, 'of which there was none in Hampstead.' Dutifully LM took her ration book to the West End, bought a microscopic piece of steak, submitted it to her culinary art and blandly offered Katherine 'a tough strip of leather which she could not chew, and to save hurting my feelings . . . threw . . . into the fire.' For LM this was a hard, grinding time. She felt her incapacity, and 'existed as a wraith within a private citadel.' In Rhodesia her old father, Colonel Oswald Baker, had finally turned his artillery about, and blown himself to kingdom come. Here at The Elephant her proud mistress was clinging to life only with the help of an oxygen cyclinder. A year passed. As the summer of 1919 fell away and, imperceptibly at first, the hours of daylight dwindled, the full terror of the situation began to advance: Katherine could not survive another English winter.

So in September Murry took the two women to San Remo, deposited them in a hotel and hastily returned to London. Within days the hotel manager sidled up. The ladies should understand that no one was more distressed than him, but he had his other guests to think of, and in short would they like to leave as quickly as possible and pay for the room to be disinfected. The two lonely women retreated to a small chalet, the Casetta Deerholm at Ospedaletti, where their feelings, never exactly quiescent, were soon wrought to Strindbergian intensity.

> My deadly deadly enemy has got me today and I'm simply a blind force of hatred. Hate is the *other* passion . . . you come up against something which says: 'Hit me, hit me, hate me, hate – feel *strongly* about me – one way or the other, it doesn't matter which way as long as I make you FEEL.'

Why did LM break the big fruit dish? And the thermometer? Why did she eternally come back from the post office with the cruel catch-phrase 'No, Katie, no letters!' And anyway, why was LM here with her in Hell, and Murry far away in Elysium? In short, why did LM live and breathe and cumber the earth? Katherine entertained dark fantasies. 'I . . . dreamed she'd died of heart-failure and I heard myself cry out, "Oh, what heaven! What heaven!" ' She looked at her revolver and plotted mayhem. 'I see myself at the top of the stairs and she at the bottom and then to know she'd never stare at me again.' But there was no escape. The wind and the roaring sea encapsulated them in their misery. By day their anglophobe Italian neighbours seemed like gaolers: by night they were a sinister threat. In the pitch black, the doorbell rang menacingly. *'Qui va là ?'* quavered LM. No answer but the moaning of the wind. *'Qui va là ?'* shrieked the daughter of Colonel Baker, emphasising the strength of her feelings with a cannonade of pistol shots.

Qui va là indeed! Did the Italians for one moment imagine that Katherine Mansfield was *their* rightful prey?

Chapter 5

Piotr Demianovich Ouspensky

In Finland, at ten o'clock on an August evening in 1916, Piotr Ouspensky had a telepathic experience which was unusually structured. He was sitting, Turkish fashion, on the wooden floor of Madame Maximovitch's country house. To his right and to his left sat Dr Stjoernval and Andrei Zaharoff; directly opposite him, enigmatic and smiling, was Gurdjieff. Suddenly, in his chest near his heart, Ouspensky heard the sound of Gurdjieff's voice. The question it posed provoked in Ouspensky a very strong emotion and he answered aloud.

'Why did he say that?' asked Gurdjieff. 'Did I ask him anything?' Not least remarkable in the ensuing scenario is the control of Stjoernval and Zaharoff, as Gurdjieff sat silently and Ouspensky answered him with mounting intensity. They had been manoeuvred into the embarrassing situation of men who eavesdrop on half a telephone conversation. An extended conversation. An intimate converation. Only there was no telephone and the communication was taking place across a distance of four or five feet. Piotr Ouspensky was thirty-eight years old, and the dialogue concerned conditions he must now accept or cease being Gurdjieff's pupil. Abruptly he sprang up; 'I went into the forest, I walked about there for a long time in the dark, wholly in the power of the most extraordinary thoughts and feelings.' Again Gurdjieff's voice vibrated in his chest, and this time, deep in the forest, Ouspensky replied mentally.

Piotr Demianovich Ouspensky was born in Moscow on 5 March

1878. His mother, like many ladies of the Russian intelligentsia, painted, read French novels in the original and diverted herself with artistic questions. His father Demian Ouspensky, an officer in the imperial survey service and a gifted amateur mathematician, died when his son was still young, leaving behind him certain papers on the fourth dimension, which have been irretrievably lost.

'From the age of three', wrote Ouspensky, 'I remember myself quite clearly.' He remembered Moscow; the coronation of Tsar Alexander III; the lights and the fireworks. And Zvenigorod. 'I remember the river there, boats with a smell of tar, hills covered with forests, the old monastery.' Above all, he remembered his remarkable grandmother and her house on Pimenovskaia Street, where the artists and thinkers gathered, and the icons painted by his grandfather glowed in the candlelight. Here Ouspensky and his younger sister would pore over his little picture book *Obvious Absurdities,* which showed a man carrying a house on his back and a carriage with square wheels. It was the book's title which baffled the boy. What differentiated these scenes? 'They looked exactly like ordinary things in life.'

Two terrifying and alluring ideas came very early to Ouspensky. First, a suspicion of hidden laws underlying and unifying the world of obvious absurdities: 'A stick pushed under a stone,' exulted the boy, 'a penknife, a shovel, a see-saw, all these things are one and the same, they are all "levers".' The second was *déjà vu,* the haunting, the irresistible conviction that he had been here before. This vision his sister shared. Conspiratorially the two children would perch at their nursery window like two seasoned critics in a theatre box, watching a familiar play. All too well they could predict what would be enacted in the street below. But they never told the grown-ups because 'They don't understand anything!' So in 1888 when the *famille* Ouspensky visited the Paris exhibition, the boulevards seemed perhaps more familiar to the children than the adults.

Soon brother and sister were to part. Ouspensky exchanged his comfortable room for a hard bed and a red blanket at the Second Moscow Gymnasium. To his house master, a lanky German with a ginger beard, the new boy seemed doubtless to be the standard kit, a jumping, running, standing-still problem, packaged like all the rest: grey overcoat with black fur collar, dark blue cap with the silver school badge of laurel leaves. Turn the child upside down and shake him and his pockets would disgorge nothing exceptional: a watch, a silver twenty-kopeck piece, a penknife, a candle, a pencil and a burning-glass. But differences there certainly were. To begin with, Ouspensky's nose for obvious absurdities did not exactly make for discipline. Nor did his reductionist vision of authority figures: 'the tall German is made up of large and small levers!' The boy's passion for natural history, biology, physics and mathematics was not catered for in the classical curriculum. *'Cupio, desidero, opto, volo, appeto* . . . Damn!' To cap it all Ouspensky 'knew' with a kind of fatalistic relish exactly how and when he was going to get into hot water. But foreknowledge did nothing to prevent his being expelled. 'By the decision of the Master's Council, the pupil Piotr Demianovich Ouspensky is excluded from the number of pupils of the Second Moscow Gymnasium.'

Ouspensky was about fifteen when the Gymnasium signalled its heartfelt *vale* and he climbed into a sledge and was driven away. His mother was overwhelmed and, solely because she was, so was he. Navigating by his interest, Ouspensky now embarked on an ambitious programme of self-education. He studied biology and psychology. He absorbed Nietzsche. Retracing his father's voyages, he pursued mathematics with special regard to the fourth dimension. He made a study of dreams. He enrolled as a 'free listener' at Moscow University but quickly decided that 'professors were killing science in the same way as priests were killing religion.' Precocious, self-willed, eclectic, intellectually arrogant, Ouspensky grandly dismissed the educational establishment. At seventeen he was an anarchic polymath. 'I particularly distrusted all forms of academic science and took a firm decision never to pass any examination and never to take any degrees.' He never did.

When Ouspensky was eighteen his mother died. Overcome with remorse, he suddenly had the impulse, the freedom and the material resources to begin his *Wanderjahre*. He went north to remote Orthodox monasteries, south to the university cities of Europe and even east into the Caucasus. He was a passable horseman, and he carried in his saddle-bags cheap revolvers to repay the ruinously generous hospitality of Circassian chieftains. Simultaneously he pressed forward with his interior explorations. By the age of twenty-one Ouspensky arrived at the conclusion that dreams continue into life; that the frontier between dreams and the waking state is poorly charted.

In the family Ouspensky the names Piotr and Demian passed

alternately from father to son, generation by generation. The Demians were austere world-deniers: the Piotrs zestful embracers of life. Piotr Demianovich Ouspensky was both. Ascetic and gourmet; equally susceptible to the charms of a new mathematical theory or a barefoot girl; equally intoxicated by high-proof vodka and the fourth dimension – the young Ouspensky was polarised in two directions at once. He succeeded in combining an impetuous, adjectival romanticism with an almost glacial classicism. Even his face was *coincidentia oppositorum*. The high Slav cheekbones were set on a square Teutonic skull above a neckless torso. The hair was blond to the point of albinism. The eyebrows and obstinate jaw suggested a bear-like strength, but the lips were precision-engineered, and the delicate pince-nez alighted on his nose like a dragonfly. A strange suitor this.

We do not know the name of the girl to whom Ouspensky laid passionate siege in 1901; we do not know why he was repulsed. But we may conjecture. In a glittering world of counts and princes, Ouspensky was a commoner. Life in salon and theatre, under the crystal chandeliers, appealed to him not at all. He was hopelessly short-sighted. He suffered from an embarrassing disease called 'lack-of-roubles'; the great Moscow restaurants, the Yar and the Stryelna in Petrovsky Park, were closed to him. He was an orphan; had no patron, no preferment, no career. Any mother would have told you he was just not a good bet. And so he emerged bruised from his first grand affair.

The year 1905 was crucially important to Ouspensky. He was twenty-seven and drifting. By day he contrived a living as a journalist; through the dazed summer evenings he drank heroically. 'One night I remember I got home with the left sleeve of my overcoat missing. How I lost it, and where, I have never discovered, although I have given the matter very careful thought.' Obvious absurdities were everywhere. Ouspensky detested socialism but 'could only work on "left" papers because "right" papers did not smell good.' It was a time of descent; the vast empire itself was creaking and groaning. In September the trains stopped running and a general strike spread like contagion. In October the Tsar signed a liberal proclamation guaranteeing civil rights, freedom of speech, conscience and assembly; and the *okhrana* arrested Ouspensky's sister for 'revolutionary activities' and immured her in the Boutirsky prison.

Ouspensky was close, almost telepathically close, to his sister. Exert himself as he might, there was nothing he could do now to save her. How was it that her own sense of *déjà vu* had not armoured her? Why, if a man glimpsed the steel trap, understood it would infallibly spring on him, did he still reach for the bait? He himself had known he would leave the Gymnasium in disgrace; knew it and in effect connived in its fulfilment. And his mother was dead. Desperate to make some meaning, Ouspensky now seized on his master-idea, the theory of 'eternal recurrence'. It had an honourable genealogy in Heraclitus, Pythagoras and Nietzsche; it was tenable in mathematical terms of the fourth dimension; elegantly it explained both *déjà vu* and the inutility of *déjà vu*. It was simple, ominously simple:

> This means that if a man was born in 1877 and died in 1912, then, having died, he finds himself again in 1877 and must live the same life all over again. In dying, in completing the circle of life, he enters the same life from the other end. He is born again in the same town, in the same street, of the same parents, in the same year and on the same day. He will have the same brothers and sisters, the same uncles and aunts, the same toys, the same kittens, the same friends, the same women. He will make the same mistakes.

This idea of eternal recurrence struck Ouspensky with the force of a revelation. Straightway he began to sift its implications in a haunting autobiographical novel. *The Wheel of Fortune*.[1] The scene is set in Moscow, at a country *dacha* and in Paris. The time is 1890 to 1902. The hero Ivan Osokin, by the agency of a magician, goes back twelve years to his troubled schooldays, his early manhood and loves. All will hinge on his predestined meeting with the beauty Zinaida. . . . Seeing his life unwind like a film, Osokin struggles to remember and understand; and by understanding to break the iron circle – to amend his fate. So, in literary form, Ouspensky embarked on a search which, with dogged persistence, he would carry through to his last days.

The next faltering step came in 1907 when Ouspensky contacted a banned organisation – the Theosophical Society. The tide of clandestine occultism now at flood in imperial Russia had an aspect that was extravagantly, decoratively absurd; but was it any more impossible than the world of obvious absurdities? Ouspensky had no doubt. See him sitting in the editorial office of the *Morning* with a leading article on the Hague Conference to grind out:

> Pushing aside the papers I open a drawer in my desk. The whole desk is crammed with books with strange titles, *The Occult World, Life after Death, Atlantis and Lemuria, Dogme et Rituel de la Haute Magie, Le Temple de Satan, The Sincere Narrations of a Pilgrim,* and the like. These books and I have been inseparable for a whole month, and the world of Hague Conferences and leading articles becomes more and more vague, foreign and unreal to me.
>
> I open one of the books at random, feeling that my article will not be written to-day. Well, it can go to the devil! Humanity will lose nothing if there is one article the less on the Hague Conference.

And in fact if Ouspensky were actually to write what he thought, 'The paper would be seized in the streets by the police, and both the editor and I would have to make a very long journey.' It is a matter of dispute if his sister made that same long journey to Siberia or remained walled up in Boutirsky. It is a matter of agreement that she died a prisoner in 1908 while the politicians' vapouring at the International Peace Conference still hung in the air.

For Ouspensky, Moscow had become oppressive and claustrophobic. He felt keen relief when his assignments took him south to European capitals. During the Theodore Roosevelt presidency – the golden age of the Model T Ford – he visited New York. But essentially it was the Orient which plucked at him like a magnet. At least one intellectual Muscovite ridiculed his expectations:

> 'Do you really believe that there still remains something unexplored in the East?' he said. 'So many books have been written about the East, so many serious scientists have given up their whole lives to the study of every small piece of land there, of every tribe, of every custom. It is simply naïve to think that anything miraculous and unknown has remained in the East. I could more easily believe in miracles on Kuznetsky Most.'

Ouspensky listened; then accompanied by his friend Sherbakov he left for Constantinople. He climbed the hill from the bridge across the Golden Horn, up the steps of the Yuksek Kalderym, through a courtyard bounded by old green plane trees and ancient tombs, and into the *tekke* of the Mevlevi dervishes.[2] Their music, their turning ceremony, their very faces, affected Ouspensky profoundly. 'I saw them for the first time in 1908. Constantinople was then still alive. Later it died. *They* were the soul of Constantinople though nobody knew of this.' Embarking next at Smyrna, Ouspensky arrived in Egypt. 'Yellowish-grey sand. Deep blue sky. In the distance the triangle of the Pyramid of Khephren, and just before me this strange, great face with its gaze directed into the distance.' In front of the Sphinx of Gizeh, Ouspensky experienced a sense of annihilation; his whole life was too transient for the Sphinx to notice. 'I did not and could not exist for it. And I could not answer my own question – do I exist for myself?'

It was not to Moscow that Ouspensky returned but to St Petersburg, that deep aquarium where the strange fish swam: Diaghilev, Nijinsky, Rasputin; Mamontov the Maecenas of the opera, Artzibashev the sensualist, Volinsky the symbolist critic; *prima ballerina assoluta* Kschessinka, the Tsar's mistress and the Madame du Barry of the coming revolution. Surely mathematicians rather than architects had formulated those frozen palaces; surely some deranged dramatist had contrived this theatre of obvious absurdities. 'Petersburg lived a restless, cold, satiated, semi-nocturnal life,' wrote Alexei Tolstoi. 'Phosphorescent, crazy, voluptuous summer nights . . . green tables and the clink of gold.' As for Ouspensky, he had a tiny room on the corner of Nevsky Prospekt and Liteynaia Street. There was a chair, a bed, a table and a packing-case stuffed with occult books. And that was that.

Tsar Nicholas ruled from his palace at Tsarskoye Selo, attended by glittering Cossacks of the Escort, elite of the Imperial Guard, and the Regiment of His Majesty, the Sacred Legion: the intellectual capital however was a certain night-club. There, in an atmosphere of bonded friendships and ruptured vodka glasses, the intelligentsia cocked a hind leg at the establishment. At eleven o'clock the imperial ballet and imperial opera companies took their bow; the blasé audiences dispersed, and anyone of rank in the intellectual fraternity made a bee-line for the Errant Dog.

Ouspensky's entry onto the stage of the Errant Dog and his friendship there with Volinsky marked the beginning of a period of intense activity. The aged Leo Tolstoi lunched with him, spoke of the Russian freemasons and drew little diagrams of the fourth dimension on the tablecloth. Ouspensky studied the Tarot, theosophy, Alexandrian Christianity, the French magical revival,

Russian Orthodoxy, neo-Platonism, Jacob Boehme, the monks of Athos. Above all, Ouspensky studied himself. Employing variously fasting, meditation, breath-control and drugs, he ran a positive gauntlet of experimental mysticism. His zeal fervent, his classifications rigorous, his detachment scientific, Ouspensky nevertheless emerged disappointed from this passage. Yes, he had won fugitive access to a world of mathematical relationships, of hieroglyphs, of Boehme's 'signature of things'. Yes, he now knew more about symbolism than Volinsky ever would. Yes, he had a strange vision of the Long Body of man, a human life extended in time. But real, objective, bankable facts, he had none.

In 1912 Ouspensky published the book which made his name, *Tertium Organum*. A KEY TO THE ENIGMAS OF THE WORLD, screamed the title page, THE MYSTERY OF SPACE AND TIME, SHADOWS AND REALITY, OCCULTISM AND LOVE. ANIMATED NATURE. VOICES OF THE STONES. MATHEMATICS OF THE INFINITE. THE LOGIC OF ECSTASY. MYSTICAL THEOSOPHY COSMIC CONSCIOUSNESS. THE NEW MORALITY. BIRTH OF THE SUPERMAN. This certainly was large advertisement. Yet the charge of sensationalism cannot be made good against Ouspensky himself. His theme is audacious, but in the text proper it is elegantly, even austerely argued. Building upon Kant's *A Critique of Pure Reason* and C. H. Hinton's *A New Era of Thought,* Ouspensky erects a capacious structure of meta-logic which can accommodate not merely the perennial mystical experience, but those quirky modern paradoxes in sub-atomic particle physics. To read him on time and dimensions is to encounter a mind original, alive and *engagé*. His phenomenology of consciousness, based on direct experiment, is a sight more convincing than Husserl's or Heidegger's. Ouspensky stands, a myopic Canute, with the tide of logical positivism splashing round his boots, and he actually turns it back. In *Tertium Organum* he does for Europe what Ghazzali did once for Islam: he renders mysticism intellectually defensible.

Rewards and consequences were quick to follow. Ouspensky entered 1913 with a modest literary fame. If he volunteered an opinion or called for vodka, people at the Errant Dog sat up and took notice. Even when somewhat mellow himself, his reputation and transparent disinterestedness were enough to reconcile and to sober troublemakers. Restaurant commissionaires and even policemen took to ringing up 'Piotr' at the first hint of bother. A widening circle brooded over his writing. His revelational booklet *The Symbolism of the Tarot* drew him into correspondence with Orage; in Moscow his *Tertium Organum* fell under the eyes of George Ivanovitch Gurdjieff; and in Petersburg it won him the company of Anna.

Anna Ilinishna Butkovsky was twenty-nine. She still retained something of the *ingénue,* yet with a distinct patina of sophistication. She had already visited Rome, Paris, Vienna, Berlin and Prague; studied for the degree of Doctor of Letters; met the obligatory cardboard officer; married in haste and repented at leisure; consoled herself with the writer Evreinoff; and now was pursuing music at the *conservatoire.* Every day on the stroke of noon she would meet with Ouspensky at Phillipoff's Café, where (in conformity with Ouspensky's original system of management-by-exception) Alexei the waiter served repeated cups of the strongest coffee *à la Varsovienne* until positively forbidden. 'Better to say "No" once,' explained Ouspensky, 'than to have to order five or six times.' They talked about music, alchemy, Vivekananda, Wagner, the Holy Grail. Long years afterwards she recalled 'the gentle, poetic radiance of his St Petersburg days.' They were more than a little in love, and not merely with each other – their grand passion was for 'the Miracle', the evolution of consciousness. 'We shall find the Miracle, I know it,' said Ouspensky. 'I never feel, I *know*.' But by now there was something else he knew: nothing substantial could be achieved alone. Even the shared search with Anna and Sherbakov was not sufficient. Hospitality must be given to an exhilarating dream: the idea of entering an esoteric school with a real teacher. Could he conceivably make contact with the vanished schools, of Pythagoras, of Egypt, of the builders of Notre-Dame? The notion was at least experimentally tenable. Fantastic, yes – but so was the very idea of such schools. It was Anna who brought him back to earth. 'Why don't you go to India?' Ouspensky adroitly secured an open commission from three Moscow papers to write Indian colour pieces, but just as plans were maturing, his travelling companion Sherbakov died. 'The meaning of life,' Ouspensky had written, 'is in eternal search. *And only in that search* can we find something new.' Bereaved for a third time, he set out alone.

Energetic and romantic, Ouspensky was a pioneer 'esotourist'. Passing through London in the second half of 1913 he looked up Orage, but quickly crossed the Channel and was standing by the slender spire of Notre-Dame where the twelve Apostles descend to the four quarters of the world. 'They can be seen only if one knows of their existence,' wrote Ouspensky, 'like so many other things in the world.' In Egypt he penetrated the Great Pyramid by candle-light. In Ceylon he was seen and pierced by the blue sapphire eyes of a reclining yellow Buddha. He met the yogi philosopher Aurobindo. At Adyar he sat with Annie Besant, president of the Theosophical Society, conferring on a white llama skin. It is perhaps unnecessary to add that he saw the Taj Majal by moonlight; scent of jasmine, mewing of peacocks. It would be easy, too easy, to be supercilious about this considerable journey and the hope which prompted it. But the actual experience was Ouspensky's, and perhaps we cannot enter into its nuances so facilely. As an experiment it proved cathartic; the traveller sloughed off much of his romanticism. At least he apprehended now that 'whatever the name of the school: occult, esoteric or yogi, they should exist on the ordinary plane like any other kind of school: a school of painting, a school of dancing, a school of medicine.' Twice on the journey Ouspensky heard the voice of the dead Sherbakov. Was it conceivable that the Miracle would speak to him in Russian accents on Russian soil?

Great events were to enforce an answer. The war found Ouspensky again in Colombo; immediately he embarked for England *en route* for home. The seasoned traveller who arrived back in Russia in November 1914; the author of *Tertium Organum*; the cogent speaker who could draw a thousand people to his lecture on the miraculous in the Petrograd town *duma* – this was now a pupil worth Gurdjieff's acquisition. On Friday 13 November, *Golos Moskvi*, 'the Voice of Moscow', carried an anonymous feature entitled 'Round about the Theatre' describing the scenario of a completely unknown ballet, *The Struggle of the Magicians*. Surely it was no accident that the scenario was set in India, offered a complete picture of oriental magic, fakir miracles and sacred dances, and that it 'belonged to a certain "Hindu" '. Ouspensky recoiled from the jaunty tone of the copy, 'but as Hindu writers of ballet scenarios were, to a certain extent, rare in Moscow, I cut it out and put it into my paper, with the slight addition that there would be everything in the ballet that cannot be found in real India but which travellers go there to see.' In Easter 1915 he was recompensed: the sculptor Merkouroff disclosed to Ouspensky that the 'Hindu' he had

gratuitously advertised was in fact a Caucasian Greek named
Gurdjieff. Mr Gurdjieff now extended an invitation to meet him.

Ouspensky had never been exactly well disposed to authority
figures; the Second Moscow Gymnasium could vouch for that. He
was now thirty-seven, a newspaper man, a Petersburg sophisticate,
broadly travelled, absurdly well read, an original thinker, an author
lionised in his own expanding circle. He went with fastidious reserve
to meet this unknown Greek, anticipating a mixture of superstition,
self-suggestion and defective thinking. Nevertheless, he went.

> My first meeting with him entirely changed my opinion of him
> and of what I might expect from him.
>
> I remember this meeting very well. We arrived at a small café in
> a noisy though not central street. I saw a man of an oriental type,
> no longer young, with a black moustache and piercing eyes, who
> astonished me first of all because he seemed to be disguised and
> completely out of keeping with the place and its atmosphere. I
> was still full of impressions of the East. And this man with the
> face of an Indian raja or an Arab sheik whom I at once seemed to
> see in a white burnoose or a gilded turban, seated here in this little
> café, where small dealers and commission agents met together,
> in a black overcoat with a velvet collar and a black bowler
> hat, produced the strange, unexpected, and almost alarming
> impression of a man poorly disguised, the sight of whom
> embarrasses you because you see he is not what he pretends to be
> and yet you have to speak and behave as though you did not see it.'

It was a pivotal meeting on which depended the orientation of
Ouspensky's entire life. Characteristically Gurdjieff strewed
brambles in his path. Item: pupils must preserve strict secrecy. Item:
pupils must each pay him 1,000 roubles a year. Item: it was quite
superflous for Ouspensky to tell him his traveller's tales.

> 'You know,' G. said once, 'when you went to India they wrote
> about your journey and your aims in the papers. I gave my pupils
> the task of reading your books, of determining by them *what you
> were*, and of establishing on this basis what you would be able to
> find. So we knew what you would find while you were still on
> your way there.'

But for Ouspensky there was something which overrode all these
contrived hurdles. It was not simply Gurdjieff's being, his 'feline

grace and assurance', the quality of his silence. No, it was his answers when he broke that silence. 'In his explanations I felt the assurance of a specialist, a very fine analysis of facts, and a *system* which I could not grasp, but the presence of which I already felt.' Ouspensky shared with others, before and after him, the sensation that Gurdjieff had put him on the palm of his hand, weighed him and put him back. Without explicitly saying so, Gurdjieff gave Ouspensky to understand he would accept him as his pupil. Whether Ouspensky would accept Gurdjieff as his teacher was never in question. He saw him the next day, and the next, and the next. When finally Ouspensky's profession compelled him back to Petrograd he went breathlessly to Anna Ilinishna and without a 'good-morning', or even pausing to sit down, said, 'I have found the Miracle.'

If Ouspensky's new role as a pupil was exhilarating, it was also chastening; Gurdjieff gave no quarter:

> 'If you understood everything you have written in your own book, what is it called?' – he made something altogether impossible out of the words 'Tertium Organum' – 'I should come and bow down to you and beg you to teach me. But *you do not understand* either what you read or what you write. You do not even understand what the word "understand" means. . . . If a man knows how to make coffee well or how to make boots well, then it is already possible to talk to him. The trouble is that nobody knows anything well.'

Ouspensky was soon nicknamed 'Wraps Up the Thought'. Whenever he lapsed into philosophising, or meandering rhetorical questions, he received a cold baptism.

> Er, er . . . it is difficult . . . well-nigh impossible . . . for civilised humanity with its deeply-rooted ideas, to assimilate new ones . . . er . . . Perhaps we are disciples of Auguste Comte; or we may become attached to the ideas of Thomas à Kempis . . . or possibly we are influenced by reading about the Rosicrucians, or by the doctrines of Theosophy. . . . We are all products of our destructive civilisation.

On this Gurdjieff commented, 'He's exactly like a cow going round and round a new gate without being able to find the way in.' In engaging with Gurdjieff, Ouspensky had set out with the burning personal aim of knowing the future, even to the day and the hour of his death; but in Gurdjieff's terms such a far-off aim was neither practical nor apropos. 'If today is like yesterday.' he pointed out dryly, 'tomorrow will be like today.' The incident at the Sadovaya restaurant, opposite the Gostinoy Dvor, is very indicative. 'I promise to answer now any question you care to ask,' Gurdjieff assured a downcast Ouspensky. As programmed, Ouspensky asked about eternal recurrence. Gurdjieff's answer in itself was highly interesting, but the coda perhaps even more so. Certainly it offers one clue in deciphering the Gurdjieff–Ouspensky relationship.

> You see how easy it is to *turn* you; but perhaps I was merely *romancing* to you, perhaps there is no recurrence at all. What pleasure is it when a sulky Ouspensky sits there, does not eat, does not drink. 'Let us try to cheer him up,' I think to myself. And how is one to cheer a person up? One likes funny stories. For another you must find his hobby. And I know that Ouspensky has this hobby – 'eternal recurrence'. So I offered to answer any question of his. I knew what he would ask.

But Ouspensky, whose bad mood had vanished, dismissed the psychological explanation and clung to the philosophical: 'G.'s chaff did not affect me. He had given me something very substantial and could not take it back.' Perhaps he had.

The Gurdjieff–Ouspensky transaction was authentic, even awesome. In a period measured in months Gurdjieff generously uncovered to Ouspensky data and ideas which had cost him twenty years to search out. This material is outside our compass, yet it constitutes the hidden dimension of any biography. Decidedly this was not the infatuation of a naive philosopher with a clownish shaman. Ouspensky's own account *In Search of the Miraculous* leaves no latitude for debate: Gurdjieff was not less well informed than his eminent pupil, he was better informed; his thinking was not less disciplined, it was more disciplined. Ouspensky paid by his devotion, high intelligence and seriousness. Often enough it was Ouspensky who precipitated Gurdjieff's frightening storms.'You want a fourth, eighth dimension – three are not enough for you. Mystics indeed! The best thing for you all would be to be put in gaol.' But equally it was Ouspensky who rushed to recuperate the situation. Of all that first Petrograd group – Charkovsky, Zaharoff, Dr Stjoernval, Nicholas and Anna Ilinishna – it was Ouspensky who, with an almost photographic memory, registered the teaching for posterity. And in 1916 it was Ouspensky who was given that strange series of telepathic experiences in the house at the forest's edge.

By now the war was sucking more and more millions into its vortex. Ouspensky, still very much a connoisseur of obvious absurdities, noted,

> two enormous lorries on the Liteiny loaded to the height of the first floor of the houses with new unpainted wooden *crutches*. For some reason I was particularly struck by these lorries. In these mountains of crutches for *legs which were not yet torn off* there was a particularly cynical mockery of all the things with which people deceive themselves.

In October 1916 the author of *Tertium Organum* was himself mobilised and shoved into the uniform of the Guards Sappers but, even aided by his magnificent pebble glasses, he could with great difficulty perceive three dimensions, and accordingly in January 1917 he was released. Ouspensky and Anna Ilinishna were now married, but perhaps surprisingly not to each other: she chose an English businessman, while Ouspensky chose one Sophie Grigorevna, an incisive, Junoesque matron, with dark, chestnut hair, imperious eyes, and a grown-up daughter. Over all their lives, as over Gurdjieff's work, brooded the coming revolution. Ouspensky writes of his presentiment in a metaphor of astonishing brilliance:

> One felt that something was bound to happen and that very soon. Only those upon whom the course of events still appeared to depend were unable to see and feel this. The marionettes failed to understand the danger that threatened them and did not understand that the very same wire which pulls the villain with a knife in his hand from behind a bush makes them turn and look at the moon. A marionette theater is worked in the same way.

In March 1917 Nicholas II, last of the Romanovs, was constrained to abdicate. The tragedy of Ouspensky's sister had left him with no feeling at all for the dynasty, but equally he had not the slightest illusions about the Bolsheviks and what they really presaged. A strange semblance of normality, a strange calm, enveloped Petrograd like a cocoon, but Ouspensky was quite undeceived. 'Tramways, railways, post,' he assured a friend, 'all these are working, thanks to inertia alone. But inertia cannot last for ever. You will realise that the fact of our walking here and that nobody is assaulting us is abnormal. It is made possible by inertia alone.' Gurdjieff meanwhile had vanished and news of him was inconclusive. The little group at Petrograd waited and waited. 'At last – it was already early in June – I received a telegram from Alexandropol: "If you want to rest come here to me." – That was G.!' Within two days Ouspensky had left the capital. Within a week he was sitting with Gurdjieff, and Gurdjieff's father and mother, in the Caucasus.

Ouspensky has left us a charming vignette of his fortnight in Alexandropol; the wild Tartar ravine; the panorama of Mount Ararat; the Armenian church with its image of the Virgin. He remembers Gurdjieff's extraordinary consideration for his father, a robust octogenarian with the statutory pipe and astrakhan hat. Concerning the revolution, 'the great agitation of minds in Russia', the liquidation of his entire enterprise there, Gurdjieff took the long view: 'wait five years and you will see for yourself how what hinders today will prove useful to us.' Precisely five years later he was to acquire the Château du Prieuré. Meanwhile he talked cryptically of returning to Petrograd 'to see the Nevsky with hawkers selling sunflower seeds.' In the upshot it was Ouspensky he sent back to Moscow and Petrograd, calling the groups to new work with him in the Caucasus.

Gurdjieff's Essentuki 'intensive' was a revelation to Ouspensky, and there is a striking incident conveying the degree of his commitment. In November 1917 he and five others were wintering with Gurdjieff on the Black Sea shore, twenty-five miles north of Tuapse. 'You ought to know that,' Gurdjieff replied to a complicated question from Ouspensky, 'it was spoken of in the lectures in St Petersburg. . . . if you now heard that somebody was giving the same lecture at Tuapse, would you go there on foot?'

'What is there to think about?' responded Ouspensky. 'Of course I would go without a word.'

This passage has a curious double-edged significance. Clearly there is no subtracting from Ouspensky's willingness to face twenty-five miles of darkness, snow, rain and wind. But what magnet would have drawn him along that road? The hope of hearing 'someone', anyone, lecturing on an inconsistency in the 'table of hydrogens'. And there he sat in the same room as George Ivanovitch Gurdjieff.

In fact Ouspensky was already in the throes of an agonising reappraisal: 'I had for some time begun to separate G. and the *ideas*. I had no doubt about the ideas.' This first estrangement of Gurdjieff and Ouspensky remains a perplexing enigma. It is all too easy to assume it was Ouspensky who brought matters to a head. Ouspensky was a writer, a philosopher avid for real ideas systematically advanced within a private elite group. All this had miraculously corresponded with the segment of Gurdjieff's life from 1915 to 1918. But Ouspensky was not religious by temperament, won no place in the sacred dancing, and was thrown off balance when the current of the work changed direction. Which brings us back to Gurdjieff. Surely he, if anyone, monitored the relationship; if anyone consented to the growing breach, he did. And why? Perhaps we will not enter so easily into Gurdjieff's thinking and its time-scale; or riddle out the paradox of a man whose music is so full of compassion and who resolved 'to press the most sensitive corn of everyone I met.' Ouspensky's own explanations merely deepen the mystery. 'I do not in the least mean that I found any of G.'s actions or methods wrong or that they failed to respond to what I expected. . . . I had nothing to say against G.'s methods except that they did not suit me.'

What must follow was as painful as a syllogism, and Ouspensky's formidable mind was now at extreme tension. Gurdjieff was 'the Miracle', the unique source of those ideas he found so telling. But if teacher and pupil had not the same orientation and specific gravity, was not this the moment for Ouspensky to go? Forty years old, without apparent means of earning his bread, he found himself in the remote Caucasus far, far from the Errant Dog, at the outset of a bloody civil war. His wife and step-daughter were with him. Painfully he brooded over a giant decision, the possibility of an unforgivable error; his wish to know the future now had a traumatic immediacy. The first Cossack raid took place on Essentuki, and Gurdjieff prepared for an improbable journey. One may query the wisdom of Ouspensky's final decision but never its courage. He resolved not to go with Gurdjieff but, equally, not to leave before him. Just one week after Gurdjieff's departure, Cossack patrols cut the railway line; then the pendulum swung and revolutionary forces swept into Essentuki with robberies and 'requisitions'. A fortnight later, the massacre of hostages signalled a period of terror. 'I must confess I felt very silly,' concludes Ouspensky dryly. 'I had not gone abroad when it was possible in order to work with G. and the final outcome was that I had parted from G. and stopped with the bolsheviks.'

It was absurd.[3]

Notes

1. Drafted in 1905 as *The Wheel of Fortune,* Piotr Ouspensky's only novel, substantially autobiographical, was published in Petrograd in 1915 under the title *Kinemadrama*. The English translation, styled *Strange Life of Ivan Osokin,* first appeared as a limited edition in 1947 shortly before the author's death.
2. Among the many special influences assimilated by the young Gurdjieff, Mevlevi music and religious exercise must have numbered. Today when the Mevlevi tradition labours under almost insuperable difficulties in its native Turkey, amicable relations have been maintained between certain Mevlevi and certain members of The Gurdjieff Society. The great *Ney* player Aka Gunduz Kutbay and other Mevlevi instrumentalists helped with music for the film *Meetings with Remarkable Men,* scripted by Peter Brook and Madame Jeanne de Salzmann.
3. Ouspensky's direct contact with Gurdjieff lasted four years. He first met Gurdjieff and became his pupil in Moscow in April 1915 at the age of thirty-seven. Throughout the ensuing two years, Ouspensky, living in Petrograd, exerted himself to maintain contact with Gurdjieff, living in Moscow. In February 1917 Gurdjieff left for Alexandropol, where Ouspensky joined him for a fortnight in June. With brief intermissions, Ouspensky was now with Gurdjieff from July 1917 to July 1918 in Essentuki, Uch Dere and Tuapse. However, well before the end of this third year he had become estranged, and he intentionally parted from Gurdjieff at the beginning of August 1918. Ouspensky next met Gurdjieff in June 1920 in Constantinople, where, during a fourth and final year, the relationship was tentatively resumed. In August 1921 Ouspensky came to London. From this point the two men, living in different countries, met only briefly, and in January 1924 Ouspensky formally severed his connection with Gurdjieff.

    Drawing on this four-year experience, Ouspensky taught Gurdjieff's ideas, in the form that he had received them, for a quarter of a century, until he abandoned 'the system' a few months before his death in 1947. His book *In Search of the Miraculous* will remain for ever the definitive record of this particular mode. Gurdjieff himself changed the form in which he taught, as soon as a new understanding had been reached. In this connection it is perhaps worth recording that Jeanne de Salzmann (who befriended Katherine Mansfield in her final months) participated in all the stages through which Gurdjieff's work passed during thirty years, following him from Tiflis to Constantinople, Berlin, Hellerau, Fontainebleau and Paris, where he died in 1949.

Chapter 6

John Middleton Murry

There was a song Katherine Mansfield used to sing, pulling a long, ridiculous face:

> I am an unlucky man
> I fell into a coalhole
> I broke my leg
> And got three months for stealing coal.
> I am an unlucky man
> If it rained soup all day,
> I wouldn't have a spoon
> I'd only have a fork.

Could she possibly have been thinking of John Middleton Murry?

Consider for example the incident at the Closerie des Lilas. It happened in his green and salad days before he met Katherine. Picture a tender spring evening in Paris: Murry sits at the café table deep in thought; he is trying to work out how to ditch his first mistress, the young and naive Marguéritte. 'Then I . . . walked slowly away, still in my dream, down the Boulevard St. Michel. I had not walked for more than two or three minutes when I clapped my hand to my pocket: I had left my wallet behind.' At one stroke Murry had lost everything, including his fare back to England. But no! Not quite everything. He felt in his trouser pocket and found a big five-franc piece. It seemed prudent to consult the oracle: 'heads it would go well with me, tails it would go ill.' In the deserted street he spun his last coin high in the air; 'it glittered in the moonlight, tinkled on the road, and rolled firmly and decisively towards the open gutter under the kerb.' He was penniless.

For his epoch Middleton Murry incarnated the Higher Seriousness. In all his kaleidoscopic shifts and turns – a literary critic in his twenties, a religious in his thirties, a socialist in his forties and a pacifist in his fifties – one constant is evident: the stupefying seriousness of his self-depiction. Murry's stigmata are somehow stigmata of special relevance. Yet by his rotten luck, his *naïveté*, his stinginess, his timidity, his *Angst*, his elaborate self-justification, his ridiculous embroilment with powerful, even violent, characters, Murry emerges as a figure of farce, under cruel arc lights of a surrealist stage. He is absurd. And in his absurdity he is human.

But to begin this rare history at its beginning.

John Middleton Murry entered the world on 6 August 1889 at Peckham, near the Old Kent Road. 'I was', he reflects, 'a beautiful baby.' His father however had little opportunity to study his appearance; the breadwinner had left every morning by eight o'clock on his way to Somerset House. Completing there his full day's stint as a poor and subjugated clerk, he hurried on to a penny savings bank, where he ruined his eyes over their ledgers; and it was not until the small hours of the morning that he re-entered his little front door, more dead than alive.

John Middleton, the object of all this devotion, was to put it bluntly a nervous child; at seven he could still not get to sleep without a knotted towel for company. At the church concert he was cast as Little Boy Blue in a waxworks show and – carried on-stage like a cardboard figure – was required to blow his own trumpet with stiff mechanical movements. Until he was thirteen John was an only child. His father was fiercely ambitious on his behalf but not perhaps more ambitious than the boy himself. He creditably squeezed every drop of knowledge out of his prime book of reference, *Cassell's Penny History*; at the age of two he would read the daily newspaper to the less literate patrons of the Ordell Arms; at seven his impromptu essay on Gothic architecture received fifty marks out of fifty. Then, almost effortlessly, he won a scholarship to Christ's Hospital School and, putting on his yellow stockings and dark blue gown, was swallowed up in the alien world of an English public school. Classicism and cricket were evidently the twin keys to success in this new milieu, but Murry did not progress equally in both domains.

Connor was the name of the boy who dropped stone dead, struck by lightning, the moment Murry bowled a ball to him. 'A thin line of mucus was between his lips, and an odd bead of solder on the hinge of his spectacles.' It was beginner's luck, and in future Murry concentrated heavily on the classics.

> He settled *Hoti's* business – let it be! –
> Properly based *Oun* –
> Gave us the doctrine of the enclitic *De*,
> Dead from the waist down.

His reward was glittering. He became a classical Grecian of the third parting, with a scholarship to Brasenose College, Oxford. At the age of twenty-one the cadaverous undergraduate was a virgin, precociously literate, a social *déraciné,* and, according to his tutor, quite inhuman.

In the winter of 1910 Murry came up against the problem of women. It was one he was going to give a lot of attention to for the rest of his life. He had made an excursion to Paris, where he quickly found himself receiving the standard proposition. *'Tu veux coucher avec moi?'* Murry considered the matter gravely: 'I wanted the experience of physical love; but I did not want the experience of venal fornication.' Solemnly he responded, *'Si tu veux boire avec moi, bon, mais coucher, non. Je suis sérieux.'*

Eventually he lost his virginity to Marguéritte, a simple French country girl in a little black velvet hat with a bunch of cherries at her ear. *'Tu es heureux?'* she whispered afterwards. Silence in the darkness. Intuitively she moderated the terms of her enquiry: *'Tu n'es pas triste?'* But Murry was *triste*. He was in love of course: it stood to reason. But he certainly would not want to introduce her to his mother. He was in the grip of Oxonian post-coital blues; he felt 'he had simply collapsed, disgraced the regiment, betrayed the caste into which he had been adopted.' At Easter 1911 he said *au revoir* to Marguéritte for the last time. He hesitated, he agonised, and then he simply cut out. 'I never wrote to her again; nor did I read the letters she wrote to me.' Instead he went to a prostitute in Oxford. 'In about a week I felt downright ill. And then, to my horror, I discovered that I was. I had contracted gonorrhoea.' It was all very disheartening.

The domain of letters suddenly seemed to Murry an altogether safer billet than the domain of life. The first edition of his literary review *Rhythm* came out in the summer of 1911, whilst he was still up at Oxford. 'Both in its purity and its brutality it shall be real,' promised the prospectus, in Caslon type on art-paper. Precisely what success *Rhythm* had in brutalising its subscribers is difficult to gauge. Certainly it led Murry himself to Katherine Mansfield, Frank Harris, Gaudier-Brzeska, D. H. Lawrence, and finally to the bankruptcy courts in Carey Street, where he arrived wearing pepper-and-salt trousers, bowler hat and monocle, and looking for all the world like Bertie Wooster.

On 11 April 1912 Murry moved into Katherine's flat at Clovelly Mansions and nothing was ever quite the same again. Katherine was the woman who would not go away. Successively lover, wife, pen-pal and exasperating invalid, by her death she became a convenient and tractable symbol, his avenue to substantial royalties, and at last a clouded subliminal memory. But did Murry, to begin with, really want to come over this steep place? Katherine explained their conjunction with devastating simplicity: 'I had been the man and he had been the woman.' She certainly harboured no illusions that she could transform Murry into a rogue male. After all, the editorial champion of brutality had by his own admission, 'a very timid, girlish, love-seeking sort of soul.' His liaisons were supersaturated with the emotions he supposed he ought to feel. 'Of the torment of physical passion for its own sake', he reported, 'I know nothing.' His master faculty was 'To caress and yet be a spiritualised rubber glove at a seance, to make love but as though from the Great Beyond.' It was not every girl's cup of tea, but then Katherine Mansfield was not every girl.

Dan Rider's bookshop in St Martin's Lane was the first literary forum where the editor of *Rhythm* was taken half seriously, and here he fell in with Frank Harris, already at fifty-seven the grand old man of British pornography. Small wonder Murry was seduced. Frank Harris in his brown-strapped buckskin shoes with the Cuban heels, his gold watch-chain lying weightily across his Queensberry waistcoat, his Eton tie classically knotted beneath a butterfly collar and pinned by an emerald stud, his wicked straw boater set at the optimum angle of attack, fascinated the attention like a glittering bluebottle. And the man inside the package! The ferocious Kaiser-Bill moustache, the randy bloodshot eye, the 12in. forearms, 14in. biceps, the dangerous mulberry face, the gravel-deep voice, the swart hair erupting from nose and ears and clotted over the low Neanderthal forehead. You could certainly see what he meant when he said, 'Christ goes deeper than I do, but I have a wider experience.'

Murry ached to present Katherine to Frank: it was to be a sweet, a triumphal moment. At last Katherine was persuaded to attend. 'Our talk as we waited for Harris', remembers Hugh Kingsmill, 'was desultory like the talk on the battlements of Elsinore before the arrival of Hamlet's full throated father.' But Murry was not a lucky man; Harris burst apoplectically into Rider's bookshop waving, of all things, the June number of *Rhythm*. Derisively he read out the first three items from the contents list:

> 'Who is the Man?'
> 'Drawing'
> 'The Shirt'

'The Shirt!' he echoed, and crashed the list down with a devastating laugh. 'Drawing of a man in a shirt, eh? By God, Murry, this paper of yours is going to make a stir.'

With this theme of the man in the shirt Harris felt on very familiar ground, but as he developed his Rabelaisian interpretation, calculated to strip the paint from the Forth Bridge, Murry burst into tears and ran out of the shop.

'Good God!' said Harris, dumbfounded.

'He'll kill himself!' prophesied Katherine, and rushed after him.[1]

But Murry did not kill himself, and the July edition duly appeared. 'Who is the Man?' Why, it is Harris himself! And this incidentally is Murry's critical judgment:

> It will always be the truth about Frank Harris which I shall endeavour to declare to the world . . . how Frank Harris is the greatest writer of short-stories England has ever possessed, how 'The Bomb' is one of the greatest novels ever written in the English language . . . how Frank Harris is the greatest creative critic whom the world has known; how he has seen where his greatest predecessors in criticism, Coleridge and Goethe, have had but a half-vision.

Almost immediately afterwards Murry discovered that *The Bomb* was practically a transcript of an actual event in Chicago, and that Harris's story 'An English Saint' had been plagiarised from Stendhal. The honeymoon was over.

Is it not evident that Murry's intellectuality blinkered him? With men of feeling, men of action, he simply collided. He met individuals of unusual stature, he even attracted them, but he retained the friendship of none. And yes, he had a rare propensity for traumatic experiences. Take Gaudier-Brzeska. When Henri Gaudier-Brzeska first submitted his extraordinary drawings to *Rhythm,* Murry, sensing disaster like a keen and eager bird-dog, immediately wrote an invitation. Would the artist care to take supper with him and Mrs Middleton Murry at Clovelly Mansions? With pleasure, came the reply, but might he perhaps bring his sister with him? It was no wonder the *pot au feu* burnt to cinders as confessions were exchanged. Gaudier-Brzeska's name was not Gaudier-Brzeska and his sister was not his sister. He was Henri Gaudier: she was Sophie Brzeska. He was twenty, she was forty and they were in love. Come to that, countered Katherine, she was not Mrs Middleton Murry, she was Mrs Bowden. And she and Murry were lovers. It was all very exhilarating.

Gaudier fairly vibrated with life. He had cruel, alert, finely chiselled features and eyes like Genghis Khan; he seemed a channel for a demonic force. Murry quickly caught 'the image of a panther, crouching to the ground almost one with the earth, sinuous, swift and strong.' Sophie his mistress was small, angular and animated, with elfin eyes and high cheekbones. To begin with it was all roses, roses! Murry thought them a lovely and noble pair: Gaudier undertook to model Murry's head; Katherine gave Gaudier an Indian knife; they talked of going to live on a Pacific island together; Gaudier seized Murry in a grip of steel and hugged and kissed him. Suddenly far away on the edge of Murry's mind 'passed a sort of presentiment that it would need but a little to set him murdering instead of hugging me.'

In the sober light of day Katherine too found reservations. Underneath the elfin charm of Sophie, she sensed something hungry and avid. How true were Katherine's feelings: Sophie Brzeska was indeed 'a woman who was bodily ill and mentally diseased, whose life had been a succession of continual emotional crises; of terrors, intuitions of evil, forebodings of madness, outbursts of rage, meditations of suicide and intimations of her own greatness.'

But, after all, what need for Murry and Katherine to fret? They would soon be far removed from all vexatious London associates; off to live in the gingerbread cottage they had leased at Runcton near Chichester. It was Gaudier who dropped the bombshell: 'Sophie will *live* there – it will do her good. And I shall be able to come every week-end, even if I have to walk.' What could a chap say? Gaudier's elemental enthusiasm, his passionate simplicity, did not allow a man like Murry the least possibility of refusal. Glumly, rebelliously, Katherine spent September cleaning, painting, staining and polishing in preparation to receive the demented Sophie at her cottage; finally she wrote to say that all was ready. Gaudier's reply was bombshell number two. He and Sophie wanted nothing more to do with the traitorous Middleton Murrys.

When it emerged, Gaudier's explanation had an irony worthy of Hardy's pen. 'I met you at a dangerous turning, the brains burned by the recent summer, thirsty for good friendship, only with one drawback: poverty.' It was thirst for good friendship which had made Gaudier set out on a surprise visit to Runcton: it was poverty that made him leave the train half-way. Thirty miles he walked, dusty, hungry, stinking with sweat, carried along by his vision of fellowship at journey's end. Trudging in at the garden gate, he heard Katherine's voice through the window. She felt that Sophie wanted to drag her into a morass, fasten her tentacles round her and suck her dry. Sophie was too violent. Katherine did not, could not, really like her: she pitied her. Without a word the penniless Gaudier turned about, and set off back to London. From now on he became Murry's implacable enemy and bitterest critic: *Rhythm* was full of putrid trash; Murry had no courage, discrimination or honour; he didn't even have the decency to return Gaudier's book of poems by Jehan Rictus. Murry was highly alarmed, but the thin purple book was nowhere to be found. He rushed off a letter suggesting Gaudier buy another copy for which he enclosed the money. Unfortunately Murry forgot to put the postal order into the envelope. Gaudier replied saying that Murry was vile beyond imagination, and Katherine worse.

When Murry moved back to London, doors locked and bolted were not sufficient to keep Gaudier out. In May 1913 he caught up with him. 'I should like to throttle you,' proposed Gaudier, squeezing his hands round an imaginary throat, 'but you're not worth murdering.' So he contented himself with slapping Murry's face. Murry wrote off immediately to Katherine. 'Of course I'm not worth a twopenny damn now . . . all this business simply does for me darling. . . . But it won't last much longer now I've had a good cry.' Back in their studio Gaudier and Sophie performed ritual murder. Murry's head, superbly modelled in hardened clay, was set on two bricks. 'Murry is so small, raise poor Murry up a bit,' crooned Sophie. Bricks were then launched at the target until Murry was resolved into a little heap of greyish dust.

Already, as if blasted by sympathetic magic, Murry's literary foundations had begun to crumble. Charles Hoskin, alias Godwin, alias Charles Granville, alias Henry Charos James, alias Stephen Swift, the slippery publisher of *Rhythm,* went bankrupt. Worse and worse, he had left the £150 printing order in his luckless editor's name. 'It might as well have been four million,' protested Murry. A man with a bowler hat and yellow gloves called round from the printers to give Murry a writ and take his furniture away. Katherine threw her entire allowance into the balance but it was no good. The last edition of *Rhythm* appeared in March 1913; resurrected in May as the *Blue Review* it failed after three issues. His living gone, threatened by Gaudier, harried by the printers, embarrassed by LM, Murry came to feel that his real destiny lay across the Channel.

By December 1913, Murry and Katherine were established in Paris at 31 rue de Tournon. Earning his keep? Why, that would present no difficulty: he would simply review French books for *The Times Literary Supplement.* Murry arranged for Katherine to have private French lessons from his friend Francis Carco, while he settled down to his writing. He submitted a leading article on Stendhal: it was returned. He wrote six critical pieces on 'The Present State of English Letters', but the present state of English letters did not permit their publication. Quickly the little store of capital melted away. In February 1914 a cold day dawned when all Murry's *argent* was *disparu.* Suddenly England seemed the lesser of two evils, had he only the money for the fare. A painful solution occurred to him; he must sell his furniture – it was largely LM's furniture anyway. Unhappily, it being *mardi gras,* the only establishments open for business were the brothels. It was very distressing. With pepper-and-salt trousers and monocle, Murry descended like Orpheus into the underworld, until the glyph LA MAISON EST OUVERTE TOUTE LA NUIT, read backwards through glass doors, was for all time imprinted on his sensitive retina. Back at no. 31, the decrepit concierge had died that same morning. A respectful hush fell upon the house, but the unfortunate Murry, accompanied by miscellaneous brothel-keepers, must clatter his impedimenta down the grim Balzacian stairs, past the scandalised landlady, and out into the carnival streets to the tune *'C'est dégoutant'.*[2]

Within weeks of his return it seemed that Murry might be lost to England yet again. A strange invitation reached him in London: would the distinguished reviewer care to consider a post in St Petersburg in the imperial library of Tsar Nicolas? Murry was tempted and then thought better of it, but the unsung melody is perfectly haunting. It was 1914. Would Murry have met Ouspensky in literary circles at Phillipoff's or the Errant Dog? Surely, surely. Would Katherine, with her enabling question, have found her way to Gurdjieff's Moscow apartment on the Bolshaia Dmitrovka? It is idle to speculate; history took a different course. And, bearing in mind the unfortunate scenes of Murry's flight from Paris, it is some consolation to have been spared the spectacle of his retreat from Moscow.

During the next years two events of comparable gravity brought themselves to Murry's attention: the one was the First World War, and the other was D. H. Lawrence. Murry and Lawrence had first celebrated their discovery of each other in June 1913. Now back from Paris with his tail between his legs, Murry received the benefit of a full Lawrentian analysis. Instinctively Lawrence struck home to the heart of Murry's malaise – it was Katherine. If Murry went on working himself sterile to get her chocolates he made a big mistake; on the contrary the manly thing to do was to take her money to the last penny. Murry raised himself to his full height of 5 ft 8½ in.: 'my code did not allow it,' he said. And he meant it. On 13 July 1914 Lawrence and Emma Maria Frieda Johanna von Richthofen were married in a registry office behind Harrods; and Katherine and Murry were witnesses. Impulsively Frieda gave Katherine the wedding-ring of her former marriage. In this matter of rings, Professor Weekley's[3] loss was John Middleton Murry's gain. He put the ring to good service when he married Katherine four years later; it is buried with her at Fontainebleau.

A splendid year, 1914. D. H. Lawrence got married. Edgar Rice Burroughs wrote *Tarzan of the Apes*. Shackleton pushed off to the Antarctic. Vaughan Williams composed his *Lark Ascending*. Charlie Chaplin starred in *Making a Living*. John Middleton Murry called on H. G. Wells, wearing cuff-links of ginger-beer wire. The consumptive Gavrilio Princip shot Archduke Ferdinand.

And suddenly the *belle époque* was over.

Anyone who had read Bernhardi's *Deutschland und der nächste Krieg* might have guessed a war was coming. Murry had not only read it, he had reviewed it, but the war caught him short. Before he had time to take stock, he found himself caught up in a common enthusiasm; the first night of the First World War he spent outside the French embassy chanting *A bas les Allemands,* and the next day he enlisted in a cyclist battalion at Putney. And then his natural discretion reasserted itself. It was well enough to review Bernhardi; it was well enough to write editorials about brutality: it was quite another thing to balance a bicycle and pedal towards the sound of the guns. Princip had acted at a very inopportune moment: 'just when I was counting on a holiday in Cornwall.' Murry sped to his doctor. His enlistment had been overhasty; his health was not at the moment robust. The medical certificate posted back to the enlistment centre exceeded his wildest expectations. 'It said I had had a severe attack of pleurisy, that I now had a tenacious catarrh, and ended: Query T.B.' Despite the tenacity of his catarrh, Murry breathed again.

Christmas came. Murry and Katherine were at a party where no one, simply no one, could carve the roast sucking-pig. Murry devised a very special dramatic production: Katherine should play herself; he should play himself; and Mark Gertler the painter should play the role of his successor. Katherine entered into her part with tigerish enthusiasm, and so did Gertler. 'I got so drunk that I made violent love to Katherine Mansfield! She returned it, also being drunk.' It would plainly have gone the distance there in the music room in front of everyone if Lawrence hadn't broken it up, shoving Murry aside with passionate severity. Was he blind? How dare he expose himself?

Everyone agreed that Murry was going through an indifferent patch. 'Standing or sitting, his posture was crumpled. He seemed to be bending over himself, as though he were his own mother.' His chief solace was day-dreaming with Lawrence about their mythical island Rananim, to which all would escape from their several miseries. 'Oh, but we are going,' confirmed Lawrence. 'We are going to found an *Order of the Knights of Rananim.* The motto is "Fier" or the Latin equivalent. The badge is so: an eagle, or phoenix argent, rising from a flaming nest of scarlet, on a black background.' Their programme spoke for itself. 'It is communism based, not on poverty but on riches, not on humility but on pride, not on sacrifice but upon complete fulfilment in the flesh of all strong desire, not in Heaven but on earth.' But Katherine punctured the dream, ironically tabling a mass of geographical detail. She, after all, had actually been to a South Sea island. About this time Katherine left the Knights of Rananim for Corporal Francis Carco, her sometime French teacher: history must judge her choice of company. Murry and Lawrence meanwhile found their lives becoming more deeply interfused. It started one raw February evening when Murry turned up at Lawrence's Greatham cottage in the dark. Lawrence took one look at him, briskly diagnosed influenza, took his clothes off, shoved him in bed and went to work. Precisely, Murry said afterwards, like Lilly's treatment of Aaron in *Aaron's Rod*. 'He rubbed every speck of the man's lower body – the abdomen, the buttocks, the thighs and knees.' It was not at all to Murry's taste, but what could a chap do?

Along the western front the young men were dying. On 5 June 1915 Henri Gaudier-Brzeska fell in the bloody battle of Neuville St Vaast. On 7 October Leslie Heron Beauchamp exhaled his final breath at Ploegsteert Wood. At last Murry decided that he too must go to France – to the Riviera. So he went with Katherine down through the enchanted woods to Bandol, to the Villa Pauline with its almond tree, its tiled terrace, its wide view of the sea. This was more like it: here he could concentrate on writing his critique of Dostoevsky. The battle of Verdun sounded literally miles away. Why, in this amber light even Katherine seemed quite embraceable. 'I,' reports Murry, 'who was wont to explore myself with such sick and sensitive fingers, forgot myself entirely.' But escape from the past was not so easily effected. In March 1916 Lawrence discovered two bleak, God-awful cottages at Higher Tregerthen in north Cornwall. 'Really you must have the other place,' he wrote. 'I keep looking at it. I call it . . . Katherine's tower.'

We do not know if Murry's jaw actually dropped with delight at receipt of this summons: we do know that when he arrived in St Ives he bought six chairs at Benny's sale-room and painted them a dull, funereal black. It was indeed a solemn moment. With Murry and Katherine, Lawrence and Frieda all in one company, the high ideals of Rananim were about to be put to the proof. A queer – one might almost say Dostoevskian – current electrified them. Desperately Murry bargained with Lawrence. 'If I love you, and you know I love you, isn't that enough?' It was not enough. Lawrence required 'some inviolable sacrament between us – some pre-Christian blood-rite in keeping with the primeval rocks about us.' But Murry didn't want a primeval blood-rite, and he didn't want any massage either. Meeting this resistance, the high-voltage charge in Lawrence short-circuited and earthed itself in Frieda. One evening the Murrys' door burst open to admit the child of Baron von Richthofen in exuberant flight. 'He'll kill me!' she screamed. 'I'll *kill* her!' confirmed Lawrence in white-hot pursuit. It was a view to which Murry, sitting on his black chair, subscribed. 'That he would have killed, her, I made no doubt. . . . I had no impulse to intervene.' By night, Lawrence lay moaning in delirium. Murry was 'an obscene bug that was sucking his life away.'

At this critical moment an emissary from Lord Kitchener arrived unexpectedly to present his credentials at the court of Rananim. Katherine records the incident with quiet fatalism. 'A policeman came to arrest Murry the other day, and though Murry staved him off he will have to go I think.' Go he did; but not towards the bugle's call. The enlisted bicyclist of the Middlesex Regiment mounted his machine and made tracks for the dovecots of south Cornwall. What really hurt was the break with Lawrence. 'I . . . pedalled off, with the feeling that I had said goodbye to him for ever.' But Cornwall could not furnish perpetual sanctuary. Summoned to Bodmin for medical examination, and warned he could be conscripted as a navvy, building breakwaters at Aden, Murry was brought to a desperate and brilliant expedient: he went to ground in the War Office itself. The corridors of Watergate House were certainly drier than the trenches, but they proved a dismal anti-climax after Higher Tregerthen. 'I was obsessed for days with the notion of climbing on to the plinth of one of the lions in Trafalgar Square and shooting myself as a protest against the horror.' It was an obsession he succeeded in overcoming. Meanwhile he cut a dubious figure in department M17: he was an undischarged bankrupt and his facial expression suggested he was about to be hanged. Often he felt pretty rum. 'My wrists seemed to have turned to damp string and my knees to water.' He gave every scrap of attention he could to the hostilities, consistent with writing *Cinnamon and Angelica,* his verse play about fairies. Scarcely surprising that he was reported as a security risk, but quite unjust. Indeed there is something almost stoical in Murry's stance: cut-off, out-gunned, reeling under a barrage of vexatious memoranda, he fought the Great War to the last drop of his ink.

With Armistice Day there arrived a moment of general stock-taking. Rupert Brooke was dead. Julian Grenfell dead. Wilfred Owen dead. H. H. Munro dead. T. E. Hulme dead. Siegfried Sassoon shot through the lung. Robert Graves hit by 8 in. shell fragments. Gaudier-Brzeska blown to kingdom come. The authorities pondered: the sacrifices of so many young men of literature must perforce receive recognition. A happy thought struck them. Was not there actually some censor chappie down in the War Office who scribbled a bit about condiments in his spare time? In due course John Middleton Murry was awarded the OBE.

The First World War was over, but a new and microcosmic struggle had already begun; it was one in which Murry would find honours less facilely won. By 1918 Katherine Mansfield had recognised her mortal wound of pulmonary tuberculosis. In the circumstances, Murry, his handkerchief to his lips, took no joy in the little ceremony at South Kensington registry office. The marriage to him 'was only part of the nightmare.' Katherine's best, her only, hope lay in entering a sanatorium. The doctors all said so. 'Do *you* want me to go?' she asked Murry. He said he did not. Both of them turned the situation upside-down: to enter a sanatorium would kill her; to stay out would get her well. 'There was no escape,' writes Murry. 'We were trapped. And I was caught in a web of strange and subtle falsity.' Katherine's hundreds upon hundreds of letters to Murry are susceptible of many interpretations, but by their very existence one thing stands clear: Murry's basic and all too human response was to distance himself. He consented, with an almost indecent haste, to her removal. A sanatorium might not be quite the thing, but it would do her good to travel. 'She was by nature homeless and vagrant.' When they had been together, her cough had irritated him. With distance between them, he could handle her fatal illness as an intriguing abstraction: it was a symbol of universal suffering; it was part of a necessary educative experience. It was anything in fact but his wife dying, a vital young woman struggling for air. It became part of his credo that she could not live; 'at the bottom of my heart lay always the black, cold stone of unfaith.' He was devastated, naturally. It was a tragic, tragic business, the final confirmation of his terrible luck. As he consoled himself with other women, Murry scientifically noted down some gratifying side-effects. 'Nothing more powerfully prepares a man's instinctive and unconscious nature for passionate love than prolonged contact with hopeless illness in a loved one.'

Things were bad of course. Very bad. But he must not grumble. He must simply stick it out.

Notes

1. My recapitulation of the affair in Dan Rider's bookshop derives from Hugh Kingsmill's lively work, *Frank Harris* (Jonathan Cape 1932).
2. Here I am heavily indebted to Murry's own vivid account in *Between Two Worlds*.
3. Ernest Weekley (1875–7 May 1954), husband of Frieda for fourteen years and father of her three children. English etymologist on the staff of the University of Nottingham for forty years. According to Aldous Huxley 'possibly the dullest Professor in the Western Hemisphere.'

1 Gurdjieff's Institute for the Harmonious Development of Man programme design 1923

2 George Ivanovitch Gurdjieff
13 January 1924

3 Katherine Mansfield *c.* 1921

4 John Middleton Murry
   an unfortunate

5 LM the 'perfect friend'

6 Piotr Demianovich Ouspensky
'a very fine man'

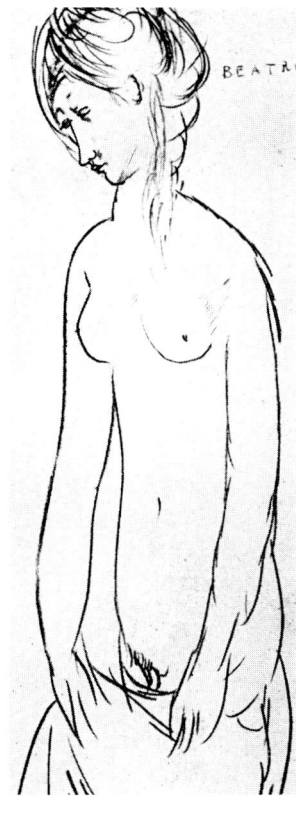

7a Beatrice Hastings
mistress of Orage but not
of herself

7b Alfred Richard Orage
who touched many lives

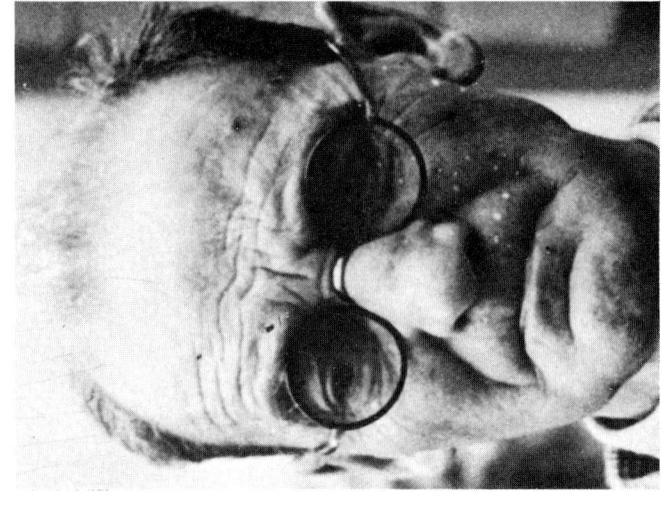

8b 'We have no illusions'
John Middleton Murry

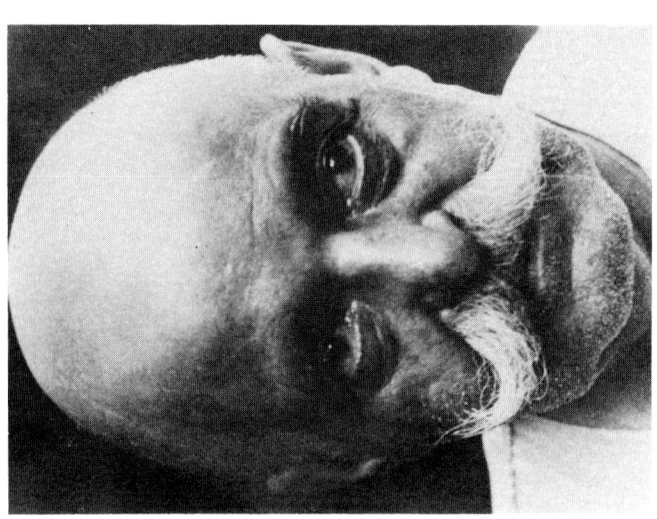

8a *Beelzebub*'s author

Chapter 7

Alfred Richard Orage

If you have tears, prepare to shed them now, for there is something satisfyingly Dickensian about the beginnings of Alfred Richard Orage. His father, William, fecklessly drank and gambled away his little farm in Cambridgeshire; retreated in poor order to the village of Dacre in Yorkshire; took up schoolmastering; sired young Alfred – born on 22 January 1873 – and, as if drained by this final call on his dissipated energies, died at about the age of forty. Mrs Orage – Sarah Ann McQuire that was – brought her four children home to Fenstanton on the old straight Roman road that runs from Huntingdon to Cambridge. Here in the parish where the rude forefathers of the Orages slept, she and her family could all manage well enough, for poor William had left an annuity of fifty pounds. Alas! The firm of lawyers entrusted with the capital failed, and payment with it. Mrs Orage squared her shoulders. Somehow, by taking in washing, she reared up the new generation: Florence and William and Edith and little Dickie. They were all decently, grindingly poor. They lived in a world without options, and when Alfred Richard was ten, he was sent to be a farm labourer. But here fate intervened in the shape of Howard Coote, son of the local squire. 'I at once saw my father and the schoolmaster, and we agreed that it was a thousand pities to try to make a ploughboy of Alfred.' Accordingly Coote paid the tearful Mrs Orage a peppercorn allowance to keep the child at school, and thus the talents of A. R. Orage, the man whom T. S.

Eliot would later describe as 'the best literary critic of that time in London', were permitted to flower. Coote was happy, Mrs Orage was happy, the world was happy. God bless us all, said Tiny Tim.

So Orage makes his debut as a meritocrat. All his life he had a nose for excellence in others and a drive to excel himself. At school he was quickly debarred from competition *pour encourager les autres,* special reserved prizes being instituted for him. Although a fall from a haycart snapped his thigh-bone, he recovered to become a formidable runner. He haunted Coote's private library and somehow ingested unlikely gobbets of Ruskin, Matthew Arnold, Carlyle, Morris and Herbert Spencer. In the cottage, by candle-light, he read *The Arabian Nights.* At the vicarage he grappled with French lessons. He walked the ten miles each way to Cambridge to study at art college, and here, like a mirage, he glimpsed the shimmering, beckoning university world he was never to enter. Soon the village school saw him in the progressed role of pupil-teacher, and he had at last the satisfaction of contributing to the family budget. In 1892 Coote sent him for a year's teacher training at Culham College, near Abingdon, and while here he fell precipitately in love with two London girls.

The young Orage had in fact dashed down to the capital to pursue the first of his quarries, and immediately committed himself to another – her friend Jean Walker, a promising Scottish student at the Royal College of Art. With Jean stuck exasperatingly in London, Orage ground his teeth a little as he took up his first post in a Leeds Board elementary school. His first term drew to its close. The year 1893 was dying, and so was Mrs Sarah Orage, her energies eroded away by a lifetime's uncertainties and drudgery. Christmas came to Fenstanton, and the four children stood at the graveside of their washerwoman mother. The family were still in black when Orage returned again at Easter, but now the leaves were green on the trees and Orage wore a flame-red tie. What precisely did that tie mean to Orage? We cannot be sure, but we know what it meant to Squire Coote. It meant socialism, Keir Hardie, red revolution. It meant ingratitude.

Orage was twenty-one and he had indeed become a socialist. Quick! Let it be quickly said that nothing around today bears much resemblance to socialism of the 1890s. Orage himself remembered it with wry affection as, a cult, with affiliations in directions now quite disowned – with theosophy, art and crafts, vegetarianism, the 'simple life', and almost, one might say, with the musical glasses. Morris had shed a medieval glamour over it with his stained-glass *News from Nowhere*. . . . And Bernard Shaw . . . had hung it with innumerable jingling epigrammatic bells – and cap. . . . I added a good practical knowledge of working classes . . . and an idealism fed at the source – namely Plato.

The revolutionary shibboleths of liberty, egality and fraternity took on rather special meanings in Orage's mouth. The world was swarming with people rampant to burst social constraints but, as Chesterton discerned, Orage was 'emancipated from emancipation'. From the beginning his priority was an inner liberty. Egalitarianism, the very kernel of theoretical socialism, played precisely no part in Orage's scheme of things. He advocated, 'the Hierarchy . . . the classification of children, schools, institutions, yes the whole State, in the ancient Platonic way of iron and brass and silver and gold.' Orage was no brave-new-world man: he was a golden-age man, steeped in Plato and the *Mahabharata*. 'To go back is to go forward,' he wrote. He was indeed to prove a brother to many struggling writers, but his fraternity was crowned by his natural aristocracy. Altogether A. R. Orage was a pretty rum sort of socialist.

Regularly now he wrote to Jean Walker; regularly she replied. He proposed; she accepted. But did the disgruntled Coote accept? It was a very good question. He, after all, was Orage's benefactor of the past and still the fount of his hopes for the future. Coote did not, could not, accept. All the world knew that a protégé subverted by socialism is downright ruined by a premature and injudicious marriage. But Orage had the bit between his teeth and in 1896 he married anyway; and his vision of the dreaming spires of Oxford faded and resolved into a five-shilling-a-week cottage at the end of Ingle Row. There were big sunflowers in the garden, 'and the walls of the interior were decently covered in brown paper.' Orage had settled for a young wife and a start on his journey. As he said himself in after years, *'Ce sont les premier pas qui Coote.'*

No children appeared, to play in the sunflowers. The young couple fed their interest in theosophical and mystical literature. Already Orage had leapt into the river of ideas and was swimming madly against the stream. He cultivated his natural gifts for public speaking and for setting the cat amongst the pigeons: he urged the merits of Plato, from Theosophical Society platforms, while at Leeds Plato Group he dwelt infuriatingly on the insights of the *Mahabharata*. He visited Bradford, where incongruously the Hermetic Order of the Golden Dawn had a temple. Few who listened to Orage could have guessed the hit-or-miss character of his early religious experience at Fenstanton. All he could remember was 'booing through the keyhole of a Methodist meeting in which a revivalist was singing "Where is my wandering boy tonight?" '

In 1900 two young men met in Walker's bookshop in Briggate. The one was Orage; the other was Holbrook Jackson, a Fabian socialist in theory and a capitalist lace merchant in practice. Orage lent Jackson the *Bhagavad Gita* and Jackson lent Orage Nietzsche's *Thus Spake Zarathustra*. 'Next morning,' recalls Jackson, 'he walked from his cottage at Chapel Allerton to mine at Headingly with a new light in his eye. He had spent the night with *Zarathustra,* and the time for action had come – and the Leeds Art Club was born.' The ideas of Nietzsche struck Orage with the force of a revelation. 'We . . . developed supermania,' confesses Jackson. 'He wanted a Nietzsche circle in which Plato and Blavatsky, Fabianism and Hinduism, Shaw and Wells and Edward Carpenter should be blended, with Nietzsche as the catalytic. An exciting brew.' The surprising thing is not that the Leeds Art Club should be founded, in this flush of enthusiasm, but that it throve; that it could attract Yeats and Chesterton and George Bernard Shaw to lecture. What was the secret? Jackson is generous in his analysis. 'The attraction was ultimately Orage, not Plato, or Nietzsche, or Blavatsky, or whatever it might be at a particular moment.'

Eulogies are somehow self-defeating. Orage would be no less interesting if he had been an ill-favoured dog in the manger; in fact there seems an almost embarrassing consensus about his charisma. To begin with he had 'an intellect with a cutting edge that went through pretensions like butter.' Jacob Epstein attests that, 'Orage was a man of extraordinary mental vigour. He had a magnetic personality.' The Nietzschean Ludovici recalls an 'intellectuality that radiated from every part of his being, particularly of course his eyes.' But if we are really talking about magnetism and radiation, 'intellectuality' is perhaps not quite the right word; Jackson found a better, 'you were conscious of his aura; you felt his presence so much that you forgot details.' Bechhofer-Roberts remarked his effortless control: 'Every one of his gestures was graceful; in all the years I was to know him, I never saw him do or say anything gauche.' Selver summed it up this way: 'I can avouch that whenever Orage made his appearance, wizardry came into action. The Orage magic was no mere legend.'

And physically? Physically Orage was tall, well-knit, lithe, dark-haired. His hat was of soft felt; his boots were patched even on the uppers.

> He wore a plain hand-woven silk tie, sometimes blue, but oftener an orange or flame colour. His hair was straight and worn short except for a long tuft which sometimes strayed over his forehead. His eyes were hazel, lively, and challenging, and in moments of excitement they seemed to emit a red glint. It was a feline face and there was something cat-like in his movements.

If men found Orage a compelling figure, 'women in his presence were liable to develop what Marchbanks in *Candida* calls "Prossy's complaint" '. Orage on Nietzsche was particularly devastating.

> His gospel, always preached with his tongue in his cheek, that every man and woman should do precisely what he or she desires, acted like heady wine on the gasping and enthusiastic young ladies who used to sit in rows worshipping him. They wanted to do all kinds of terrible things.

And yet when challenged to uncover their thoughts, they were strangely reticent.

'At least,' said one elegant beauty, dropping her eyes, 'I have always tried to do my duty.'

'What a pity,' smiled the lecturer. Perhaps some of the women threw themselves at Orage, and perhaps he did not object that much. The circumstantial evidence is strong. Jackson ran into him unexpectedly on Whitby beach and found him burning poems and love letters; not the odd, isolated letter – Orage had a bonfire going. All in all, it was not surprising that Jean Orage consoled herself increasingly with Jackson.

Why did Orage come south? It was not just that his marriage was on the rocks. It was not simply that a Leeds Board elementary school wore any man's idealism pretty thin. It was not just that he earned less than a bricklayer; that Jackson got more in half a week than

Orage in two months. No, it was more a sense of destiny; the exasperation of a virtuoso whose stage has become too cramped. On 29 November 1905 Orage stayed at Harrogate. In the visitors' book, under the heading *Where to?* he wrote 'God only knows!' But again fate was about to intervene. 'A coal merchant of Pudsey, a Mr Joseph Smith of blessed memory, gave him £60 with which to begin a new life.' Orage did not hesitate: he caught the London train. His only luggage was his three-volume translation of Nietzsche. It was fortunate for her that poor Jean Orage had her needle. She fades genteelly from the scene, stitching away in William Morris's firm of decorators and revolving in theosophical circles.

Orage was thirty-three when he came to London. The case was altered with him now: he was out of work for the first time in twelve years; single for the first time in nine. Living precariously at Hammersmith, eating in Express Dairies and ABCs, embarrassingly dependent on the charity of his friends, Orage was busy revaluing his values. Now he was equally in revolt against high-Victorian scientism and theosophy; equally dismissive of 'every pat little complacent scientific description of man' and of the 'rigmarole and abracadabras' of occultism. People who identified with these were 'caught and devoured people'. But how not to be caught and devoured? Already he had one clue. 'We decline into animal consciousness, when we are not observing ourselves.' But this merely regressed the question. How to obtain a capacity to observe oneself? Simply to wish it was not enough. Orage himself had given seven years to the study of Nietzsche; by now he had even written two books on him, but his personal Nietzschean discovery was chastening, 'Do what you will and you will find out how little you *can* will.'

Now Orage's life was to be revolutionised by two bizarrely contrasting individuals he encountered in theosophical circles. The first was Dr Wallace – Dr Lewis* Alexander Richard Wallace – a Scot with 'white silky hair, a drooping moustache to match, a rosy face and a general air of self-depreciation, no matter whom he was talking to'. The second was Mrs Beatrice Hastings, brown-eyed, dark-haired, vivacious, amoral, venomously articulate, 'capable of singing in all registers, at times high soprano, at others mezzo, tenor, baritone and even bass, an indomitable brawler and fire eater'. Both

---

*pronounced Louey

persons felt a certain urgency. Dr Wallace had time to make up for long, lonely years sheep-farming in New Zealand. His point was this: sheep had provided him with ample, more than ample, funds, but not perhaps – he did not wish to dogmatise – with companionship at his own intellectual level. Mrs Hastings, 'married to a pugilist but no longer availing herself of his protection', wanted some action. Dr Wallace sought a magical son: Beatrice Hastings a demon lover. Alfred Richard Orage, his aura positively radio-active with understanding, seemed almost too good to be true.

Unexpectedly, Holbrook Jackson, with a final dismissive reference to the 'yoga-stricken mugwumps of Leeds' moved south to London and was cordially received by Orage. One day the literary grapevine brought the two friends exhilarating news. A moribund journal, the *New Age,* was up for sale. The printer had been patience itself but he could stand no more. The prize for anyone who could foot his long-outstanding bill was instant proprietorship, instant editorship. Jackson sprinted for funds to George Bernard Shaw but the great man demurred. 'Raid the City first,' he said: disingenuous advice, for the two provincials carried precisely no clout in the City. Suddenly Orage had an inspired thought. Dr Wallace! Was not Lewis Wallace now somehow connected with merchant banking? Dr Wallace was approached. Why yes, he would be felicitated to assist Orage; if he could help somebody as he went along . . . and perhaps – he did not wish to push himself forward – a few of his own little pieces in the magazine? He volunteered the first £500. Now Shaw, with a keen sense of having been outflanked, also surrendered up £500 – initial royalties from *The Doctor's Dilemma.* Shaw's letter and Wallace's arrived by the same post at the little room in Nassau Street shared by Orage and Jackson. Yesterday they were unemployed, provincial nobodies: today they had £1,000 and were proprietors and editors of an established London journal.

When Orage and Jackson's first edition appeared on 2 May 1907, the *Fabian News* announced the birth of a new socialist journal to be run 'strictly on Fabian lines.' Fabian lines! Orage had a wider conception – visionary, evolutionary. Here was a man who spoke of 'pentecostal art', who wished 'that literature may become, as once it was, the handmaid of the Spirit sacramental in its nature, and divinely illumining for the darkling sight of men.' This was idealistic stuff. But it wasn't Fabian; it wasn't commercial; and it didn't suit Jackson one little bit. After a few months the two men parted amicably. In January 1908 a fresh order went out to the printer: pale orange octavo letter-paper headed, 'The NEW AGE, A Weekly Review of Politics, Literature & Art. Editor & Managing Director: A. R. Orage.' The 'desperado of genius' had arrived.

More than 15,000 *New Age* pages he was to edit between 1907 and 1922. Who were his contributors? Well, there were over 700 of them, and they were not pigmies either. With the touch of a Machiavelli, Orage quickly provoked and fomented a first-class literary row. 'Bernard Shaw and Belford Bax, the "Shaw-Bax", lammed into G. K. Chesterton and Hilaire Belloc, the "Chester-Belloc".' For issue after issue the two monsters roared and grappled through the columns of the *New Age*. ('Poor old Shaw,' said Beatrice epigrammatically, 'his trouble is his brains have gone to his head.') Grand, grand names were to follow. And while the *New Age* wrestled its way upward, thirty or more rival periodicals, many better connected and flusher with capital, went down the drain – among them Middleton Murry's *Rhythm, Blue Review* and *Signature*.

Contributors sometimes alluded to the *New Age* as the *No Wage*. Orage was a man of principle, and one of his principles was not to pay. On the contrary, it became a standing joke that each contributor should remit him five guineas per article.

'Did so-and-so pay yet?'

'I must write for it,' Orage would answer.

Boiled right down, he just did not have the wherewithal. Price a few pennies, a four-figure circulation and no advertisements was hardly a money-spinning formula. Fortunately Lewis Wallace kept the printer at bay with a monthly cheque of £100. He felt it was the least he could do. Clearly the editor with his patched boots was not salting away anything himself: what he got 'wouldn't pay the average stockbroker's annual cigar bill.' And if someone was really in need, Orage showed another side. 'At any rate, he did more to feed me,' said Ezra Pound, 'than anyone else in England. . . . Orage's 4 guineas a month . . . wuz the SINEWS, by gob the sinooz.'

So if Orage did not bait his hook with guineas, just how did he land the big literary fish? It had to do with freedom of expression. If an articulate man came to Orage and 'the ginger was hot in his mouth' he was allowed *carte blanche*. 'During twelve years' association with the *New Age*,' one contributor reflected, 'I doubt if even a comma was altered.' Orage gave people and ideas the benefit of the doubt; he 'was something of a mystery man in Fleet Street, where hardly anyone believes what they write.' Orage could believe three impossible things before breakfast; he did it from policy. 'The graveyards overflow with editors who could not bring themselves to believe the unbelievable.' If the *New Age* at times carried provocative, even crack-brained material, not least the effusions of Dr Wallace, it was tilting at something no less absurd: the received opinions of Edwardian England. Orage made his writers feel part of a grand cultural transformation. 'You cannot appraise a revolution in guineas.' It was inevitable that Orage's editorial reputation should march with his reputation for inconsistency. But he kept a philosophic touchstone. 'Through all his mutations he was true to one master – Socrates.'

And if Orage did grow a little like Socrates, certainly Beatrice Hastings was type-cast for the role of Xanthippe. By 1907, when she took up with Orage, she was twenty-eight and very bad news; a burning man-eater in the forests of the night. What the hammer? What the chain? In what furnace was thy brain? Did the electricity actually crackle, anode to cathode, between her and Orage? And in dark hotel rooms, posing as brother and sister, what recriminations, what dreams, what slow beginnings, what seismic climaxes? On 30 November 1907 the *New Age* carried her very first contribution: an unsigned review of Orage's *Nietzsche in Outline and Aphorism*. Soon the trickle became a torrent. She wrote frenetically, cruelly, brilliantly, week by week, two or three pieces in every issue. Who was Cynicus? Who was Robert à Field? Who was G. Whiz? Who was writing those vitriolic pieces on poetry, women's rights and Christianity? Who was Orage's editorial assistant and scarlet woman? A single answer: Beatrice Hastings! Nor did Orage himself escape her contempt. 'Until I came in, the "New Age" editorially, was a *rag*.'

By February 1910 Orage had welcomed Katherine Mansfield into the tiny dog-box *New Age* office, with its battered roll-top desk, cartoon-draped walls, its coat hooks, its files; 'the whole seeming to occupy rather more than all the available space.' Orage was thirty-seven, Beatrice thirty-one and Katherine twenty-one. Across the years one senses their instant shock of recognition and attraction. Orage and Katherine were both provincials, dissatisfied, fiercely ambitious, searching for meaning. As to the girls, their *élan* was equal and their writing styles superficially alike; in appearance they were almost congruent, could even be mistaken for each other. Both were sexually ambivalent, and between them they could take any man apart.

For a time their three lives seemed to coalesce. Beatrice and Katherine collaborated in several acidic pieces in the *New Age,* including parodies of their elders and betters. They could be seen together at Orage's improvised literary salon in the basement of the Chancery Lane ABC. And what was graver, they were observed together using cigarettes. For better or worse, Orage and Beatrice launched Katherine into the literary *demi-monde*; they stood at her sick-bed in Rottingdean; swept her off for intimate week-ends at Pease Pottage, near Crawley; helped her find the flat at Cheyne Walk. And in 1911, when Katherine became pregnant, who monitored her abortion? LM, for one, had no doubt: 'it had all been horrible. I am sure that Beatrice Hastings had been in some way responsible.' History unfortunately leaves us no record of any four-handed conversation by Orage, Beatrice, Katherine and that good grey goose Dr Wallace. Assuming they ever stood at a general rendezvous, what would they have talked about? If occultism was the highest common factor, New Zealand wool seems the lowest common denominator. Katherine haled from Wellington, Beatrice was the daughter of a Hackney wool dealer, and sharp necessity had driven Dr Wallace out to the sheep more times than he cared to remember. And Orage? Well, Orage could illumine the woolliest subject; he 'was the only real *causeur* in London.'

Katherine and Orage made an excellent beginning, but in the literary laboratory sweetness and light are highly unstable elements. Already by 1912 John Middleton Murry was the coming man in Katherine's life. The spring number of *Rhythm,* carrying two of her poems and 'The Woman at the Store', seemed plain talk at the *New Age*. Their friend and protégé Katherine had changed colours. Orage may have pursed his lips, but it was surely Beatrice who wrote the anonymous *New Age* review on 28 March: K. Mansfield's story showed 'no single relief of wisdom or of wit, unless the interspersed portraits of an animal and a stout, nude lady with a jet-black triangle for her nose are expressly meant to instruct and charm the reader.' The young Ruth Pitter – delicately negotiating a floor peppered with beads – learned from an embarrassed Orage that Beatrice and Katherine had gone a round or two with heavy necklaces.

Whether it was Katherine's abrupt about-face or Beatrice's

acerbity, one has the impression that Orage at this point was a bit jaundiced about women generally. Using his favourite pen-name 'R. H. Congreve' he offered *New Age* readers six 'Tales for Men only', cautionary fables about artists going under love's yoke. The poet is warned, 'From mythopoeia you will descend to symbolism, and if that is too obscure for the girl, down you will go to valentines.' Female pretensions in decor are wickedly satirised:

> There was a piano and a host of divans. Oh, divans, I thought. Divans! What a lollipop life we are in for! Turkish delight, scented cigarettes, lotusland, minor poetry, spooks – and where is the guitar? There, as I live, hanging behind the door!

The author of this male chauvinist outburst was suffering from a bad case of Beatrice-fatigue. 'Once in 1912', complains Mrs Hastings bitterly, 'he lay for three weeks in bed, nothing the matter but "flop".' Such a performance was quite unacceptable. Mrs Hastings attacked Orage in his own journal. She remarked with bitterness the 'kind of a wobbly I had as companion.' Later she reported what a rotten writer he was even when he stood up; 'what a flat, ponderous, stilted, maundering, when not coy, conceited and facetious, when not plagiaristic or outright thievish "literary" pen he had.' And another thing: his duplicity! Beneath the quotidian mask – the sophisticated, charismatic, sympathetic Orage, whom just about everybody appreciated – Beatrice had detected 'a rustic, a lout, a snob.' Her former idol was teetering, and in 1914 'humpty crashed entirely.' Beatrice grandly plucked up her skirts and made for France. 'I had wealthy relatives, was often travelling and always occupied and insatiable after new studies.' On the train to Paris she was honoured by the attentions of a French soldier, 'the very tulip of his regiment.'

So Mrs Hastings finally terminated a companionship which, if her 'memories of their past lives might be believed, had lasted through the centuries.' We have only Beatrice's account of how Orage took it. 'He wrote me . . . to Paris the craziest letter, informing me that he was Yudisthira, the god of justice, and that I was Rama in the form of a Harlot.' Who knows? Perhaps Beatrice had indeed bombed Orage temporarily out of his mind, and the characterisation is not bad anyway.

It was now that Orage made a significant encounter. 'I was already beginning to be disillusioned with the purely literary and cultural life when I met Ouspensky.' In 1913 a certain Madame Pogossky had translated into English Ouspensky's *The Symbolism of the Tarot,* and in this year a spirited Orage–Ouspensky correspondence began. That the two men met in London in 1913 is beyond doubt, but where precisely? In Cursitor Street, close-cabined, sniffing the printer's ink of the *New Age* presses? At the Sceptre perhaps, or the Chinese restaurant in Piccadilly Circus? Or did they shake hands across Russian *objets d'art* in Madame Pogossky's Bond Street shop? Or smile over a sixpenny *mazagran* in the Domino Room at the Café Royal, where 'Orage officiated with an unfailing sleight of mind as chairman of his skewbald witenagemot.'

We do not know.

Both men were intellectuals, both journalists, both responsive to Nietzsche and the *Mahabharata,* both were in search of the miraculous and both had attempted 'the perilous system of developing psychic powers by regulating the breath out of its natural rhythm.' But Orage confessed a difference. He had imbibed his theosophy in the arch-preposterous setting of Leeds; Ouspensky was outward bound for Egypt, Ceylon and India. When his ship sailed, an unlikely go-between sustained contact between the two principals: a fattish, red-faced, Russian-speaking youngster, complete with umlaut and a flair for writing facetious lampoons. This was Carl Bechhofer, a particular protégé of Orage, who subsequently took up with Ouspensky in Petrograd at the beginning of the war. So the Orage–Ouspensky connection was made and reinforced. It was soon to change the Englishman's entire orientation and to save the Russian's life.

But these episodes lay in the future. Meanwhile in Paris Beatrice Hastings had wasted no time. Working from two divans at 13 rue Norvins on the Butte Montmartre, the *'poétesse anglaise'* had conjured up a most distinguished replacement for Orage – by name Modigliani. The unfortunate painter, generally blind drunk and in direst terror of Beatrice, fled 'the monster' unsuccessfully up and down his attenuated world. Occasionally when she cornered him there were terrible *'scènes avec des revolvers et des bouteilles de rhum.'* Today the detritus of their madcap relationship is in art collections. Naked, nubile, high-breasted, the vixen-mistress of Orage is snared for ever in the sinuous line of gamekeeper Modigliani. Beatrice Hastings has joined the immortals. In the spring of 1915, while established in Francis Carco's flat at the Quai aux Fleurs, Katherine Mansfield re-entered Beatrice's world with gusto. 'At B.'s this afternoon', she reported to the discarded Murry, 'there arrived "du monde" including a very lovely young woman, married, and *curious* – blonde – passionate. We danced together. . . . I enjoyed it in a way, but B. was very impossible – she must have drunk nearly a bottle of brandy.' Katherine refused to spend the night with 'Biggy B', and everything ended in the predictable row. Beatrice bawled out that Katherine was a *femme publique*, and 'we parted for life again.' But not before Katherine had caught some of Mrs Hastings' fierce animus against male editors. 'Orage wants kicking, of course,' she wrote.

Early in 1916 Orage further exasperated his former mistress: writing pseudonymously in the *New Age*, he began to serialise a curious autobiographical novel entitled *A Seventh Tale for Men Only*. Orage figured as Doran, Beatrice as the girl 'who looked as though she had been brought up in moonlight', and there was a blow-by-blow account of their parting. Far more interesting however is Doran's triple resolution: 'to understand human life at all costs to his feelings, his tastes and his predilections; to avoid no society and to seek none; to accept the first guide that offered itself.'

About this time two dubious guides – as satisfyingly contrasted as Don Quixote and Sancho Panza – did indeed present themselves. Quixote's analogue was Dmitri Mitrinovic, 'a tall, dark, bullet-headed Serbian with the lips of a Roman soldier and an erratic, soaring mind.' Panza was represented by Major Clifford Hugh Douglas, RAF (Reserve), MIMechE. An obsessive ballroom dancer, the major in full evening dress had an uncanny resemblance to a penguin. 'He was squat and bald, with a foghorn voice, and somewhat Jewish in appearance. This detail imparted a burlesque irony to his brainless anti-Semitism.' Mitrinovic, an attaché at the Serbian embassy, had an apocalyptic, supernal vision of geo-politics as the evolution of the Universal Man. It was simple as pie, if you could set your teeth in it. 'The ultimate Aryan glory will consist in the Aryanisation of pan-humanity and the pan-humanisation of Aryandom. The English essence is the universal solvent.' Major Douglas, sometime manager of the British Westinghouse Company, had an economic theory to end all economic theories – Social Credit.[1] Unhappily, 'Douglas's ideas were so unique and his prose style so anfractuous that even those few who did understand what he meant must have been convinced that they did not.' It has been said that when Douglas was present there was little chance for anyone else to get a word in. This is to put it mildly. Major Douglas, formerly of the Royal Flying Corps, favoured saturation bombing, reducing the civilian population by the awesome tonnage of his paragraphs. Mitrinovic, with his shaved head, hypnotic eyes and two quarts of bottled beer in the pockets of his soiled frock-coat, said very little. He did not have to. 'Hardly had I shaken hands with Mitrinovic than I found myself so affected by his mere presence that I nearly lost consciousness.' When Mitrinovic did speak it was as if through a mouthful of plum pudding. 'All-bion,' he would mumble guardedly, 'Word of Mystery, Name of Strength.' With enough bottled beer inside him, he was noted for his zestful imitation of the Serbian bagpipes.[2]

For all his spectacular faults, Major Douglas was a man with a burning idea; and because the war was about empire, and empire about resources, because money was a universal constant, Orage championed Social Credit. 'Douglas and Orage *worked* for peace,' said Ezra Pound, 'whereas dozens of soupeaters merely yodel about it in hope of ha'pence.' Orage stood like some great sergeant at the bar, defending a difficult and intractable case; the advocacy fascinated but depleted him. Between 'national dividends' and 'monetary facsimiles' he ground himself down. And the world went on, and the carnage went on, and no one listened.

Orage was forty-five when the last shot was fired. 'The Great War', he wrote, 'put an end to many things and many ideas. . . . We woke from the evil dream shortly after the armistice; and in the horrible light of morning we began to count our losses.' He had watched the *belle époque* vanish; the young men go into the dark. After more than ten years as the editor of a prominent intellectual review, he knew all the fashionable ideas, the fashionable thinkers, the stories behind the stories. He knew them and was weary of them, fed to the back teeth with the literature of politics and the politics of literature. Where did all that really lead? To 'mad houses, lock-hospitals and ugly accidents.' As for himself, he might indeed be the chockstone in an elaborate edifice of lives, yet his marriage had broken, his mistress was gone, and he had no children. As his crisis deepened, one long-cherished ideal sustained him. 'He was convinced that there was a secret knowledge behind the knowledge given to the famous prophets and philosophers, and for the acquisition of that knowledge and the intellectual and spiritual power it would bring with it he was prepared to sacrifice everything and take upon him any labour, no matter how humble or wearisome or abstruse.'

His hour was coming.

Notes

1   Major C. H. Douglas's first article on Social Credit appeared in the *NA* on 2 January 1919 but Professor Wallace Martin (see *NAUO* 270) dates his alliance with Orage nearly a year earlier. A serious assessment of Douglas and Social Credit is quite inappropriate here. Put at its simplest, Douglas proposed that money should be related not to gold, but to the productive capacity of industry; and issued in quantities sufficient to enable the public to consume all consumable goods produced. It was a theory which successively captured the enthusiasms of Orage and Ezra Pound; and, piquantly enough, is today (1980) much in vogue in Katherine Mansfield's New Zealand. The death of Orage on 5 November 1934 robbed the British Social Credit Party of its only advocate of real intellectual stature and it quickly degenerated into a bizarre activism. On May Day 1938 Social Creditors burned Montague Norman in effigy; hung their shirts from coat hangers elevated on poles; marched to 10 Downing Street and shot arrows at Neville Chamberlain's windows. Money is almost as baffling a study as time, but readers with a masochistic interest in Social Credit might care to read C. B. MacPherson's *Democracy in Alberta* (Toronto, 1953). To the ordinary mind Douglas's own works, *Economic Democracy*, *Credit-Power and Democracy*, *Social Credit*, *The Monopoly of Credit* etc. are perhaps less illuminating than his extraordinary portrait by Augustus John exhibited at the Royal Academy in 1934 (Cat No. 3, *R. A. Illustrated* 115). C. H. Douglas died in 1952.

2   Rightly or wrongly Mitrinovic is here depicted in Edwin Muir's terms as 'an egregious nonsense-monger'. Surely his florid, rococo edifice of symbolism bordered on the paranoid; certainly his frequent public adventures ended in fiasco 'after a brief life of intense activity and sacrificial expenditure.' Mitrinovic was born in 1884 near Monastir in Herzogovina and had edited the Serbian literary journal *Bosanska Vila*. His 'M. M. Cosmoi' column ostensibly on world affairs ran weekly in the *New Age* between August 1920 and 13 October 1921. Despite the violence done to their intellects, Orage, James Young and Philip Mairet were all attracted by Mitrinovic's warm personality and audacious 'Panhumanism'. In 1927 he organised the English branch of Alfred Adler's International Society for Individual Psychology. Mitrinovic's final years were clouded by illness and in 1949 he sorrowfully renounced control over a great quiver of heterogeneous organisations.

Chapter 8

The Caucasus

'Possibilities *for everything*', said Gurdjieff, 'exist only for a definite time.' One morning, after a night of dangerous shooting in Essentuki, he began to reflect seriously on ways out of his impasse. Very soon newspapers in Piatigorsk, where the higher district soviet sat, carried an unusual and planted story. It seemed that a certain Mr Gurdjieff was organising a scientific field-study: his party of twenty-one would be prospecting for gold in a river near Mount Indyuk and investigating the archeology of prehistoric dolmens, prevalent in neighbouring Caucasian passes. 'The expedition intends to go to a remote wilderness, inaccessible to military activities of the civil war. Therefore this scientific work and discoveries cannot be hindered.' Considering that Gurdjieff's 'scientist citizens of Essentuki' were in fact Tsarist Guards officers, doctors, engineers, musicians and other 'enemies of the people', his dignified letter to the Soviet authorities requesting material assistance in mounting his expedition must surely qualify him for some sort of prize.

Gurdjieff's subterfuge had little or nothing to do with saving his own skin – his courage had been proved in fiercer crucibles than this – but it was imperative to preserve his teaching and extricate his pupils, especially those of military age. And as a piquant bonus, he was genuinely interested in dolmens. Gurdjieff could count on two able lieutenants: his wife Madame Ostrowska, and the phlegmatic, distinguished Dr Leonid Stjoernval, senior member of his Petrograd group. There was unwavering devotion too from Thomas de

Hartmann. But all was not roses. Ouspensky, on whom perhaps more than anyone Gurdjieff had lavished attention, suddenly elected to follow the system but not the man. Far more perplexing, Gurdjieff's old mother, sheltering with him in Essentuki, could not attempt the mountain journey. Nor could his brother Dmitri, newly arrived with his wife Anna Grigorevna and their little daughters. At least they could look after each other, but they might well be at risk when the real purpose of the 'scientific expedition' filtered back.

Among those pupils most eager to travel was S., a resourceful lawyer. It seemed therefore an inexplicable scandal when Gurdjieff directed him instead to apply for a legal post with the Soviet authorities. Within weeks S. was recruited, indoctrinated, promoted and placed in charge of the office which issued passports, *laissez-passers* and identification papers. The strands were now coming together. Equipment was pouring in from the soviet in Piatigorsk: picks, spades, hatchets, cooking pans, a big tarpaulin and two large officers' tents. Somehow Gurdjieff obtained a huge revolver, a rifle, three carts, two horses, a mule and a little donkey called Mashka. Ouspensky, pursuing with an iron logic his resolve to separate, loyally exerted himself in the preparations. He it was who reminded Gurdjieff that alcohol was essential 'to wash the gold'. Promptly Gurdjieff requisitioned, and astonishingly received, two casks of virtually unobtainable alcohol. The clinically pure stuff was decanted into bottles labelled 'Medicine for the treatment of cholera': the denatured variant, rendered drinkable by filtration through hot bread and baked onions, was marked 'Medicine for the treatment of malaria'. Gurdjieff was ceaselessly active. Those who remained behind must be carefully provided for. Those who were travelling must be hardened, carrying stones in home-made rucksacks: 50 lbs for the women, 70 for the men. They must be taught how to walk in the mountains, how to march by the North Star. They must be warned of the dangers and given a rule of absolute obedience. At the same time the Bolshevik authorities must be manipulated. The railways were wholly given over to desperate troop movements, yet Gurdjieff somehow succeeded in drumming up two railway wagons to start the expedition on its journey. At last all was completed. Gurdjieff instructed S. to issue Soviet passports to the entire party – and join him.

It was surely a strange affair, that morning departure from

Essentuki. Despite the war, despite the rich administrative confusion, a band was playing in the park and crowds were strolling in the August sunshine. Standing out from the abundant and variegated military uniforms, the colourful dresses of the women and the black *bourkas* of the old men, were some costumes even more surrealistic. Men in tunic-like linen shirts, and girls in shapeless blouses and skirts; strung from their belts, little cooking pans, hatchets and bottles of medicine against malaria. Their leader was the 'scientist' wearing the astrakhan hat, and identifiable by the large black-and-red fireman's belt, a donation from the Piatigorsk soviet. In Gurdjieffian historiography Essentuki is crucially important: it is less a place than a high psychological event. Lectures remain from that time, and very haunting music. But no record captures the final moment; equipment, ideals, dry goods, carpets, mules and Guards officers' wives, cross-pollinating in two deplorable baggage cars. We do not know if eyes strained back to the villa on Panteleimon Street. We cannot guess what Gurdjieff said to his mother and Dmitri; what final glance passed between Ouspensky and his teacher. We only know the train whistled and slowly pulled away, and the band played on.

In Maikop the engine died without resurrection. Not only was the line encircled by fighting Cossacks and Red Army contingents, but a freebooting group called the Green Guards had actually torn up the railway bed. Gurdjieff's expedition walked to a farm two miles from the town, deserted and masked by a wood. It had sweet-smelling hay in the barns and an enormous oak tree giving shade. When the Bolshevik press-gangs came by, there was a wonderful spot to hide in the tall grass by the White River. And yes, there was a diving-board there. Above them and far away the strange bathers could hear rifle-fire; sometimes the shots would smack into the mountain and stones splash down into the river. Once a Bolshevik soldier rode by with an officer's epaulette hanging from his saddle like a scalp. But no one disturbed the scientists, and in the third week White forces recaptured Maikop.

The next day, under the great oak tree, Gurdjieff incongruously served home-made chocolate biscuits to some middle-aged ladies from the local theosophical society. By now their affable host had in his pocket a very singular piece of paper. On one side was the Bolshevik endorsement:

The bearer, Citizen Gurdjieff, has the right to carry everywhere a revolver – calibre. . . . number. . . .
Certified by signature and seal affixed:

Secretary:
SHANDAROVSKY

The President of the Soldiers' and Workmen's Deputies:
ROUKHADZE

Place of issue: Essentuki
Date of issue: . . . .

On the back of the selfsame bit of paper was a new White Army certification:

A certain Gurdjieff is authorized to carry a revolver numbered as indicated on the reverse side.
Certified by signature and seal affixed:

For General Denikin:
GENERAL HEYMAN

Chief of Staff:
GENERAL DAVIDOVITCH NASCHINSKI

Issued in Maikop.
Date: . . .

Just four days later the Bolsheviks recaptured Maikop, but Gurdjieff and his party were one jump ahead. With carts and horses they trudged through harvested cornfields, negotiated narrow trenches, pushed through the White River, waist-deep in water. Five times on their journey they crossed Bolshevik and White Army lines, and for both they had conformable papers. At each hair-raising confrontation the problem lay in making a snap judgment: which sentries and which certificates? Gurdjieff himself orchestrated the flourish of documents, by twirling the right side of his moustache or his left. His differential calculus was unerring, and he reduced the Byzantine complexities of the civil war to purest binary.

At the village of Hamishki the road ran out and the hard times began. The carts were useless now; from here on everything must go on an animal's back or a man's. Neither species enjoyed the new dispensation, but Mashka the donkey was overtly rebellious. It seemed impossible to get a load onto her; she had a knack of sucking in air until the straps were buckled and then expelling it until the load slipped on the loose girths.

It is unnecessary to exaggerate the rigours and difficulties of this mountain-crossing to the sea. Clearly it was not of the same order as the prodigious journeys of The Seekers of Truth; yet Gurdjieff did not dub it their 'Way of Golgotha' for nothing. From a facilely Euclidean standpoint Maikop is sixty miles from the coast, but even a crow could not fly there straight. For a man with a 70 lb pack there are gradients to climb, passes to find and unravel; there are swamp plateaux, deceptive valleys and the green prairie of Luganaky rising twenty miles to the mountains; south-eastward is Elbrus, 3,000 ft higher than Mont Blanc. Gurdjieff and his pupils toiled through virgin forest, grassland, stands of rhododendron and oleander; uphill and down, by day and by the stars, in torrid sunshine and torrential downpour.

At Babakoff, which they reached in a cloudburst, Gurdjieff was excited to learn of a solitary dolmen in the woods. Next morning hunters took him up to the mysterious box, 7 or 8 ft square, scooped from one massive rock and closely shut by a flat stone lid. Carved in its south-east side was a perfect circular hole. Quite how young Olga de Hartmann contorted her way through its 11 in. diameter exercises the imagination, but she was poorly rewarded. No inscriptions, no artefacts were inside. Gurdjieff took measurements, calculated a line of advance, projected it by a succession of sticks, and cut into the forest. Soon another complete dolmen was unearthed from grass and undergrowth. Then a third. The pupils were surprised and the hunters astonished. But the latter had their own rich moment. The dangerous slope declining from the hill of the dolmens provoked a question on the best technique to negotiate it. 'By sliding on your arses,' counselled the hunters gravely. Indeed from Babakoff it was all descent, through a region of paradisal beauty. Down, down they marched, the scientific expedition, and in the evening they saw the lights of Sochi reflected in the Black Sea, and went into the town and took rooms in the best hotels and dressed for dinner and looked at each other amazed. Two hard months they had been on the road from Essentuki. 'Sing the Bell Song from Lakmé,' said Gurdjieff to Madame de Hartmann.

As Gurdjieff intended, the walk from Maikop had exposed everyone in merciless profile; it was clearer now which pupils he could carry with him into the future, and which pupils must part. Nor were occasions for severance lacking on either side. By the sweet irony of history, the White Army had just recaptured Essentuki and every question was re-opened. Painfully each of the company revalued their values, weighing against their esoteric aspirations the claims of relatives and the dictates of money. Some went to Essentuki, some to Maikop, some to Kiev. Andrei Zaharoff, who despite misgivings had made the journey, now parted from Gurdjieff for the last time. Petrov left. Joukov left. In the end only the Stjoernvals and the de Hartmanns remained. Nor is there the slightest evidence that Gurdjieff was perturbed by these developments.

Gurdjieff spent every evening in Sochi gambling in the Circassian officers' club. It is easy to assign one reason: the Moscow industrialists and aristocratic Petrograd *émigrés* who frequented the place were – many of them – still in substantial funds, while Gurdjieff, a formidable card player, was not. But his chief motive lay elsewhere. He needed to know when the process of reciprocal destruction would embroil the town; and the Circassian officers' club was a treasure-house of unlicensed military intelligence. When the moment came, in the bitter January of 1919, Gurdjieff was ready to take ship. Suitcases in hand, Gurdjieff and his diminished company wavered up the narrow, shifting planks. The steamer – cramped, verminous, jam-packed with refugees, its fuel barely sufficient – fought its way south against a head-wind. A night and a day Gurdjieff and his people were on the open deck, and the pier at Poti, white with frost, was a welcome sight. That night they slept in an empty compartment at the railway station, and at eight on the next evening, in appalling cold, arrived in the capital of Georgia.

Tiflis in 1919 was less one city than a trio of distinct towns. The well-scrubbed German enclave, founded by Württemberg millenarians, was more like Hellerau than Tiflis. Chauvinist Georgian claims to be 'the centre of the world's culture' relied on the Russian quarter, on the south-west bank of the Kura. Here were the sybaritic hotels, the well-lit leafy avenues, the fashionable clubs filled with chocolate soldiers and slippered Armenian usurers. Here were the dubious underground wine shops, the Rose of the World, the Heart's Desire and the Bid Me Goodbye and Go. Here was a theatre with a revolving stage, an opera house as large as the Opéra-Comique in Paris. Here was the Chimerion, decorated with Sudeikin's modernist paintings, where negro ragtime singers competed with gipsy violinists, and the dancer Lydia Johnson 'sent all Tiflis mad for a month'. Last of the triple segments, but the first to engage Gurdjieff's attention, was old Tiflis, which lay in a declivity east of the Russian quarter, in another world. So neighbourly were the wooden houses here, so portentous their superstructure of balconies, that the sun's rays never struck direct into the Tartar bazaar. Ageless women, regressed behind veils, behind grills, stared down, unsatiated by their looking. Below in the dark, airless, rat-infested labyrinth, moved a current of operatic yet uncompromising masculinity.

Gurdjieff arrived in Tiflis with five dependants, no money and a temperature of 104°. Inevitably pupils and relatives would muster to him, and the situation was going to get worse not better. Immediately he 'was compelled to run about the city in order to find at any cost some way out of this desperate situation.' He went first to the Tartar bazaar. The fashionable trade was in second-rate rugs and *kilims,* funnelled away quick as you like to Constantinople, where the reckless buying of bored and undiscriminating Allied officers had created a false market. For Gurdjieff this situation was heaven-sent. Style, provenance, knots, symbolism, repair technique and market values – Gurdjieff really knew his carpets. Linguistically and psychologically he was the perfect middleman, born to thrive; and as to risk capital, he had friends and relatives. Gurdjieff bought his first rug cheap and sold it dear. He mobilised assistants; some washed the rugs and some repaired them. In three accelerating weeks Gurdjieff launched into trajectory a weighty business. And yet paradoxically he continued to live in straitened circumstances. How so? The answer basically lay in his capacity to garner dependants. He felt a compelling responsibility to pupils who had left everything and followed him; and to his own kith and kin who had barely escaped from Armenia with their lives. Even when Gurdjieff's delight in exaggeration is borne in mind, we glimpse the scale of his problem in the statement, 'I now had to provide a means of livelihood for nearly two hundred people.'

And some of them were rather special. There was Alexandre de Salzmann, painter, inventor, forest ranger, lighting director, associate of Rilke, Dalcroze and Kandinsky, 'a former dervish, former Benedictine, former professor of jiu-jitsu, healer, stage-designer . . . an incredible man.' With him his wife Jeanne de Salzmann, an accomplished teacher of Dalcroze eurhythmics. There was

Olgivanna – Olga Iovonovna Lazovich Milanoff Hinzenberg – not a nomenclatural *tour de force* merely, but a graceful beauty, grave-eyed, slender, dark hair parted in the middle; the daughter of the chief justice of Montenegro. As if to offset these, there was the stolid pipe-clenching figure of Pinder, Major Frank Pinder of British Intelligence, responsible for the security of the Batum-Baku oil line. To this company was happily added Gurdjieff's brother Dmitri, who arrived unannounced from Essentuki. The de Hartmanns' fortunes, meanwhile, had revived with gratifying absurdity. In Sochi, Thomas had been modestly content to supervise Mashka the donkey: in Tiflis after precisely one day he was implored to become professor of composition to 2,000 musicians enrolled at the conservatory. His wife Olga Arcadievna, whose horizons had so recently been bounded by the inside of a Caucasian dolmen, suddenly found herself singing Michaela at the opera house.

By now the centre of gravity of Gurdjieff's own activity had shifted. The Tartar bazaar carpet period had been succeeded by the Russian quarter 'cultural' period. A revolutionary experiment had begun: under the guise of culture, Gurdjieff was exposing aspects of his work quite publicly. It went absolutely against the grain of his earlier life. The knowledge he had sought for, found, synthesised, had been acroamatic knowledge, from hidden monasteries. The dances he had encountered, remembered, reconstructed were sacred temple dances. In Moscow, in Petrograd, in Essentuki, his pupils had been hand-picked and bound to secrecy. 'There are things which are said only for disciples.' Why then did Gurdjieff reverse the flow? Why in Tiflis in 1919?

'Before beginning any work in Sacred Gymnastics you must learn how to turn.' So the new dispensation began. It was not the words which were new, it was the audience. Gurdjieff was speaking not to his own pupils but to a row of pretty young girls in Greek costumes, pupils of Madame de Salzmann at the Dalcroze school. Dalcroze eurhythmics were sponsored by the Georgian government: Gurdjieff was not. Stage by stage, almost by infiltration, he began to present his own extraordinary and quite discrete material. Audiences at the Tiflis opera house first saw the sacred dances as an extra item in a Dalcroze demonstration; next as a programme in their own right. Extrapolating from these performances, Gurdjieff made projections for a permanent centre of work. Five pupils were present when he exposed these plans: the de Hartmanns, the de Salzmanns and the faithful Dr Stjoernval. 'What name would you give such an institute?' queried Gurdjieff rhetorically, as they took the sun on the verandah. The pupils pondered. 'Finally as if we had been squeezing a tube of toothpaste, the word "harmonious" came out.' In this way was born the Institute for the Harmonious Development of Man.

Gurdjieff's worn, faded coat had been turned inside out and resewn by Madame de Hartmann. Gurdjieff himself was preoccupied with the less tractable problem of turning the entire situation inside out. The new Institute's accommodation was poor; very well, it would be abundant. His work was completely unrecognised; in future the government, no less, should sponsor it. A city which held itself to be the capital of world culture presented special opportunities. The Georgian Menshevik social democratic government and the local authorities of Tiflis were accordingly requested to provide suitable accommodation for the Institute of Mr G. I. Gurdjieff, whose unique system 'was already in operation in a whole series of large cities such as Bombay, Alexandria, Kabul, New York, Chicago, Christiana, Stockholm, Moscow, Essentuki and in all departments and houses of the true international and labouring fraternities.'

The government duly reacted: Mr Gurdjieff would appreciate that the housing situation was acute but certainly he would be found accommodation 'worthy of such an important establishment of general public significance.' He would be found it when opportunity offered; when the mayor of Tiflis had completed the necessary enquiries. Meanwhile protocol must be observed: social priorities weighed. What ultimately galvanised the administration was a biting cartoon in a satirical magazine the *Devil's Whip*. Gurdjieff and his pupils were shown sitting round an old stove, bang in the middle of Erivan Place, the main square of Tiflis. 'They have finally moved,' read the caption. The drawing itself was well achieved, which, considering it was by Alexandre de Salzmann, was not surprising. Immediately the authorities assigned Gurdjieff a two-storey house across the Kura, complete with a large hall on the ground floor. From these premises – 'unsuitable in every respect,' said Gurdjieff – a prospectus was issued carrying the preamble, 'With the permission of the Minister for National Education, the Institute for the Harmonious Development of Man based on G. I. Gurdjieff's system is being opened in Tiflis.' Surely the ballet *The Struggle of the Magicians* was never rehearsed under more astonishing auspices. As for the rest of the prospectus, it was a strange document, both true and untrue. To begin with, half the tutors nominated were not even in Tiflis.

Then perhaps it is time to resume the story of one of these absentee instructors – Piotr Ouspensky.

The whistle which signalled the departure of Gurdjieff's train in August 1918 must have seemed to Ouspensky to punctuate his life with awesome finality. Now he was alone. Alone that is except for his wife Sophie Grigorevna, her daughter Madame Lenotchka Savitzky and Lonya the new baby boy. Ouspensky did not wish to walk the streets of Essentuki ambushed by violence and strange memories; he resolved to get through to Novorossiysk, but immediately the line was cut. Bolshevik robberies and 'requisitions' now began; in Piatigorsk General Russki, General Radko-Dmitrieff, Prince Ouroussov and many others were shot, after being made to dig their own graves. When the wave of terror hit Essentuki, Ouspensky somehow contrived to find a succession of academic hiding places. His first post was that of schoolmaster. It is not clear if he bothered to mention his expulsion from the Second Moscow Gymnasium, but in the revolutionary circumstances prevailing, that would probably have counted in his favour. When his own confiscated books reappeared at the school, along with every other confiscated book in Essentuki, Ouspensky went promptly to the commissar and asked to be made librarian. The commissar inquired what a librarian was, which Ouspensky explained, terrifying the poor man by adding that he had written books himself. The next day comrade librarian Ouspensky discontinued his teaching duties, put up on his door a notice 'Essentuki Soviet Library' and began to read for the duration. It was at least an arrangement which gave him privacy; indeed not another soul set foot in the library for the six months of its existence. So there he sat, the author of *Tertium Organum*. Slowly the year turned and the rains of Ouspensky's improbable autumn curdled to snow, ponderous ectoplasmic flakes materialising out of the grey sky. With his finger he traced symbols in the frosted window-pane, and peering out could scry the future no further than three or four feet. It was not until January 1919 that Denikin's Cossacks cut their way into Essentuki. Ouspensky's verdict on this passage in his life was the expression of a supreme detachment. 'For me and my family,' he wrote, 'things turned out comparatively favourably. Only two people out of four got ill with typhoid. No one died. Not once were we robbed. And all the time I had work and earned money. Things were much worse for others.'

Liberty was most welcome, but it could not bring a solution to all Ouspensky's physical and metaphysical problems. He stalked his house, dividing his attention between Gurdjieff's mathematical symbol the enneagram and the infant grandson crying lustily in his arms. Ouspensky was firm in his resolve to separate from Gurdjieff. When he left Essentuki for the last time it was not south towards Tiflis but north towards Rostov-on-Don. On 19 May the White Russian general Denikin had launched his spring offensive, and in June, with his usual keen sense of absurdity, Ouspensky followed the drum. In the coming months fine filaments of influence were to link Ouspensky with Orage in London and Gurdjieff in Tiflis; Ouspensky, Zaharoff, Major Pinder and Bechofer-Roberts were being swept to an unlikely conjunction.

From Rostov Ouspensky moved to Ekaterinodar capital of the Kuban, a city which appears temporarily to have robbed him of his equanimity. 'It has practically no history at all, its reputation being based only on the fevers which rage there,' he wrote.

> In short, in normal times, it is the most God-forsaken place one can imagine. . . . The only noteworthy edifice is a most hideous monument of Catherine II with its gnome-like figures of Potemkin and Cossacks round its base. . . . I do not think there exists a worse smelling spot on earth. . . . What a blessing nasal catarrh would be now!

Ouspensky's acerbity may doubtless be excused by his desperate material plight. 'I personally am still alive only because my boots and my trousers and other articles of clothing – all "old campaigners" – are still holding together. When they end their existence, I shall evidently end mine.' Ouspensky makes no mention of the postal services in Ekaterinodar, but they must have been holding up at least as buoyantly as his trousers. Far away in Cursitor Street, Orage was astonished to learn through the mails that he had two friends in the Kuban capital, neither known to the other; the first was Ouspensky and the second was Major Pinder. Ouspensky was destitute, while the major, now head of the British Economic Mission to Denikin's Volunteer Army, was less embarrassingly placed. Orage's concern for Ouspensky took a characteristically practical form: he immediately commissioned work for the *New Age,* and better still he urged

Pinder to take Ouspensky on to his staff. So a very special freemasonry secured Ouspensky a post writing press summaries for the British Mission, and if Pinder himself had personally to foot the bill, well, *sagesse oblige*.

The Russian press had much to offer a connoisseur of the absurd. Grim, horrible privations, alarums, excursions, were overlaid with a tinsel gloss of 'Hague Convention' idealism. The thinking journalist took refuge in a mordant gallows-humour. A nice example of the *genre* is the satirical conversation-piece 'A New French Course'.

> Q. How much does a pound of butter cost where you are?
> A. I do not know how much a pound of butter costs where I am because I am not fond of articles of luxury. Such products as butter excite me, and I try not to look at them.

If one did not know better, it would be tempting to identify the pen of Ouspensky himself in this fragment. Certainly his five letters to the *New Age* must have caused some hard swallowing over London breakfast tables. There was a queer, unsettling, interdisciplinary, trans-historical viewpoint. The warring nation-states were defined not in their own terms but as 'big two-dimensional creatures . . . about on the level of the zoophytes, slowly moving in one direction or another and consuming one another.' Ouspensky's letters were unequivocally anti-Soviet, but even here his analysis was distinctive. 'In reality Bolshevism . . . is something very old, that at different times has borne different names.' He certainly could not swallow it, but nor had he the slightest faith in fashionable antidotes. In a passage of Swiftean savagery, festooned with topical examples like penditive hand-grenades, he explodes the very notion of political utility. Everything interacts mechanically 'according to one general rule, which I may call the Law of Opposite Aims and Results. In other words, everything leads to results that are contrary to what people intend to bring about and towards which they strive.' Perhaps Ouspensky was speaking from personal experience.

The first of his letters, penned in the unfortunate milieu of Ekaterinodar on 25 July 1919, appeared in the *New Age* on 25 September, and was translated by none other than Orage's protégé Carl Bechhofer-Roberts. Few casting directors would assign the role of rescuer to the fat, red-faced, unheroic figure of Bechhofer, but the man must be given his due. Fired by the material he had translated, he relinquished Cursitor Street and plunged into the maelstrom of the Russian civil war, not simply from journalistic ambition but to 'assist friends who were suffering there.' By the time Ouspensky's second letter was published in November, Bechhofer was with Gurdjieff, broiled to a fine lobster pink in the hot baths of Tiflis; and when the third, fourth and fifth letters appeared in December, he was freezing half to death with their author Ouspensky in a barn in Rostov. Why is the Bechhofer fragment so important historically? Why does it make such piquant reading? Because he had no axe to grind. Because he blundered right into a complex situation, and through it and out again, without gathering the least notion of its structure. Because he encountered Gurdjieff and Ouspensky, Zaharoff and Pinder, without divining the real nature of their connection. Because his memoir *In Denikin's Russia* will gain an immortality for reasons not dreamt of in his philosophy.

From Batum, Bechhofer arrived in Tiflis, where in a fashionable café he met 'a curious individual named Georgiy Invanovich Gourjiev ... surrounded by this strange entourage of philosophers, doctors, poets and dancers. He was not exploiting them; on the contrary, several of them were living on his diminishing means.' Bechhofer, a man obdurate against all 'higher thought', was pleasantly surprised by Gurdjieff: 'instead of talking theosophy to me, as I had feared, he was good-natured enough to show me some sides of Tiflis that not all visitors see.' In effect Gurdjieff led Bechhofer over a sensory assault course: he fattened him like a Strasburg goose on strange Georgian and Persian delicacies, in an obscure underground restaurant, 'through the windows of which one looked out over the swift and muddy waters of the Kura river'; he delivered him into the iron hands – and feet – of a Persian masseur in the sulphurous baths of Tiflis. Wined and dined, parboiled and soaped, scraped and pummelled, processed to a turn; Bechhofer was summoned at last to the percussive splendour of evening rehearsals of *The Struggle of the Magicians*. The durable young journalist distilled from these experiences a sense of the very special options open to Gurdjieff:

> If he really wanted to go anywhere, were it even to his mysterious monasteries in Thibet – in one of which, he said, echoing an Indian tradition, Jesus had studied! – I cannot say who would be able to prevent his going.

It was in fact not Gurdjieff but Bechhofer who next took the road.

The correspondent of *The Times* and the *New Age* reached Rostov-on-Don in December with his priorities very clear. 'In a few minutes I was knocking on the door of my friend Mr Ouspiensky.' The author of *Tertium Organum*, the once fashionable *habitué* of the Errant Dog, had fallen on evil days. Certainly it was good that Ouspensky had never set much store by possessions. When he answered the door to Bechhofer that cruel winter, his inventory comprised:

> the clothes he was wearing (principally a rather ragged frock-coat, a remnant of former fortunes), a couple of extra shirts and pairs of socks, one blanket, a shabby overcoat, an extra pair of boots, a tin of coffee, a razor, a file and whetstone, and a towel. He assured me he considered himself exceptionally fortunate to have so much left.

Bechhofer's education in Russian social realities had begun. Ouspensky 'received me cordially and at once invited me to share his room. I said I would not trouble him, but would go to a hotel. He laughed.' Rooms in hotels were a pre-Revolutionary phenomenon. 'These are not like the old days,' explained Ouspensky gently, 'when you and I used to meet in Petrograd, and even make appointments two or three days in advance.' As if to prove it, Ouspensky was ejected from his quarters within twenty-four hours and, with Bechhofer in tow, removed to accommodation above a barn. 'In any other place, at any other time,' laments Bechhofer, 'I would have turned up my nose at the rooms. They were small, very cold and draughty, and excessively inconvenient.' To get to them they had to ring the porter's bell; he then reluctantly emerged, drove off a couple of ferocious dogs, unbolted the gate and let them in. 'Sometimes when the porter was busy or asleep or drunk, one could spend a quarter of an hour outside in the snow, or inside one's own door, with a chorus of barking dogs for company.' These dogs only reinforced Bechhofer's assessment that his title to the rooms was precarious: he owed them to Ouspensky, who shared them with Zaharoff, who had been lent them by a White Russian officer, who had requisitioned them from the landlord. Security, or the nearest thing to it, came in an unlikely form. Miraculously Zaharoff obtained a permit to buy 1½ tons of coal from government stocks at a knockdown price. Ouspensky and Bechhofer queued three hours to pay, and Bechhofer, surmounting big difficulties, picked the stuff up at the depot. It was a moment of jubilee. As a solid fuel or a solid currency, 1½ tons was a lot of coal.

The fire was banked high for the evening's celebration. Month after month Ouspensky had subsisted on a diet of bread, coffee and a slice of sausage, but this night was special. 'We had found', admits Bechhofer, 'a quantity of spirit in one of the cupboards . . . and, despite Zaharoff's protests, Ouspiensky proceeded to transform it into vodka with the addition of some orange peel.' According to Ouspensky's political analysis, soon vindicated, either they themselves drank the spirit or the Bolsheviks would. 'People have been drinking since the beginning of the world,' pointed out the author of *Tertium Organum* philosophically, 'but they have never found anything to go better with vodka than salted cucumber.' It seemed to clinch the point. So there they sit, as if exposed by the fire's spluttering flare and caught by some historical fixative: the cheeky, resilient Bechhofer; the shy, inarticulate bachelor Zaharoff, his handsome face marked out for the terrible disease which will soon kill him; and Piotr Demianovich Ouspensky in his ragged frock-coat, with his glass of home-made vodka, his 1½ tons of coal, and his 2½ tons of knowledge.

The nostalgic ambience mellowed Ouspensky and he spoke of mad, vanished St Petersburg nights: Bechhofer was tempted into speculation. 'Where shall we be in a month's time?' he pondered, but his question was not judged very practical by either of the two older men. 'You may wonder as much as you like,' said Ouspensky, 'but you will never find better vodka than this.'

An answer to Bechhofer's question was marching inexorably from the north; the Volunteer Army's long retreat on Rostov, in which 200,000 died, had drawn the Bolshevik forces to the city perimeter. 'The panic had already begun,' reports Bechhofer. 'Every one was losing his head. The wildest rumours were going around; and wise people were thinking only how to escape. . . . We had to scatter our forces.' By Christmas 1919 the railway station was thronged with frightened, screaming people. Only the super-profiteers could enter the cruel black market for tickets; and only a tiny minority with special contacts could fight their way on board. Bechhofer managed it through the British Railways Mission; Ouspensky through the British Economic Mission. For Zaharoff, just sacked from the official propaganda section, it was suicide to remain in Rostov. Resolved at all costs to get through to Gurdjieff in Tiflis, he managed at the eleventh hour to find a place on a train, through his brother-in-law, a railway engineer. It was too late. Zaharoff was already marked by smallpox, and in the opening days of the new year he died miserably and alone in Novorossiysk. He was one of Gurdjieff's six pupils in the first Petrograd group. As for Major Pinder, when Rostov fell on 8 January 1920, he was captured, summarily tried and condemned to death.

Ankle-deep in mud, Ouspensky somehow extricated his wife and family from Ekaterinodar and got them away to the coast. They were not alone. A multitude of starving, disease-ridden, ragged scarecrows limped bloodily through the snow into Novorossiysk: desperate, defenceless, civilian refugees and the pathetic leavings of Denikin's Volunteer Army, driven into the sea by the sabres of Budenny's cavalry. In this melancholy port Zaharoff had died, and here Ouspensky came. British and French warships, jostling agitatedly in the harbour, popped their blind, impotent salvoes over the grey horizon into the Euro-Asian land mass; and the ice splintered from their turrets. Old men gave up and died. Young men tried to swim to the ships or rush the evacuation point, but they were driven back by bayonets. The worthless confetti-currency could not buy passage; nothing could. Uselessly mothers bartered their last jewellery trinkets while their daughters prostituted themselves. Other families, clinging together to the last, knelt praying on the white foreshore. That Ouspensky passed through this hell was due solely to his British connection, which is to say it was due *au fond* to Orage.

Well before the red curtain came down on Novorossiysk on 27 March 1920, Ouspensky and his family were undergoing rigorous quarantine in Turkey on the island of Prinkipo. Yesterday was black, tomorrow was unknown. 'But when from the ship I saw in the mist the minarets of Stamboul and the Galata Tower on the other side, the first thought that came to me was that I should soon see the dervishes.' Ouspensky never set foot in his native country again; indeed he felt it had ceased to exist.

> No one was left of those who were with me when I was first in Constantinople. *And there was even no Russia.* For during those last three years the ground had fallen away behind me. It was a quite inconceivable period, when there was no *way back*. . . . To no place that I had left was it possible to return. From nobody from whom I had parted did I have any news.

Resourcefully Ouspensky began to build a new world. He could scratch a living teaching mathematics to children and English to Russian *émigrés*. He encountered Mikhail Lvow, whose friendship he had shared with Leo Tolstoi. He began to give lectures on ideas. But there is a sense that he was waiting: Ouspensky waiting for Gurdjieff.

George Ivanovitch's Christmas in Tiflis was not traumatic like Ouspensky's but it was pretty spartan. His meal, shared with the de Hartmanns and the de Salzmanns in a cold bare room, consisted of rice porridge with honey and dried fruit. It was perhaps not a time for those with Armenian blood to celebrate. In the first raw months of 1920, Gurdjieff's sister, her husband and all but one of their children were slaughtered by invading Turks at the frontier village of Baytar. In the spring, pitiful survivors from Gurdjieff's extended family struggled into Tiflis more dead than alive. And so, astonishingly, did Major Pinder. By what daring shifts, what act of clemency, what bureaucratic confusion or diplomatic wire-pulling he escaped the death penalty is not recorded. Against an unpropitious political backcloth, intensive work was proceeding on the ballet *The Struggle of the Magicians*. Gurdjieff spurred on his pupils by assuring them it would be performed in the state theatre. Which state seemed problematical. The existential issue confronting Gurdjieff was weightier than a ballet performance. 'I decided not only to liquidate everything in Tiflis, but even to break with everything that up till then had tied me to Russia, and to emigrate beyond its borders.'

But where? That was the gigantic question. Bechhofer had rightly discerned that Gurdjieff was a man with special options. He could go east into Turkestan or west, via Constantinople, into Europe. His choice and strong predilection was there in microcosm in Tiflis itself: he had only to enter the Tartar bazaar to feel at home linguistically and culturally; he had only to visit the German quarter to experience alienation. Going absolutely against his natural inclination, Gurdjieff arrived at his decision: he would bring his work west. A time may, or may not, come when his choice will seem widely significant, even momentous. Certainly it was critical for key individuals in this biography. Quickly Gurdjieff dissolved the Institute in Tiflis and came down to the Black Sea port of Batum with thirty followers and twenty rare carpets. All but two of these carpets, representing his entire material assets for an unknown future, were illegally confiscated by Georgian customs officials; but the small company successfully found passage to Constantinople. It was June of 1920 and Gurdjieff slept on deck. The sea was calm and full of dolphins.

In Stamboul Gurdjieff began to rehearse the sacred dance, The Initiation of the Priestess, which Katherine Mansfield would watch on the night she died.

Note

1   The initial half of this chapter relies substantially on the unique and moving first-hand account given in *Our Life with Mr Gurdjieff* by Thomas de Hartmann (Cooper Square Publishers, New York, 1964; Penguin Books, 1972). Thomas Alexandrovitch de Hartmann, pianist, composer and painter, and intimate friend of Gurdjieff, was born on his family estate at Khoruzhevka in the Ukraine on 21 September 1886. Growing up in St Petersburg, he studied composition with Taneyev and Arensky, and pianoforte with Anna Essipova-Leshititsky at the *conservatoire*. By coincidence *The Pink Flower*, his first significant work, was premièred on 16 December 1907, nine years to the day before Rasputin was murdered. Between 1908 and 1911 de Hartmann lived in Munich, where he became a friend of the painter Wassily Kandinsky (as did another of Gurdjieff's pupils, Alexandre de Salzmann). Thomas de Hartmann was Gurdjieff's direct pupil for twelve years from 1917 to 1929, when, at Gurdjieff's instigation, he left the Prieuré and settled in Garches near Paris. In 1925, as Gurdjieff was beginning the first draft of *Beelzebub*, de Hartmann, in his fortieth year, completely abandoned his achieved style of composition, and began to grapple with polytonality and other radical modern devices. (His action foreshadows the grand renunciations of Orage in 1931 and Ouspensky in 1947.) At Colet Gardens, London, on 9 March 1950, Thomas de Hartmann gave an impromptu talk, recalling Gurdjieff's influence on his composition for Movements and sacred dances. 'It is not "my music" ', he said. 'It is his. I have only picked up the Master's handkerchief. Mme de Salzmann remembers that time.' Laurence Rosenthal has described the collaboration between Gurdjieff and de Hartmann as 'unique in the history of music.'

Chapter 9

The Alps

On 7 February 1920 Katherine Mansfield received a letter from her old friend D. H. Lawrence. 'I loathe you,' it read. 'You revolt me stewing in your consumption. . . . You are a loathsome reptile – I hope you will die.'

In these words Lawrence judges and is judged. But is his picture consistent with the facts? What of the powerful current issuing from Katherine's pen: long, intimate, sensitive letters; shoals of ephemeral book reviews for Murry's magazine the *Athenaeum*; collaborative translations of Tchekov; to say nothing of her short stories? As late as June 1920 she could still write convincingly to Murry, 'You see we are both abnormal: I have too much vitality – and you not enough.' And what of the humour of her self-depiction?

VERSES WRIT IN A FOREIGN BED

Almighty Father of All and Most Celestial Giver
Who has granted to us thy children a heart and lungs
   and a liver;
If upon me should descend thy beautiful gift of tongues
Incline not thine Omnipotent ear to my remarks on
   lungs.

Of course she was suffering. The terror of her situation emerges with brutal immediacy in her private journal:

The nasturtiums blaze in the garden: their leaves are pale. On the

lawn, his paws tucked under him, sits the black and white cat. . . .
I cough and cough and at each breath a dragging, boiling,
bubbling sound is heard. I feel that my whole chest is boiling. . . .
Life is – getting a new breath: nothing else counts.

Murry, the man she had chosen to lean on, the man whom fate, accident, type or polarity had drawn to her, construed the case in his own special terms. He did not, in the circumstances, wish to make too much of it, but her cough jarred on his spine. Her illness was a calamity which drew its delegated authority from its impact on him. 'I can so imagine', wrote Katherine sadly, 'an account by him of a "calamity". "I could do nothing all day, *my* hands trembled, I had a sensation of *utter* cold. At times I felt the strain would be unbearable, at others a *merciful numbness*." '

Murry was disembarrassed of Katherine in September 1920, when she left Hampstead and, with LM, made the long journey south to Menton for her health. Not everyone has given unqualified endorsement to the choice of resort: 'It was Menton . . . which killed her. Menton with its still, enervating pine-laden climate fatal for consumptives.' Here Katherine rented the Villa Isola Bella, a house on two levels. Pale, crumbling primrose, the villa clung to the hillside overlooking the sea; across the cobalt-blue bay of Garavan, she could see the yellow Saracen walls. Heraldic in the garden was a big silver mimosa, and a vast magnolia rich in buds. Behind Isola Bella rose the orange-grey massif of the Alpes-Maritimes.

Soon the postman was labouring up the hill with his satchel full of restoratives. Constable had published Katherine's collection *Bliss and Other Stories,* and Murry, who had stayed on at Portland Villas looked after by Violet the maid, sent her the reviews. Almost all were favourable, some were ecstatic. Walter de la Mare praised her 'devotion to truth'. It is evident that Murry added his *gauche* increment of comfort. 'Your card,' she writes to him, 'with the cutting *re* tuberculosis came today. What a splendid letter it was! "Advanced stage" and now "splendid health". What that means to read!' Her irony is not deliberate, but surely it is there. Katherine was striving for a self-observation which was '*Dead* true – and by dead true I mean like one takes a sounding.' It did not admit such easy mail-order optimism.

The eye which Katherine cast on the world was wry, sardonic, curiously detached:

L.M. is also exceedingly fond of bananas. But she eats them so slowly, so terribly slowly. And they know it – somehow; they realise what is in store for them when she reaches out her hand. I have seen bananas turn absolutely livid with terror on her plate – or pale as ashes.

Since housekeeping and cooking duties were soon in the capable hands of Marie, a local *bonne femme,* LM had indeed little to do except eat bananas, make French knots in her bedroom and distract Katherine with questions like, 'What is milk a metre?' or 'Can you tell me a book that will explain what makes the sea that funny yellow colour so far out? What is the *authority?*' Katherine gave her a copy of *Bliss* inscribed, 'In spite of what I have said – and shall say – you have been a perfect friend to me.'

This is a friendship which has received some critical attention. Its basic structure is not in much doubt, but the inevitable Freudian embellishments would scarcely have satisfied Katherine herself. 'I am amazed at the sudden "mushroom growth" of cheap psychoanalysis everywhere. And I want to prove it won't do – it's turning Life into a *case.*' Poor Katherine. Armchair psychologists have had a field-day with her fiction, her relationships and even her opium-heightened dreams: there was the night Beatrice Hastings materialised, dead drunk; ' "You don't take me in, old dear" said she. "You've played the lady once too often, Miss – coming it over me." And she shouted, screamed *Femme marquée* and banged the table.' Then Oscar Wilde appeared in a vision, very shabby:

> He wore a green overcoat. He kept tossing and tossing back his long greasy hair with the whitest hand. When he met me he said: 'Oh *Katherine!*' – very affected. . . . 'You know, Katherine, when I was *in that dreadful place* I was haunted by the memory of a *cake.* It used to float in the air before me – a little delicate thing *stuffed* with cream and with the cream there was something *scarlet.* It was made of pastry and I used to call it my little Arabian Nights cake.'

It is all grand material for theorists.

Katherine's own psychological critique was grounded in years of attempted self-observation. But 'which self? Which of my many – well, really, that's what it looks like coming to – hundreds of selves? . . . I feel I am nothing but the small clerk of some hotel without a proprietor, who has all his work cut out to enter the names and hand the keys to the wilful guests.' She longed in fact to encounter the proprietor:

> a self which is continuous and permanent; which, untouched by all we acquire and all we shed, pushes a green spear through the dead leaves and through the mould, thrusts a scaled bud through years of darkness until, one day, the light discovers it and shakes the flower free and – we are alive – we are flowering for our moment upon the earth. This is the moment which, after all, we live for, – the moment of direct feeling when we are most ourselves and least personal.

The chaise-longue on the terrace of the Villa Isola Bella was covered with a kaross made from the skins of flying squirrels, whose inconsequential lives Colonel Baker had abruptly terminated long ago in Africa. Drooped incongruously here under a large striped umbrella, devastated by Dr Bouchage's iodine injections, the stricken woman* poured out an astonishing succession of stories. She began writing in early October 1920 and by the end of December had completed 'The Young Girl', 'The Stranger', 'Miss Brill', 'Poison', 'The Singing Lesson', 'The Life of Ma Parker', 'The Lady's Maid' and the long and intricate 'The Daughters of the Late Colonel'. All this in addition to her weekly book reviews for the *Athenaeum* and her daily letters to Murry. It was achieved in the face of real bodily pain.

> Is it right to resist such suffering? Do you know I feel it has been an immense privilege. . . . And if someone rebels and says, Life isn't good enough on those terms, one can only say: 'It *is!*' . . . We resist, we are terribly frightened. The little boat enters the dark fearful gulf and our only cry is to escape – 'put me on land again'. But it's useless. Nobody listens. The shadowy figure rows on. One ought to sit still and uncover one's eyes. I believe the greatest failure of all is *to be frightened*.

At moments Katherine weighed her past in the balance, and was under no illusion that she was among the saintliest of women. 'I've *acted* my sins, and then excused them or put them away with "it doesn't do to think about these things" or (more often) "it was all experience". But it hasn't ALL been experience. There IS waste –

---

*Murry's contribution to her morale at this time was to send her a copy of Richard Prowse's *A Gift of the Dusk,* the harrowing journal of a tubercular patient in Switzerland.

destruction, too.' What was she thinking of? Her sexual peccadilloes? Her lost children? Her use of LM? Perhaps – it is just conceivable – there was a sin against the truth in Katherine's letters to Murry, with their flattery and saccharine endearments: Precious dearest darling Heart; My Tiny; My Little Lion; My Beautiful Bogey; Darling Precious little Husband; My precious little Paper Boy; Betsy; Darling little Fellow. As to sins, caution is indicated. The body of Katherine's letters is like a great anthill where desperate worker-ants scurry to bear away the choicest literary eggs. Anything can be proved; anything and nothing. But whether her endearments were wasted on the desert air, is far less speculative; that can be tested against Murry's confessed preoccupation. He was 'starving for some feminine warmth and tenderness. . . . *How* one is starved for it when one has spent years tending, and anxious for, a sick wife!' The *Athenaeum* set high, one might fairly say Pecksniffian, standards. 'The Cocoa-Pacifist-Stamp-Collectors Weekly'. Ford Madox Ford called it. But Murry, its editor, now dignified by an OBE and an entry in *Who's Who,* was just emerging from a complicated affair with Dorothy Brett and busy transferring his affections to Princess Elizabeth Bibesco, daughter of Asquith the wartime prime minister. Katherine's precious little Paper Boy was making his rounds. 'A man is a man,' LM prophesied darkly, 'that's a man all over'; but Katherine guessed nothing, and would not hear such generalisations. They offended against human dignity. Murry would not send her typewriter to her. That was the extent of her grudge against him. She barely had strength to hold a pen any more. 'Look here, you ought to have sent me that Corona.'

On 8 December 1920 breaking-point was reached; Katherine looked at the clutter of shallow books for review and made a decision:

> It is with extreme reluctance that I am writing to tell you K.M. can't go on. The fact is she ought to have given up months ago but money was so urgent that she dared not. . . . And she is not improving as they say. In two words – and plain ones: it's a question of shortening her life – to keep on. And that she can't do.

These reviews, for which Murry had paid Katherine by the inch, were a mainstay of the magazine. His reply was candid, gratuitously candid. Confessing himself 'annihilated' by her letter, he asked his wife if her illness were in any way aggravated by his recent liaison with Elizabeth Bibesco. This high-voltage shock was Katherine's cue to feel annihilated, but on 12 December she responded in stoic terms:

> I told you to be free because I meant it. What happens in your personal life does NOT affect me. I have of you what I want – a relationship which is unique but it is not what the world understands by *marriage*. That is to say I do not in any way *depend* on you, neither can you shake me. Nobody can.

That same night, cocooned in her mosquito net, Katherine began the second half of that incredible *tour de force* 'The Daughters of the Late Colonel'. We still have the thirty-two quarto pages, beaten out in four hours, which LM rescued from the waste-paper basket. The pen hops, skips and jumps across the paper, tumbling through the margins to the final flourish and date '13 XII 1920'. Dawn was grey in the east. 'It is finished,' Katherine cried. 'Celebration with tea!' And the faithful LM appeared with tea, 'the pale morning light gleaming through the golden sprays of the mimosa trees, which grew tall and fern-like outside the terrace.' Secure in her work, and concentrated on perfecting a style which she regarded as merely embryonic, Katherine could not be shaken.

But at least there are those who must be given credit for trying. Next to enter the lists was Princess Bibesco herself. LM recalls her 'letter blaming Katherine for her treatment of Murry: how could she, a sick woman, away in France and quite unable to make any kind of life or happiness for Murry, how dared she try to hold him, to keep him tied etc, etc.' These events, the glib milestones of literary biography, tested the sick woman to her extreme:

> There is no limit to human suffering. When one thinks: 'Now I have touched the bottom of the sea – now I can go no deeper,' one goes deeper. . . . I do not want to die without leaving a record of my belief that suffering can be overcome. . . . One must *submit*. Do not resist. Take it. Be overwhelmed. Accept it fully. Make it *part of life*. . . . Life is a mystery. The fearful pain of these letters will fade. I must turn to *work*. . . . Oh Life! accept me – make me worthy – teach me. I write that. I look up. The leaves move in the garden, the sky is pale, and I catch myself weeping. It is hard – it is hard to make a good death.

But the gravity of her situation only heightened Katherine's perception of sights and sounds, and fed her inner question. 'Let me remember when I write about that fiddle how it runs up lightly and swings down sorrowful; how it *searches*.'

Alarmed at the possibility of unfortunate scenes, Murry braced himself to visit Menton. With the best will in the world, he could not feel his wife's depression had a scrap to do with his infidelity. No, 'there was no doubt that the root of the trouble, apart from the phthisis itself, was overwork.' What could one do? But LM recalls his arrival:

> He went up to her room and was there for a long time. Then as I went up to my own room, I met him coming downstairs, almost slipping down. I tried to speak but he went on past me, and left the house.

Justifying, explaining, hotly embarrassed, Murry crossed and re-crossed the Channel three times. To be contested by a princess and the most famous woman writer in England was not ungratifying, but trying to placate them both was likely to sprain his brain. For a time it seemed as if the prime minister's daughter would secure the prize. Murry swore that nothing on earth should ever come between them. Duly the *Athenaeum* of 14 January 1921 featured a short story by a new literary discovery – Elizabeth Bibesco. It also signalled the end of Katherine Mansfield's contributions. In the upshot it was not the charms of the princess but the will-power of the frail, fated New Zealander which prevailed. Early in February Murry relinquished his editorship and went to live with his wife in Menton. 'I explained to Elizabeth that I was completely in love with Katherine, that she was seriously ill, and that whatever she wanted me to do, I must do – however hard or unjust or against the grain it might be.' Lawrence put a different construction on Murry's resignation. 'I hear the *Athenaeum* lost £5000 a year under our friend the mud-worm. I hear he is – or was – on the Riviera with K. – who is doing the last-gasp touch.'

There were only two bedrooms at the Villa Isola Bella, so, by custom long established, LM was invited to quarter elsewhere. 'It was a new and interesting experience for me,' she writes. 'A peasant home with great yellow pumpkins hanging over trellis-work arches, and wonderful Italian pasta for dinner; I learnt all the names for the many different varieties.' If we look beyond Ida's gastronomic evolution, it is difficult to identify the benefits of Murry's residence. Certainly Katherine wrote no more stories at the Villa Isola Bella. The soap-opera endearments which she and Murry exchanged through the mails, and the *cinema vérité* of their relationship at close quarters were in cruel contrast. She had said she did not depend on Murry. Very well. Faced with a charge of twenty francs for his wife's carriage to the surgery, the former editor of the *Athenaeum* asked her for eleven francs, an equipartition based on a notional two-franc tip. 'I suppose,' meditated Katherine, 'if one fainted he would make one pay 3d for a 6d glass of salvolatile and 1d on the glass.' But if Murry was not generous with money, he was perhaps over-generous with his confidences. Yes, he *had* considered taking rooms with Dorothy Brett; yes, Elizabeth Bibesco *was* still in love with him, and he had letters to prove it. 'You have withstood her gallantly so far,' wrote the princess, 'how can you give way now. . . . How can I exist without your literary advice?' It was, as Katherine said, a very fascinating question. What she found more difficult to shrug off was Murry's basic attitude to her illness. Not only did he 'accept' it, but 'it even suits him that I should be so subdued and helpless. And it is deadly to know he NEVER tries to help. But I was not born an invalid and I want to get well.'

In March LM broke off her practical and theoretical studies of pasta, and made the wearisome journey north to London. Her charge was to liquidate the establishment at Portland Villas and to scour the streets for Katherine's beloved cat Wingley, whom Murry had lost. 'I found him', reports the incomparable LM, 'a few streets away sitting on the top of the wall with a bevy of enemies or admirers round him and looking rather dishevelled.' But by now a sterner task had fallen on her broad shoulders. 'I feel', wrote Katherine on 10 March, 'Switzerland might be much the best place. Would you go and look at it for me.' Like Keats, like Tchekov, like Aubrey Beardsley who lay ominously nearby in Menton cemetery, Katherine must resume the doomed perambulations of the consumptive. The Villa Isola Bella was, she said, blazed in poker-work on her heart, but it had done nothing for her health. Indeed she was conspicuously worse than when she arrived. Tuberculosis was not only seated in both lungs but in her throat, where the affected gland had to be excruciatingly drained. The enervating summer was advancing and Katherine longed for the crystalline air of mountains. Her relationship with Murry was at stalemate, and 'the South is not made *pour le grand travail.*' In Switzerland lay hope. 'I shall try to find that man Spahlinger and see if his treatment suits me.'

Murry was not, Katherine told LM, someone 'to expect from or count on. If he comes along – he comes and that's all.' Wingley, the dear kitten Wingley, was a different proposition. 'But all these train journeys – arriving at hotels – and so on? Would it be torture for cats? I feel the cat's first need is a settled home; a home that never changeth.' Murry was to prove no encumbrance. 'He is v. willing not to come.' Rather he would 'spend the summer in the English country with a bicycle'; he would take up Sir Walter Raleigh's invitation to lecture at Oxford on 'The Problems of Style'; he would seize an occasion to meet Thomas Hardy. Opportunities abounded.

On 4 May 1921 Katherine left her Villa Isola Bella for the last time, while Murry went his way. By now Katherine was barely ambulatory. 'I can only walk from the kerridge to the door and from the door to the kerridge.' All the practical arrangements were, as usual, down to LM, who had returned to the villa in April. 'I had to arrange everything beforehand: reserve seats, obtain foolproof tickets and visas, pack every little comfort she might need, and fill the picnic basket. One essential item was a small square clock.' Time. It had begun to count now: hours, days, months, breaths, heartbeats. 'The journey to Geneva took no time. My watchet seemed to be racing the train.' Then at Clarens, much to Katherine's delight, the station cuckoo clock struck seven. Surely in taking to the high ground she was gaining on her pursuer. 'Ever since early morning those mountains that I remembered from last time had been there – huge, glittering, with snow like silver light on their tops. . . . Only to breathe was enough.' But the Spahlinger option proved a false dawn – 'I hear today that Spahlinger costs 14 horses to begin with!!!!' – and for weeks the two women languished precariously in hotels. 'I am posing here as a lady of weak heart and lungs of Spanish leather.' Miss Mansfield had come a long way from Tinakori Road, Wellington, and the case was altered with her. 'On my bed at night, there is a copy of Shakespeare, a copy of Chaucer, an automatic pistol and a black muslin fan. This is my whole little world.' It was now that she heard of Montana-sur-Sierre, a village of fabled curative powers, far up the Rhône valley in the canton of Valais. Here – somehow or other – LM brought her, to the Chalet des Sapins. The Shangri-La quality was undeniable: a high place on the green forest's rim, far above the burdensome world. Southwards through the pine trees, across the Rhône trench, rose the white company of the Valais giants: Pigne d'Arolla, Mont Collon, Dent Blanche and Matterhorn.

In the Murry–Mansfield equation, geographical distance is in inverse ratio to emotional protestation. 'How intimately I have *grown in* to you lately,' writes Murry, safe beneath the dreaming spires of Oxford. Audiences were flocking to hear his consideration of the problem of style, 'especially the young ladies,' as Gertler remembers. On 24 May came his coveted meeting with Hardy, and the two connoisseurs of bad luck fell on each other's shoulders with instant recognition and satisfaction. 'The old man was everything I had dreamed – everything,' wrote Murry. But then suddenly they were over: the lectures, the lionising, the days of wine and roses. Murry's fame was waxing, but paradoxically his practical options had narrowed sharply. He had no home in England, and no job since the *Athenaeum* had folded. Of course there was always the Chalet des Sapins. Fully furnished, and the climate excellent against catarrh. And drawbacks? Well yes, there were certain domestic difficulties, but when had he been a man to shrink from difficulties? He really did love her in his fashion and it was not as though it was for ever. He began to buy Alpine equipment.

Is Murry to be given no remission? Does no ordinary human sympathy go out to this timorous, awkward, cerebral, industrious, ineffectual man, trapped in a rotten situation; whose young wife was dying, and of an acutely infectious disease? That which LM might extend naturally, Murry must syllogise to attain. Perhaps neither Alpinists nor biographers have made enough of his ascent to Montana. Few could describe his long and exhausting approach by *wagon-lit,* or his austere base camp in a hotel at Sierre perched 1,765 ft above sea level. No monument celebrates his desperate 2,000 ft solo assault, made at the height of the summer season, up the sheer face of the funicular railway. History records only the bald fact that on 9 June 1921 he tumbled into the Chalet des Sapins more dead than alive and went to bed.

Precisely four months earlier Katherine had written to another man in her life – Orage. Her thanks are generous and straightforward, but surely beneath them lies an unconscious appeal for help.

>
> Villa Isola Bella
> Garavan
> Menton A/M
>
> 9
> ii
> 1921
>
> Dear Orage,
>   This letter has been on the tip of my pen for many months.
>   I want to tell you how sensible I am of your wonderful unfailing kindness to me in the 'old days'. And to thank you for all you let me learn from you. I am still – more shame to me – very low down in the school. But you taught me to write, you taught me to think; you showed me what there was to be done and what not to do.
>   My dear Orage, I cannot tell you how often I call to mind your conversation or how often, in *writing,* I remember my master. Does that sound impertinent? Forgive me if it does.
>   But let me thank you, Orage – *Thank you for everything*. If only one day I might write a book of stories good enough to 'offer' you. . . . If I *don't* succeed in keeping the coffin from the door you will know this was my ambition.
>   Yours, in admiration and gratitude
>
>   Katherine Mansfield
>
> I haven't said a bit of what I want to say. This letter sounds as if it was written by a screw driver, and I wanted it to sound like an admiring, respectful, but warm piping beneath your windows. I'd like to send my love, too, if I wasn't so frightened. K.M.

It was a good letter to receive. And timely. If the pages of the *New Age* are a fair barometer of Orage's private thinking, he was himself in something of a pickle. Certainly the magazine had moved down market since the period of Katherine's contributions. The editorial mix was so redolent of the Mad Hatter's tea party as to be almost unique in English letters. There were the obscure and bombastic economic outpourings of Major Douglas upon Social Credit. There were the equally obscure rhapsodies of Mitrinovic, who, under the bravura *nom de plume* 'M. M. Cosmoi', contributed a weekly column on the psychic functions of the races, full of towering abstractions, jaw-breaking neologisms and exalted metaphysical allusions. 'I am not qualified to assess their value,' confesses Paul Selver, 'and my only safe comment upon them is that, by comparison, the ponderings of Dr Wallace were models of lucidity.' Dr Wallace must not be forgotten. Never perplexed for want of an opinion, never happy with three words where thirty-three would do, the silken-moustached benefactor was proving a contributor for all seasons. He entertained immortal longings and was writing a book called *Cosmic Anatomy*; he was pro Social Credit; his piquant articles on Psycho-Egyptology challenged the findings of Freud. Competing to get him onto their couch was a whole panel of distinguished psycho-analytical contributors, including Dr J. A. M. Alcock, Dr Mary Bell, Dr James Carruthers Young and Jung's protégé Dr Maurice Nicoll. In the end they managed to set their hands on the collar of Edwin Muir the assistant editor, also adjudged a suitable case for treatment. 'It would be impossible', comments Professor Martin with dark ambiguity, 'to discuss the introduction of psycho-analysis in England without reference to *The New Age*.' Mitrinovic, in a formulation of uncharacteristic simplicity, summed it up another way: 'London is Looney-bin, no?'

To what extent can Orage himself be disentangled from this literary thicket? He seems impaled on too many spiky allegiances, while the sun of the *New Age* is luridly setting. And yet. And yet. Orage was nobody's fool, and he could look back on an extraordinary achievement. His bitterest critics could not laugh away a magazine which had featured Arlen, Belloc, Bennett, Bierce, Brooke, Chesterton, Ellis, Galsworthy, Gogarty, Harris, Hulme, John, Pound, Read, Shaw, Webb, West and Zangwill; which was the first to mention Freud, the first to publish Mansfield and Murry, Aldington and Muir; which produced material from Gaudier-Brzeska, Wyndham Lewis, Epstein and Picasso. Nor was Orage himself so naive that he failed to sense the extravagance and incompatibility of his columns in this strange *Götterdämmerung* period. He did not follow Douglas all the way; he broke off his collaborative articles with Mitrinovic; his own pieces on psycho-analysis do not swallow it hook, line and sinker, but evaluate it in the context of St Thomas Aquinas, the Hermeticists and Pantanjali. There is almost a feeling that the editor is playing while the man is wrestling to break free. Certainly Orage had lost none of his thirst for self-knowledge, his legitimate and authentic interest in Oriental disciplines, or the magic power to transmit his enthusiasms to others. Evening and morning Edwin Muir chanted the mantra Orage had suggested to him. 'Brighter than the sun, purer than the snow, subtler than the air, is the Self, the spirit within my heart. I am that Self, that Self am I.' Muir had approached the exercise experimentally, and he did not keep it up for long. 'But the effect of Orage's extraordinary spiritual effort sustained for so many years', he readily conceded, 'could be felt by anyone who met him; it gave him an unspoken ascendancy.' It was an ascendancy which troubled Orage, for his wish to follow was as strong as his capacity to lead. Where could he find a more becoming allegiance?

It is difficult – no, it is downright impossible – to recapture now the mood of that far-away summer, but the very ambiance of Douglas's utopian economics and Mitrinovic's supernal equations suggests something peculiar in the air. Perhaps we who did not breathe that air cannot judge. Certainly Orage was not the only intellectual to feel a lack, a gnawing disappointment in his own *métier*, even a sort of messianic expectation. And Katherine was not the only one to cry 'Oh Life! accept me – make me worthy – teach me.' Rowland Kenney, first editor of the *Daily Herald*, and Clifford Sharp, first editor of the *New Statesman*, were opening to new perspectives. John Beresford was looking beyond his fiction. The beautiful and rich Lady Rothermere was not fulfilled by the *beau monde*. James Young and Maurice Nicoll, indeed a whole tribe of analysts and *cognoscenti*, were acutely disillusioned with psychoanalysis: it 'would never help one re-create one's own inner being.' In August 1921, Dr Nicoll made the following entry in his diary. 'Prayer to Hermes: Teach me – instruct me – shew me the Path so that I may know certainly – help my great ignorance, illumine my darkness. I have asked a question.'

One week later, Piotr Ouspensky arrived in London.

Chapter 10

Cosmic Anatomy

Ouspensky's entrance on the London stage in 1921 was so apposite, so on-cue, it seems downright miraculous. To explain it – if indeed it is susceptible of explanation – would take us on an improbable detour to Rochester, New York, where the youthful, abstracted, ashen-faced Nicholas Bessaraboff had materialised on Claude Bragdon's doorstep, with no other visiting card than the Russian edition of *Tertium Organum*. Bragdon, an ebullient occultist and dilettante publisher, knew a good thing when he saw one. In 1920, using his own savings, he launched a fastidious translation, handsomely printed and bound, onto the American market. Ouspensky's austere metaphysical work was an overnight best seller. Soon three major New York publishing houses were falling over themselves to get it. Somewhat before Bragdon and Bessaraboff turned it over to Knopf, an awkward detail had occurred to them. The two literary entrepreneurs held no translation rights, and they did not even know if the author was alive. Nervously they tried to trace him: Washington knew nothing; nor did the Red Cross; even Orage was not much help. In the bloody shambles of Novorossiysk Ouspensky's trail went dead. Meanwhile, sweltering in Constantinople, quite unaware of his book's translation, Piotr Ouspensky was grappling with problems of his own, not least the advent of Gurdjieff.

Gurdjieff was a refugee with a difference. By his cultivated attention, his verve, his address, his personal magnetism, he swept all difficulties aside. Crossing and re-crossing from Constantinople to

Kadiköy; in equal rapport with the brawny hawkers of meat cake and the seagull-boned intellectual, Prince Sabaheddin; in tram, in tea-shop, on the little bathtub ferries which plied the Bosphorus, in the Grand Bazaar, in the green musky twilight of the Mevlevi *tekke* or the faded empire splendours of the palace at Kuru Cheshme, the Teacher of Dancing moved like a man predestined. Two diamonds and two rare carpets smuggled out through the Finnish diplomatic bag: these were his only valuables on disembarkation. Immediately he set to. 'Among other things, I collaborated with an old friend and countryman of mine in the resale of a large consignment of caviar; in addition I participated in the sale of a certain ship.' Caviar chandler and ship broker, Gurdjieff also set up as a physician-hypnotist, curing hopeless cases of alcoholism and drug addiction. And did he really undertake to transform the pasha's son into a champion wrestler? It has a certain ring to it. The case of John Godolphin Bennett piquantly examples Gurdjieff's charismatic power. Captain Bennett, as head of the political branch of British military intelligence in Constantinople, received a disturbing dispatch, warning him that a certain Gurdjieff had arrived, who had been a Tsarist agent and might now be a Bolshevik agent. Alternatively he might be an Armenian agent. These nice political distinctions were quickly subsumed, for on his first interview with Gurdjieff, the head of military intelligence became his pupil. 'I had never before had the same feeling of being understood better than I understood myself,' pondered Bennett thoughtfully as he drove Gurdjieff back to the grande rue de Péra. 'It was evident that this man had a specialised knowledge of a kind I had not met with before.'

Ouspensky, whose resolve to break from Gurdjieff had just cost him eighteen months' privation and very nearly his life, now sat up night after night with him working on *The Struggle of the Magicians*.[1] At Koumbaradji Street he wrestled to formulate a dervish song, as Gurdjieff translated it from Persian.

> I saw G. the artist and G. the poet, whom he had so carefully hidden. . . . After a quarter of an hour . . . when I had completely disappeared beneath forms, symbols, and assimilations, he said. 'There, now make *one line* out of that.'

Close to the Galata Tower ran the street Yemenedji Sokak, a shadowy ravine of old wooden houses. Here at no. 13 Gurdjieff fixed his Institute for the Harmonious Development of Man; three doors away in the Grand Rabbinate he secured a room for the rehearsal of his extraordinary sacred dances and rhythmic exercises. 'I remember most vividly "The Initiation of a Priestess" ', recalls Bennett, 'in which Gurdjieff's wife, Madame Ostrowska, was the central figure.'

In the summer of 1921 Gurdjieff re-worked the political equation:

> Since at that time the wiseacring of the Young Turks began to have a particular smell, I decided – without waiting for the various delights which were bound to develop in connection with these wiseacrings – to get away with my people as quickly as possible, with our skins whole.

Gurdjieff had come a long way from Tibet. Now at the age of forty-five or more, having no facility in any European language, with the slenderest material assurances and the usual clutch of dependants, he moved west. They went by way of Sophia, Belgrade and Budapest to Berlin, then in the grip of hyper-inflation. 'It is impossible', said Bennett, 'to convey the sense of complete assurance with which he threaded his way through the complications of countries devastated by war and revolution.'

Meanwhile the admirable Bragdon had finally tracked Ouspensky down and posted him two elegant copies of the *Tertium Organum* translation plus a substantial sum in accrued royalties. Better still, Ouspensky received from Lady Rothermere just such a telegram as writers of philosophic works like to receive: 'Deeply impressed by your book Tertium Organum wish meet you New York or London will pay all expenses.' Mary Lilian, Lady Rothermere, wife of the first Viscount Rothermere, owner of the *Daily Mail,* the *Sunday Despatch* and the *Evening News,* was a flighty blue-eyed blonde, fond of rich food but anxious to nurse her excellent figure through into middle age. Sharp-witted, culturally ambitious, lavishly generous, madly unconventional and uninhibited, she 'utilized her exalted worldly position and vast wealth as a lubricant to living.' Piotr Ouspensky reached London in August 1921 to a reception of well-meant vulgarity. A fellow guest recalls her ladyship's dinner party: 'The matchboxes were of solid gold with embossed coronets on top and frightfully heavy. We ate our dessert with gold knives and forks off what looked like solid gold plates.' Fortunately the author of *Tertium Organum* had a broad catholicity of taste; hot-house grapes in

St John's Wood were just as acceptable to him as stale bread and sausage in Ekaterinodar.

Lady Rothermere is best remembered as the patron of Ouspensky and T. S. Eliot. There are quarters where her special endorsement may seem superfluous, and historically it would be difficult to exaggerate the direct impact of Ouspensky on the *New Age* circle, especially upon Orage's psycho-analytical study group. Dr Alcock wrote feverishly that their 'so-much-longed-for psychosynthesist had materialised.' When Ouspensky broached the question of an esoteric group, Orage actually telegraphed Rowland Kenney to attend. And Kenney was glad he did. His judgment on Ouspensky was this: 'I learned more from him of my own inner being and the working of the human mind in a few hours than I had learned from the mass of literature I had previously read in the course of years.' When Dr Maurice Nicoll, protégé of Jung and analyst of Edwin Muir, heard Ouspensky lecture to the Quest Society, he rushed home to his wife and, literally shaking her bed, exclaimed, 'You must come and hear Ouspensky. He is the only man who has ever answered my questions.' Mitrinovic, whose last 'Cosmoi' article appeared on 13 October, lamented the defection of his own pupils. The biographer Philip Mairet saw Ouspensky as 'one of those most uncommon and least understood of men – the magicians . . . too swift in the shallows of life, and in the depths too deep, for his enemies to touch him.' As for Orage himself, he informed Bragdon that, 'Mr Ouspensky is the first teacher I have met who has impressed me with the ever-increasing certainty that he knows and can do.'

Socially Ouspensky proved good-humoured, honest, unpretentious; delighting in Indian tea, Chinese food, Russian vodka, pre-Revolutionary courtesies and pre-Revolutionary amenities; inordinately fond of cats. As a teacher he was formidable. His demolition of contrary opinions was magisterial, his rejection of emotional persiflage uncompromising. 'Is Buddha the seventh state of consciousness?' asked one unfortunate lady. 'I don't know,' responded the author of *Tertium Organum* without even looking up; his unspoken corollary, 'and I don't care,' hung heavy in the air. When Paul Selver began to rhapsodise about the importance of Czech and Serbian poets, Ouspensky dismissed his 'remark with a sweeping gesture, as though consigning all these unspeakable rhymesters to a garbage-heap.' On becoming Ouspensky's pupil,

Dr Kenneth Walker, Hunterian Professor of the Royal College of Surgeons, mentioned his own general contentment, excellent health, enjoyable work, freedom from financial and private worries. Ouspensky sat silent. 'His expression showed no change, and I had the feeling that it would not have altered even if I had been able to say; "I've just been elected President of the Royal College of Surgeons and, last week, I rode my own mount in the Grand National and won it." ' Ouspensky's groups soon had Orage reeling at their revolutionary implications. 'Why, Kenney,' he exclaimed one evening, 'I may find that all I have regarded as the real "me", the literary man, the artist, the philosopher, all is artificial. Perhaps my real bent is cobbling old boots.'

Certainly the speed and authority with which Piotr Ouspensky stamped himself on an important segment of intellectual London in the autumn of 1921 begs some explanation. This was not the debatable romantic figure who had transited London in 1913. Ouspensky had emerged newly tempered from the crucible of revolution. His formidable mind now had at its disposal the potent and cohesive matrix of ideas imparted by Gurdjieff.

'Gurdjieff's system', proposes Colin Wilson, 'can be regarded as the complete, ideal *Existenzphilosophie.*' Its schema of multiple selves, its methodology of self-observation, its conceptual and affective link with music, curiously recall the envisionings of Katherine. Gurdjieff and Mansfield had both 'sinned', both aimed at a certain quality of impressions, and both – in different measure – thrust life and death into question.

'It is so strange to bring the dead to life again,' wrote Katherine from her high place in Montana.

> There's my Grandmother, back in her chair with her pink knitting, there stalks my uncle over the grass; I feel as I write, 'You are not dead, my darlings. All is remembered. I bow down to you. I efface myself so that you may live again through me in your richness and beauty.'

The dying writer was racing against time, stories tumbling from her pen: 'At the Bay', 'The Garden-Party', 'The Doll's House', 'The Voyage'. Across Europe the faithful LM had brought a consolation to her mistress on the end of a lead. 'Wingley our gooseberry-eyed-one has arrived,' exulted Katherine. And the year was turning, turning. 'Now a pale sun like a half-sucked peppermint is melting in the sky.' Snow came, and the vagabond cat splendidly changed from black to white. 'I long to surprise him with terrific disguises,' wrote Katherine. But to her friend Koteliansky she revealed darker, undisguisable realities:

> Do you know I have not walked since November 1920? Not more than to a carriage and back. Both my lungs are affected; there is a cavity in one and the other is affected through. My heart is weak, too. Can all this be cured. Ah, Koteliansky – wish for me!

Can an impeccable wish mobilise health? Is pathology a function of spiritual development? Is the body subordinate to the will? Already in December 1921, Katherine is moving towards these ideas.

A curious literary happening had reinforced her vision. Under his nom de plume 'M.B. Oxon.',* Dr Lewis Alexander Richard Wallace, sheep-farmer, banker, philanthropist, expert on Social Credit and Psycho-Egyptology, had written a book, *Cosmic Anatomy or the Structure of the Ego*. The final manuscript was with the publisher Watkins before Ouspensky set foot in England; in November it appeared and Orage sent a copy to Murry for review. It was not a good book: of its genre it was not such a bad book. But why of all reviewers to Murry? Murry with his entrenched hostility to occult ideas? And if Katherine were the intended recipient, why not simply send it to her in the first place? Murry said he found the book's gnostic speculations positively repellent mumbo jumbo. His scepticism only accentuated her enthusiasm. 'What saved me finally', she wrote, 'was reading a book called Cosmic Anatomy – and reflecting on it.' She entered a secret correspondence with Orage. 'Heard from China', 'Wrote to China', her notebook records cryptically. So the road that begins with Pastor Kneipp's Wörishofen and ends with Gurdjieff in Fontainebleau, is incongruously bridged by 'M.B. Oxon'.

As for Koteliansky, no doubt he did wish for Katherine; he also put her in touch with Gorki's physician Ivan Manoukhin, who had unfortunately invented 'a cure' for advanced tuberculosis by bombarding the spleen with X-rays. 'One must have a miracle,' Katherine had written in December. Suddenly, almost simultaneously, she seemed presented with not one but two escape routes:

---

*Evidently a graceful tribute to 'M.A. Oxon.', the notable Victorian spirit medium, the Reverend W. Stainton Moses.

by licensed, attested, copper-bottomed Western science, and by spiritual revitalisation. Murry was distinctly alarmed; Katherine's physical recovery was not on the programme, 'I ought to have strained every nerve to . . . dissuade her from her own determination at all costs to be "well".' In his preferred scenario Katherine gradually faded away at Montana, playing a little cribbage, writing somewhat less each day, in slow but irreversible conversion from a woman into a symbol. 'I am fleeing to Paris on Monday next,' decided Katherine, 'to see if that Russian can bake me or boil me or serve me up in some more satisfying way.' Murry was beside himself: 'The ways, at last, had really parted. . . . I felt distinctly bitter about those who encouraged her to believe in miracles whether physical or spiritual.' But Katherine had the bit between her teeth. 'I tore up and ruthlessly destroyed much,' she records on 29 January 1922. 'Whenever I go on a journey I prepare as if for death. Should I never return, all is in order.'

Katherine arrived with LM in Paris on 31 January, booked into the Victoria Palace Hotel, 6 avenue Blaise Desgoffe, and struggled to Manoukhin's clinic at the Trocadero the same afternoon. 'It will cost me *much* money,' she discovered. To be precise, a fifteen-week course at 300 francs a session. 'But he promises to cure me by the summer.' It seemed money well spent. Murry's response to the news was characteristic: would Katherine kindly indicate if he should come, or stay on at the Chalet des Sapins and finish his novel *The Voyage*. She told him to finish his novel. But something in the way she told him sent him out to buy a railway ticket. On 11 February Murry reached Paris, and immediately LM was posted back to Montana to look to the needs of Wingley.

Interesting how in one sense Katherine had the advantage of Gurdjieff. Her affairs were indeed in order. She had less than a year to live, but at thirty-three had already placed in the world a considerable body of work. He at forty-five had written no book, publicly produced no ballet, founded no school. What they shared included a sense of destiny and obligation: she to offer her last reserves to her writing; he to pass on the teaching he had received.

From Berlin, Gurdjieff had made for Hellerau, a garden city for artists and craftsmen. Four miles from Dresden, among pine-covered sandstone hills, Hellerau's chocolate-box houses squatted self-consciously behind their sweet-brier hedges, before the God-awful, colonnaded, Greco-Teutonic *Bildingsanstalt,* former eurhythmic college of Jaques Dalcroze. If Gurdjieff wanted a panoramic view of 'advanced' European thinking, he had chosen the ideal venue. Everyone who was anyone in the *avant-garde* went to Hellerau: Shaw, Nijinsky, Stanislavsky. Everyone. Gurdjieff's pupils and travelling companions Alexandre and Jeanne de Salzmann had already worked there with Dalcroze before the war. Gurdjieff's own stay overlapped those of Edwin Muir, who had just left the *New Age,* and A. S. Neill the permissive educationalist. ('My work is infinitely more important,' Gurdjieff explained to Neill.) If Gurdjieff had captured Hellerau in 1922, this nexus of 'Progressive' thought . . . well, it is an intriguing speculation. But the provincial town in no way corresponded with him: it had not the same vibration, the same scale. Gurdjieff must go on searching.

On 13 February 1922, two days after Murry reached Paris, Gurdjieff reached London. 'And did those feet in ancient times walk upon England's mountains green?' Indeed they did. Through the wintry sunshine to No. 38 Warwick Gardens they carried,

> He who in childhood was called 'Tatakh'; in early youth 'Darky'; later the 'Black Greek'; in middle age, the 'Tiger of Turkestan'; and now, not just anybody, but the genuine 'Monsieur' or 'Mister' Gurdjieff, or the nephew of 'Prince Mukransky,' or finally, simply a 'Teacher of Dancing.'

His words there had the requisite hauteur. 'I do not say nobody can control his actions. I say you can't, because you are divided.' And if example of division were demanded, there stood Ouspensky himself. Yes, he expected a great deal more from Gurdjieff's work. No, he did not conceive it possible for him to work with Gurdjieff. Yes, he would do his utmost to help Gurdjieff found his Institute in London – upon which he would leave for Paris or America. Will he, won't he, will he, won't he, will he join the dance? Ouspensky's vacillation is understandable. Inevitably – intentionally even – Gurdjieff, by his presence, created a fluttering in the Kensington dovecot. 'Now they will have to choose a teacher,' he told Pinder. And, according to their lights, each did. In its starkest terms the choice between Ouspensky and Gurdjieff lay between theory and practice. 'Mr Gurdjieff, what would it be like to be conscious in Essence?' was someone's timid question. 'Everything more vivid!' came the aphoristic reply. No, if you wanted a chalk and blackboard dispensation, Ouspensky was your man. 'But after Gurdjieff's first visit', said Orage, 'I *knew* that Gurdjieff was the teacher.'

His future pupil, his most famous pupil, was trapped meanwhile in a cruelly ironic situation. On 23 February, Constable brought out Katherine's collection *The Garden-Party and Other Stories*. It drew twice as many notices as *Bliss*. In the year of Brecht's first play, the year of *Ulysses* and *Aaron's Rod* and *The Waste Land,* review after review extolled her psychological penetration, technical command, poetic gift. The *Sketch* and the *Nation* importuned her for material; the *Sphere* demanded twelve stories and a portrait; unknown admirers sent letters to her; young and unpublished writers sought her help. What a pleasure, said one reviewer, to think of all the years of writing Miss Mansfield had before her. It was all too late. As her fame had grown, her real world had contracted. She who had looked out on the mountains now occupied two small hotel bedrooms, littered with Murry's newspapers. Her commissions went straight into Manoukhin's pocket. His X-rays, far from mending her lungs and cough, brought their own 'forte reaction': high fever, sickening headaches, agonising neuritis. Completed on 20 February, her last significant story, 'The Fly', is the expression of an extreme despair, a psychological terrain as abstract and implacable as the surface of the moon. Paris itself seemed to underscore all Katherine had lost. No irony was spared her. As she sat with Murry at the Café de l'Univers, her former lover Carco chanced by, and was appalled at her appearance. 'Her handsome dark eyes flashed with the old ardour and the old feverishness. She exerted a kind of magnetism, but she looked ill and her poor little hands, so pale and shrunken, filled me with agony.' After a few embarrassed moments he sidled from her life.

Under these pressures Katherine was beginning to disengage; to steel LM for her inevitable emancipation. The uncorked genie did not wish to be released from its bottle, but nevertheless to hear was to obey. Reluctantly then, LM decided to throw in with her friend Susie de Perrot and set up a tea-room in England. On her way home she called briefly on Katherine in Paris, and here that much-travelled animal, the lordly Wingley, made his last adieux to his dying mistress. It was not the happiest of moments for LM either. 'I felt I was once more leaving Katherine to her fate – and Murry.' So the Channel parted them. In England LM found Wingley a home that never changeth, with her aunt Mrs Scriven. In May 1922 Orage sought enlightenment, Katherine health, Gurdjieff a roof for his

Institute; Ida Constance Baker, with perhaps equal resolve, pedalled majestically along the south-coast road, urgently seeking an empty tea-room, where currant buns might be retailed to morning bathers.

LM's ride was not the only extravagant occurrence on the public highway that summer. In London a taxi squealed to a halt at the doorstep of 86 Harley Street and, when Dr Walker mildly responded to the bell, he was seized by his eminent colleague Dr Nicoll, bundled inside and driven away with quite unprofessional haste. 'Half an hour later', recalls Walker, 'I found myself explaining to a bored Home Secretary how essential it was to the welfare of British Medicine that Gurdjieff (who was only a name to me) should be granted permission to settle in London.' In vain the clamorous representations of British Medicine; in vain the silky intervention of a High Court judge; in vain the blatant wire-pulling of Lady Rothermere. The party which proposed to settle Gurdjieff at headquarters in Hampstead was up against an unbeatable combination: the home office and Gurdjieff himself. The Home Secretary perceived a former Tsarist agent: Gurdjieff perceived an irritating climate, a rebarbative cuisine and a stupefying insularity. Already his thoughts were bent on France and on Paris, 'The Capital of World Culture.'

Katherine, paradoxically, was now thoroughly disenchanted with Paris and largely disillusioned about Manoukhin. On 4 June she set out again with Murry for Switzerland. Dorothy Brett, who saw them off, marked in Katherine the evidence of a special evolution. 'She *understands* beyond all understanding – and she has won so complete a victory over herself that one could almost worship.' However, this particular journey was to tax all her equanimity; to assert that Murry was a less comfortable courier than LM is to understate. When the sick woman came to the Gare de Lyon, she found 'fifteen thousand young *Gymnastes de Provence*' and no porters; her husband, in a forgivable moment of panic, lost the luggage tickets and gave away a 500 franc note instead of a 50. The long journey was characterised by regrettable incidents and deprivations. Katherine's little square clock was left on the train, and all her baggage went missing at Randogne. Without a coat she was driven by open cart in sheeting rain to the Hôtel d'Angleterre, where Murry, on discovering he had lost his only fountain pen, sprained his ankle. Quickly letters crossed the Channel, and Ida Constance Baker – like Charlemagne faintly hearing the last desperate blast of Roland's horn – turned and raced for the mountains. By mid-June

LM and Katherine were united again; at the beginning of July Katherine descended to the Château Belle Vue hotel at Sierre, leaving Murry at Randogne. They were never again to live together as man and wife.

Monsieur Gurdjieff drew into Paris on 14 July 1922 together with his pupils, 100,000 francs, a sewing machine and substantial quantities of material, thread, needles, scissors and German thimbles. It was Bastille Day, and the raucous street celebrations were unconnected with his arrival. Immediately he hired the empty Dalcroze Institute in the rue de Vaugirard, and yet again threw his students into rehearsal for *The Struggle of the Magicians*. Now Ouspensky mustered from England to confer. We do not know the substance, the motivation or even the precise venue of their exchange. Ouspensky established his headquarters in the Hôtel Solferino in the rue de Lille: Gurdjieff had found a *pied-à-terre* in the rue Miromesnil. All we do know is that after this meeting Ouspensky and his English pupils generously opened their purses to establish Gurdjieff in France. And by much searching Madame de Hartmann came on a suitable property.

About a mile down the Seine from Valvins at Basses Loges, near Fontainebleau-Avon, stands the Château du Prieuré. History had frustrated the original purpose of its establishment; founded early in the fourteenth century as a Carmelite house of devotion, and a refuge for benighted travellers against wolves and highwaymen, it earned a less pietistic reputation as the hunting lodge of Françoise, Marquise de Maintenon, mistress of Louis XIV. In modern times it had been given to Maître Labori in recognition of his services in defending Dreyfus. It was a house with a singular past and perhaps a more singular future.

Instantly, without so much as setting eyes on this property, Gurdjieff resolved to establish there his Institute for the Harmonious Development of Man; the delicate and vital negotiations for purchase he confided to Madame de Hartmann, a girl still in her twenties. Olga Arcadievna spoke five European languages but she did not find it exactly easy to talk real estate with widow Labori. English by birth, Madame Labori was something of a Boadicea. Having buried her first husband, the pianist Pachmann, and her second, Maître Labori, she wished above everything to consolidate her position. Now this way, now that, the dubious battle swayed. A million francs! Was that not a shade too high? On the contrary; it was, if anything, too generous. Then would it perhaps be possible to rent the Prieuré with a twelve-month option to purchase? And if so, would Madame Labori have the kindness to send away her gardener? To these permutations and combinations there was no end, and they seemed to Gurdjieff to have all the exactitude of contemporary weather forecasts: 'either snow or rain or something or other'.

In Katherine's life, by contrast, precipitation-point had been reached; it was beyond all question. She moved now with speed and an awesome sense of purpose. On 7 August she secretly wrote Murry a letter to be given him on her death. On 14 August she made her will. Three days later, with her two esquires, she was *en route* for London. Katherine herself went to Dorothy Brett at 6 Pond Street, Hampstead; Murry lingered next door with Boris Anrep; LM was relegated to Chiswick. When Brett or LM called on Katherine, they would find a card hanging on her door – WORKING. 'You know,' she wrote to Koteliansky on 23 August, 'I am deeply sorry for Murry. . . . His situation is very serious but who am I to say anyone is beyond hope.' Murry was a man under a curse – such was Katherine's assessment, and perhaps it was the kindest tenable hypothesis. Thus her husband's quite surrealistic egoism was less a matter for blame than for exorcism. Even so, Murry standing anxiously before his dying wife, in his new suit, cuts a strange figure.

J.M.: 'Are the trousers full enough?'
K.M.: 'Quite full enough!'
J.M.: 'You're sure?'
K.M.: 'Certain!'
J.M.: 'They're not too full?'
K.M.: 'Not in the least!'
J.M.: 'You're sure?'
K.M.: 'Certain!'

This singular catechism took place on 28 August. Two days later Katherine had a more intelligent exchange.

A. R. Orage embraced Katherine warmly. They made an arresting couple: she, at thirty-three, emaciated, frail, borne up by a strange hope; he, at forty-nine, 'a philosopher looking like a boy in Dr Arnold's Sixth Form at Rugby who had found, beyond all expectation, a rare, white-plumed pigeon in his ink-stained desk'. Between old friends we must suppose an urgent exchange of confidences: her desperate health, his psychological crisis; the small success of Spahlinger and Manoukhin, the risible state of the *New Age*; his loss of Beatrice, her loss of Murry. Both had come a long way, yet what, truly, did it all amount to? Gradually she warmed to her theme: the dissipation of the stream of ordinary life, 'the image that suggested itself to me was that of a river flowing away in countless little trickles over a dark swamp.' Mere literature without a purpose was not enough, and as to her own stories, 'There is not one that I dare show to God.' But still she sensed the existence of another stream; of a literature which would be an initiation into truth.

> How does one know that? Let me take the case of K.M. She has led, ever since she can remember, a very typically false life. Yet, through it all, there have been moments, instants, gleams, when she has felt the possibility of something quite other.

And when she spoke like this, Orage put before her an idea: one must become more to write better. He proposed to her the names of Piotr Demianovich Ouspensky and George Ivanovitch Gurdjieff.

Predictably Murry took up an antagonistic posture to Gurdjieff and Ouspensky immediately, and without meeting either. 'I could scarcely bear to discuss the doctrines of Ouspensky with Katherine.' On 1 September, just two days after Katherine met with Orage, Murry left Hampstead to live near East Grinstead as the guest of Vivian Locke-Ellis, the poet. He was hardly to see his wife again until the day she died. It is one of those peculiar inconsistencies that, although opposed to occultism from the very highest principles, Murry spent time with Ellis in tumbler-turning. 'What shall I do to be saved?' he inquired glumly. Slowly the glass slid across the table. 'Christ's Coat,' came the enigmatic answer. The seamless garment, and the division in man.

Katherine met with Orage again on 5 and 10 September. Soon he had spoken with Ouspensky and secured her entrée to private lectures. So it transpired that on 14 September 1922 Katherine Mansfield entered the final phase of her life through the door of No. 38 Warwick Gardens. In the hall sat the Russian secretary, a lady with high cheekbones and humorous eyes. Katherine wrote her name in the visitors' book and was unostentatiously steered into a large ground-floor room. Quickly her author's eye registered the spartan *mise en scène*: the nondescript mauve-grey walls; the striped curtain; the vase on the window-sill with its three sprigs of artificial cherry-blossom. The sixty-odd seats were small and acutely uncomfortable; facing Katherine was a blackboard. At last, silently, modestly, scarcely noticed, scarcely noticing. Ouspensky entered and sat at a small table. It was half an hour perhaps after the stipulated time. Across a duster and a box of chalk, the Second Moscow Gymnasium confronted Wellington Girls' High School.

With deliberation Ouspensky extracted from his pocket a speaking note, established it an inch from his nose and gazed upon it intently over the top of his glasses, like a man sighting it for the first time. His eyes could not distinguish Katherine but she saw him: solid, impersonal, imperturbable, like a stone Buddha with close-cropped silver hair. Abruptly, without preamble, without the least forensic display or the minutest concession to his hearers, Ouspensky began to speak. His accent was so acute, 'It sounded as though he were really speaking Russian though using English words.' If he needed to consult his notes or sip a glass of water, he did so with the calm self-possession of a man on a desert island. His audience must support insupportable silences. If he could not hit on the right English word he simply smiled and said 'or anything you want.' What was central was for him to revisit Gurdjieff's ideas in methodical order. His audience, his distinguished audience, could take it or they could leave it. It was an aspect of peripheral interest to Piotr Ouspensky.

Kathcrine was impressed. Impressed enough to go back to Ouspensky's lectures on the two succeeding weeks. But, given her sensitive antennae and the imperious urgency of her need, given the tide which was running in the London groups, how could she not think of Gurdjieff? Already Dr James Young *par exemple* had thrown up his lucrative practice and plunged headlong into the feverish world of the rue de Vaugirard. Already Dr Nicoll had borrowed against expectations under his father's will, in order to contribute handsomely to Gurdjieff's funds. And now the general appetite was fed by exhilarating news: at long last Madame de Hartmann and Madame Labori had reached an accommodation. In a matter of days the Institute for the Harmonious Development of Man would indeed open at the Prieuré. Madame Ouspensky herself was off to cook for Gurdjieff's advance party. Even Dr Wallace was modestly hopeful of an engagement in the enterprise, preferably a vicarious one. Accordingly he gave Orage £250 to enable him to break free, and the editor's astonishing decision was discovered to *New Age* readers on 28 September. 'Mr Orage will shortly be leaving London in connection with work of general and special interest.' A literary epoch was over, but perhaps an authentic new age was beginning.

Against this dramatic backcloth Katherine Mansfield asked for an appointment with Ouspensky.

It was ever at his Kensington flat that Ouspensky received; thus on 30 September we may set Katherine ringing the bell of 55a Gwendwr Road, within the decent bounds of biographical licence. We may picture the advancing apparition of Ouspensky, stained vermilion in the glass panel of the front door; Katherine's stoic and tortoise-like ascent to his first-floor reception room; the little gas fire burgeoning into life. Now, across the square mahogany table, snarled with papers, books, maps, photographs, typewriter, camera and galvanometer, the dark intelligent eyes confront the impenetrable pince-nez. A strange laminate this: the girl from 11 Tinakori Road and the *habitué* of the Errant Dog; the chorus girl from the Moody Manners Opera Company and the writer of *Tertium Organum*; the author of *Bliss* and the survivor of Novorossiysk. Was Ouspensky more for 'Yèkaterina' in that moment than the apotheosis of her long love affair with all things Russian: with Dostoevsky, Bashkirtseff, Gorki, Bunin, Koteliansky and the idolised Tchekov? And was she more for him than a fashionable woman already halfway to death? To both questions a resounding Yes. Ouspensky was touched 'by the striving in her to make the best use even of these last days, to find the truth whose presence she clearly felt but which she was unable to touch.'

To tax Ouspensky directly about Gurdjieff would be indiscreet; Miss Mansfield hit on an oblique approach. Her health, she explained, necessitated her going to Paris for treatment by Manoukhin. Then could Mr Ouspensky perhaps give her the addresses of his friends in Paris: people of like individuality, with whom she could pursue and share her new interest. Quizzically he regarded her:

'Do you know what individuality is?'
'No.'
'Consciousness of will. To be conscious that you have a will and can act.'

More of their conversation has not come down to us, but we do know that Ouspensky gave Katherine the vital keys. As he showed her out, he could not think he would see her again. Her will-power –

that was surely the element he miscalculated. In scarcely a fortnight, Katherine would translate herself from the bow-windowed Victorian respectability of Gwendwr Road, to Fontainebleau.

When precisely did it begin – that alchemical operation known in Gurdjieffian historiography as 'The Prieuré'. All that last week of September, fortified by Madame Ouspensky's bortsch, James Carruthers Young, one compatriot and four Russian shock-troops were frenetically weeding the indistinguishable paths, sluicing the glass of the 'Orangerie', generally battling like demons to establish a bridgehead. Saturday 30 September – the very date Katherine spoke to Ouspensky – saw the signing of the lease and the passing of the 65,000 franc consideration. On Sunday 1 October Gurdjieff arrived; so did his main Russian contingent. 'From that day on, under specifically European conditions, quite foreign to me, there began one of the maddest periods of my life.' And it was destined to escalate, for on Monday Katherine and LM embarked for Calais and Paris.

Katherine's *grenier au 6ème* in the Select Hôtel was a poky, shabby, sunny, ten-franc-a-day, bed-and-breakfast affair. But the 'room is like the room where one could work – or so it feels.' Her attic window commanded a view over the Sorbonne. 'Large grave gentlemen in marble bath gowns are dotted on the roof. Some hold up a finger, some are only wise.' How impotent these philosophers of Western Europe to speak to her condition, and how remote from the tragi-comic crises of hotel life: *Le chat a mangé une compôte de pruneaux!* Ah, it took more than mere philosophy, this election for Gurdjieff. All must be discarded: her trembling hopes in Manoukhin; her correspondence-course marriage with Murry; her ancient bond with LM – now pale, tormented, with dark rings under her eyes. No, it would not be easy. 'One of the KM's is so sorry. But of course she is. She has to die. *Don't* feed her.' Physically a living, walking, lying-down cough, Katherine bent her will to the ideal of spiritual regeneration: 'Give it, the idea of *resurrection* the power that death would like to have. Be born again and born again faster than we die.'

Curiously enough, the first man she met from the Prieuré ('quite remarkable . . . rather like the chief mate on a cargo steamer') was Frank Pinder, who perfectly well knew what it was to be under sentence of death. Days passed. Friday 13 came and it was bad; Katherine thought she was veritably dying. Yet Saturday – gasping, kicking, struggling – somehow succeeded in dawning. Under the quilted sateen bedcover, Katherine sprawled exhausted. It was sunny and it was her thirty-fourth birthday and LM brought her a *brin* of mimosa. An unexpected visitor called: a Dr James Carruthers Young. That night he would be meeting the boat-train and Orage, her friend. Calling at the Select Hôtel *en passant*, Young lingered two hours, speaking about Gurdjieff and the Institute and the dances. To Katherine it sounded 'fabulous and other-worldly. I shall wait till I've *seen* it.' But between Mansfield and Young there was an immediate rapport.

In those extra-canonical traditions passing by word of mouth among Gurdjieff's pupils, we are afforded a tantalising glimpse of a meeting in Paris, between our principals. Dimly we discern the figure of Gurdjieff impressing on a reluctant Katherine that the South of France will be kinder to her illness than the Prieuré. 'And how much longer would I live?' she asks him. He is silent. At length she says, 'No, my aim is not to be cured of my disease. If you will let me, I will come and live the rest of my life at the Prieuré.' He shakes his great domed head but he does not refuse, and the picture fades.

It is Pinder's story, the souvenir of an interpreter. But what can we say for sure? There is Katherine's written disclaimer: 'I have no belief whatsoever in any kind of medical treatment.' And Gurdjieff certainly was under no illusions about her health: he had the detailed report of Dr Young who, in Paris about 15 October, gave her a searching medical examination; he had also, it seems some written caveat from Manoukhin; indeed he himself was a considerable diagnostician, and his study of Central Asian medicine was unparalleled. 'Not for nothing', writes Gurdjieff sadly, 'had I in my life held many conversations with thousands of candidates for a speedy departure from this world.' To save Katherine Mansfield physically was already too late a day – that was the general consensus. The thankless task of helping her in other ways, Gurdjieff shouldered consciously.

There was no delay. On Monday 16 Dr Young phoned to say her room was ready, and Katherine packed. 'One prisoner cannot help another,' she writes in her *Journal*.

> I have heard of Gurdjieff who seems not only to agree but to know infinitely more about it. . . . Therefore if the Grand Lama of Thibet promised to help you – how can you hesitate? Risk! Risk

anything! . . . I want to be all that I am capable of becoming so that I may be . . . *a child of the sun.*

On Tuesday 17 October 1922, accompanied by LM, Katherine Mansfield came to La Gare du PLM and caught the morning train to Fontainebleau.

Note

1   *The Struggle of the Magicians*, rising from its subterranean source on Friday 13 November 1914, when Piotr Ouspensky glimpses the perplexing notice in *Golos Moskvi*, flows through time and space to the rue de Vaugirard, where Dr James Young sits making costumes in the summer of 1922. And there it disappears.

   For seven turbulent years *The Struggle of the Magicians* unified Gurdjieff's thought and choreography, Mme Ostrowska's dancing, Foma de Hartmann's music and Alexandre de Salzmann's stagecraft. Created and re-created by Gurdjieff as a living, teaching, experience for participants, the vehicle of many inner exercises, it was not presented to the world at large. 'If I produce the ballet on the ordinary stage,' he said, 'the public will never understand these ideas.' In Constantinople in the summer of 1920, Ouspensky helped Gurdjieff to prepare a literary version of the scenario, and during Ouspensky's years at Lyne Place he continued editing this material. A decade after his death, Ouspensky's pupils printed ten copies of *The Struggle of the Magicians*, bound in black leather, for private circulation (The Stourton Press, Capetown 1957). Authorship is properly assigned to G. I. Gurdjieff; Ouspensky is not cited as editor; and the dedication to Geltzer is omitted. (A copy is in the author's possession.) In these forty-seven Royal Octavo pages, Zeinab, Rossoula, Gafar and the white and the black magicians seem strangely diminished. The book, separated from those vivifying influences which gave the ballet life, is like a husk from which the grain has fallen. In Paris in the archives of the *Societe d'Études et de Recherches pour la Connaissance d l'Homme* is an unpublished version of the scenario. Members of that Society, and of The Gurdjieff Society in London and the Gurdjieff Institute in New York, practise and study the Movements, dances and music of G. I. Gurdjieff.

Chapter 11

The Initiation of the Priestess

They sat together, and each kilometre to Fontainebleau brought nearer Katherine's hope and LM's devastation. On the long, alienating railway platform James Young greeted them – vigorous, handsome, cheerfully blasphemous. The horse's breath hung white in the October air as the fiacre jogged down past the bridge into Avon and out onto the Valvins road. At the verge of the wood of Gautier the cab drew to a halt before the Prieuré. Set in the steep slate mansard were seven little dormer windows, and a man looking down would have seen James Young pay the cabby his seven francs, tip him, and ring imperiously at the bell-handle with its legend '*Sonnez fort*'. Now the great wrought-iron gates eased open and shut again; Katherine Mansfield had arrived at her destination. Never afterwards in LM's long anticlimactic life, could she quite forget the low-rising contour of the Prieuré, the fountain climbing in the courtyard, and the maple leaves, suddenly, irretrievably sundered from the branch, and blown down into the crimson flower-beds.

Only brief days before, Gurdjieff himself had come here with all his self-imposed difficulties. 'When I walked through the gates of the Château du Prieuré,' he tells us, 'it was as though, right behind the old porter, I was greeted by Mrs. Serious Problem.' Somehow he must build, lecture, choreograph, rehearse, administer, counsel, and foot virtually the entire bill. Costs were prohibitive, and Gurdjieff's 100,000 francs were scattered to the last *sou*. 'Sometimes I had to work literally twenty-four hours a day: all night long in Fontainebleau and the whole day in Paris.' He was a foreigner; every communication, every botched translation, was costly in nervous energy. 'I felt more than ever the need to know European languages, while at the same time I did not have a minute in which to apply myself to learning them.' He was further preoccupied with trying to extricate his family from Armenia. And suddenly, on top of all this, there was Katherine Mansfield.

She glimpsed him first from the window of the *pied-à-terre* assigned her. 'He looks exactly like a desert chief. I kept thinking of Doughty's *Arabia.*' But the time had passed for distant sightings, for romantic and simplistic iconography. Even the longest lines of convergence must cross at last, and at lunch on that far-off Tuesday in 1922 Katherine Mansfield sat at Gurdjieff's table. How facilely, how vainly, imagination peoples the 'English' dining-room. Katherine in a black or purple dress with one small felicitous touch of colour. LM gauche and ill at ease. Orage is there for social amenity's sake and Pinder for translation. Here are the Russian Old Guard: Madame Ostrowska, Dr Stjoernval, Madame Ouspensky, the de Salzmanns, the de Hartmanns. Now Gurdjieff enters in his dark, shabby clothes, his brimless Caucasian hat of black fur, and sits in the centre chair facing the window; behind him on the mantlepiece stands a photo of his father, bearded and benign. It would be interesting to record Gurdjieff and Katherine's conversation; interesting but impossible. We know the occasion was informal, the cuisine audacious; we know her desperate eagerness to stay; we know the exacting benevolence of his gaze. At the point where the lines converge the heroine passes through the surface of the mirror. 'Mr Gurdjieff is not in the least like what I expected,' wrote Katherine immediately afterwards. 'He's what one wants to find him really. But I do feel *absolutely confident* he can put me on the right track in every way.' And now he had seen her, how much did it weigh with Gurdjieff—Dr Young's prognosis? And the problems of intensive care? And his Institute put in jeopardy by a celebrity's death? Evidently he foresaw the difficulties, set them in the balance against Katherine's need – and laid them to one side. LM's humble diary records the ending of that day. 'Last evening spent in the salon before an enormous fire of great logs. "Fire is condensed sunlight". Music and tambourines – atmosphere intensely alive.'

Katherine was like 'The Man Who Came to Dinner'. She arrived on Tuesday with just a comb and toothbrush. By Wednesday afternoon she had won an invitation to remain a fortnight, and, one week later, permission to stay indefinitely. With LM the case was different. She left on Thursday morning. Whatever it was which had begun in Queen's College in the little room overlooking the mews, it ended at the Prieuré. Twenty years it had lasted, through love and hate; always intense, always staggering under the load of Ida's implacable service. 'Came away for the last time absolutely dazed,' she recorded. 'Decided in train to go on the land or to Russia.' She wandered desolate in Paris and London; she bombarded Katherine with letters; she parcelled her off every conceivable necessary. Then in mid-November, feeling she might be 'happy with animals and simple people low down on the scale of intelligence,' she retreated to a farm on the estate of Madame von Schlumberger, a feminist. She was not happy. Anxious, lonely, baited for her tongue-tied French, castigated for the nervous way in which she churned butter, LM heard a thousand owls screeching in the leafless woods and dreamt of death. Katherine's death? Or was it conceivably her own? Over the years their very identities seemed to have coalesced. 'She *was* me,' wrote Katherine, the day after they parted.

Mrs Murry had not been twenty-four hours at the Prieuré, before Gurdjieff moved her to 'The Ritz'. Always ultra-sensitive to her surroundings, she now enjoyed a sumptuous room, with panelled walls, antique furniture, French engravings, ornate Empire mirrors and, from the second-floor windows, a wide view over the Versailles-style garden with its formal beds of geranium, calceolarias, lobelias and pink mesembryanthemum. He also gave her a job: 'eat, walk in the garden, pick the flowers and rest *much.*' It seemed a simple proposition but, as she protested, 'it's the eat much which is the job when it's Gurdjieff who serves the dish.' Perhaps only that dwindling circle who sat at his table can grasp her difficulty in all its plenitude, but graphic accounts remain:

> In all my travels I think I have never eaten food so delicious as at these dinners – food from every quarter of the world. There was soup, meat with spices, poultry, fish; vegetables of all kinds, most wonderful salads whose juice we drank in glasses; puddings and pies, fruit of all sorts, dishes of oriental tit-bits, fragrant herbs, raw onions, and celery. Calvados and slivovitz for the elders to drink, and wine for the young and the children. A speciality was sheep's head after the meat course, done in Caucasian style, delicious and

very rich. Gurdjieff would tell a guest that in the East the sheep's eyes were considered the tastiest part, and would honour him by offering him one.

It all seemed to Katherine like *Gulliver's Travels*. 'She stood in the doorway of our main dining-room' recalls Olgivanna, 'and looked at all and at each with sharp, intense, dark eyes. They burned with the desire and hunger for impressions.' So struck was the young Montenegrin that she flew straight to Gurdjieff. 'I told him what a lovely face she had and how much I liked her. "You take care of her," he said, "Help her all you can." ' When Olgivanna's first knock came at the door, Katherine was sitting in the firelight. Her face, her hair, her mouth, were striking enough. 'But the eyes!' More logs were needed and Olgivanna moved quickly to get them. 'When I left her room I leaned against the wall for a few seconds. Why had she to die? . . . Something became outlined in my mind. I understood her need.' The two women sat together, watching the shapes and faces and riddles, growing and decaying in the red core. Katherine spoke hesitantly about her writing: Olgivanna of her years with Gurdjieff – in Tiflis, Constantinople, Berlin, Dresden and Paris. 'I wish', said Katherine, 'I could have been with you then.' The moment came for Olgivanna to go. 'I put another log on the fire, and as I did so Katherine leaned forward and slightly touched my head.'

Even younger than Olgivanna, and away from home for the first time, was Adèle Kafian. She too responded cheerfully when asked to help Katherine. It was not exactly this Adèle had had in mind, on her long journey south from Lithuania to the Prieuré, but she grasped immediately what she could offer – 'I had an abundance of untried strength.' Perhaps Gurdjieff selected these helpers as much for the help they could receive; perhaps Katherine even became a kind of mother to Adèle, at the very moment she missed one. Quite simply we know Katherine was fortified by feeling she could repay. 'Dr Young, a real friend of mine comes up and makes me a good fire. In "return",' she adds proudly, 'I am patching the knee of his trousers today.' Her dignity is maintained.

Gurdjieff himself quickly integrated Katherine in the life of the Prieuré. Its heart was the kitchen, where she watched, absorbed:

Nina, a big girl in a black apron – lovely, too – pounds things in mortars. The second cook chops at the table, bangs the saucepans, sings; another runs in and out with plates and pots, a man in the scullery cleans pots – the dog barks and lies on the floor, worrying a hearthbrush. A little girl comes in with a bouquet of leaves for Olga Ivanovna. Mr. Gurdjieff strides in, takes up a handful of shredded cabbage and eats it . . . there are at least 20 pots on the stove. And it's so full of life and humour and ease that one wouldn't be anywhere else.

But not everyone perhaps would have chosen the word 'ease'. Whatever a pupil learned about himself at the Prieuré was not learned from an armchair. It has been wickedly said that, 'When Orage arrived at the Prieuré with *Alice in Wonderland* in his pocket, he found that far from disappearing down magical rabbit-holes, he was expected to dig them.' Intellectually no one was better equipped than A. R. Orage to grasp the notion of dulio-therapy: 'Be slave freely, not slave will be.' Practice was another matter. Orage had courage but he also had fifty years on his back:

> I was told to dig, and as I had had no real exercise for years I suffered so much physically that I would go back to my room, a sort of cell, and literally cry with fatigue. No one, not even Gurdjieff, came near me. I asked myself, 'Is this what I have given up my whole life for? At least I had something then. Now what have I?'

No such doubts cloud Katherine's letters: the Institute pupils were absolutely unlike people as she had known people; the advanced men and women were truly wonderful; she received such beautiful sympathy as she had never known in the outside world; her whole day was *lived* from moment to moment; at thirty-four she was beginning her education; she had learned more at the Prieuré in a week than in years *là-bas*; there was no other spot on the whole earth where one could be taught as much as one was here; 'This *is* the place, and here at least one is understood entirely, mentally and physically.'

The panegyric is a treacherous form; it invites scepticism, even ridicule. But at least, at absolute least, the Prieuré drew the invalid from her hotel cul-de-sac, the writer from her study, out into the light of day where real people collided in real events. And what a rich Aubreyesque stratum lay juxtaposed to the spiritual one. Here is the lugubrious lawyer Rachmielevitch; here is bountiful Lady Rothermere, dubiously chewing the herring which Gurdjieff has passed off on her as grilled rainbow trout fresh from the Prieuré pond. Here is Gurdjieff's admirable fox-terrier Philos, and the no less admirable Miss Merston who invariably, as she bends over to serve tea, breaks wind with a 'small sharp report, like that of a toy gun,' a phenomenon which, as Gurdjieff puts it, is 'so delicate, so refined, that it is necessary to be alert, and highly perceptive, even to be aware of this.' Here are some industrious ladies trying to grub up the roots of trees with tablespoons, while memorising Tibetan verbs. Here is Gurdjieff teaching himself to drive, like a Cossack breaking a colt, with a disgraceful crash and rupture of gears. Here is his meal of sour cream and powdered cinnamon, prepared by Captain John Godolphin Bennett, formerly of British Military Intelligence. Here are the Institute's new pigs with long golden hair, Katherine's 'very mystical pigs', and here is the man who found them in the tomato patch and went to give warning, walking 'very slowly, to avoid identifying and muscle tension,' and here is Gurdjieff who 'roared at him and leapt, so to speak, about a hundred yards to those pigs.'

Into this strange world moved a Katherine *engagée*: now in charge of the indoor carnations; now on kitchen duty, proudly occupying an entire morning disposing of three carrots. 'My hands', she complains in high triumph, 'are ruined for the present with scraping carrots.' If for a fugitive moment her dark eyes clouded with tears, it was from peeling onions, and when those eyes cleared, they saw sermons in stone and good in everything: 'Mr Gurdjieff hardly speaks a word to me. He must know me pretty well.'

But Gurdjieff's psychological acumen was not the only term in this particular equation; he had other powerful claims on his attention, not least his inescapable need to go hunting for money. Backwards and forwards he ran to Paris. There he treated intractable cases of alcoholism and drug addiction; bought and sold oil shares on margin; opened two restaurants, worked them up pell-mell and sold them at a profit. It was certainly not a regimen Gurdjieff enjoyed:

> It is worth mentioning that my external life at this period, when I was spending every night in Montmartre, provided many of those who knew me, or had seen or heard about me, with rich material for gossip. Some envied my opportunities for gay revels, others condemned me. As for me, I would not have wished such revels even for my bitterest enemy.

But wished or not wished, their effect on his programme was inevitable. See the Prieuré audience waiting for his lecture. Time passes: ten o'clock, eleven o'clock, midnight. In the small hours Gurdjieff arrives from Paris. For a long time he stands silent, confronting his students. 'Patience is the Mother of Will,' he says. 'If you have not a mother how can you be born?' The lecture is over. Put the pressure of work together with the language difficulty, and small wonder if Gurdjieff spoke less than expected to Katherine Mansfield.

Whatever else, time was always reserved for the Movements or sacred dances, and new exercises at the Prieuré were occasions of special drama. Gurdjieff himself, standing over Thomas de Hartmann almost forbiddingly, almost like a riding master, would drum out the rhythm on the piano top. Now, as if listening inside himself, he would add the sinuous melody – whistling, touching the keys lightly, humming or even singing very softly in a language of the rocky wastes and inaccessible hills. Professor Hartmann, his balding head glistening and nodding sagaciously above the battered old upright, would consolidate the theme. ('It is not "my music",' he would say years afterwards. 'It is his. I have only picked up the master's hankerchief.') The least deviation and Gurdjieff would burst out furiously at Hartmann in Russian, and Hartmann would shout vexedly back. By now the Teacher of Dancing was showing the series; if his movements were somehow feline, they had also an uncompromising precision. From place to place he went, establishing his pupils in their assigned positions. As each struggled to unriddle and practise his sequence, noisy and passionate disputes would agitate the ranks. Gurdjieff himself would quash these unlicensed debates, and 'his language on those occasions would have made even Lenin blush.' Abruptly he would shout. An eloquent silence supervened as Gurdjieff stood there before the class with his function, his obligation, his demand. Now Hartmann played the introductory bars, building in rare harmonies. In the front rank Madame de Salzmann, Madame Galumian and Olgivanna searched. And suddenly the whole class was working: each limb conforming to different contrapuntal rhythms; each posture, each gesture, each displacement with its own appointed duration and weight; each evolution manifesting in a universal language the laws that rule the secret movements of men and of the stars.

Night after night Katherine Mansfield is there to watch. Hieratic, inexplicable, she sits in the high-backed chair nearest to the salon fire. Her dress is simple and elegant. Her intent face has just enough rouge and lipstick to mock its pallor; her wide intelligent eyes do not miss a single inflexion. It is midnight. *'Kto hochet spat,'* shouts Gurdjieff, *'mojet itti spat.'* Who want sleep, go sleep. But Katherine does not move. She will be there at one, at two, a woman who can scarcely walk, absorbed in dances which lie at the very frontier of physical possibility. Did she feel their religious content, follow the inner exercises, attempt the complex multiplications? We know she did. 'She watched so eagerly,' remembers Olgivanna, 'she seemed mentally to do the movements together with the rest.' It was a strange translation: from room 52 in the Select Hôtel to Fontainebleau; and thence to Kashgaria, Tibet, the Chitral; to the monasteries of Kisil-Djan and Souxari, to the medical temple of Sari and the Sanctuary of Houdankr. An unlikely metamorphosis from cribbage to the Thirty Gestures and the Big Seven. Katherine sensed both its strangeness and its value. She writes of 'a tremendous ancient Assyrian group Dance. I have no words with which to describe it. To see it seems to change one's whole being for the time.' But the movement which had for Katherine a special message was 'The Initiation of the Priestess, a Fragment of a Mystery'. It came from a cave temple in the Hindu Kush, and Gurdjieff's wife Madame Ostrowska danced the high priestess. This is the piece which Katherine reports as follows:

> There is one which takes about 7 minutes and it contains the whole life of woman – but everything! Nothing is left out. It taught me, it gave me more of woman's life than any book or poem. There was even room for Flaubert's *Cœur Simple* in it, and for Princess Marya. . . . Mysterious.

She began to re-assess her writing.

In this she was not alone. Before her – footsore and bemused, with aching back and blistered hands, forbidden by Gurdjieff even to pluck a cigarette from the pocket of his faded corduroy jacket – stood the once trenchant editor of the *New Age*. Almost every day Orage and Katherine stole time for long exchanges and iconoclastic fancies. 'Do send *Lit. Sups.*', Katherine urged Murry. 'They're so good for lighting fires.' But essentially their criticisms began where all good criticisms begin – at home. In 'a world of Peeping Toms with fewer and fewer Lady Godivas to ride by,' Katherine felt she had been merely a camera: subjective, unconscious and *ipso facto* evil. She had a new vision: she would let the laugh be with the heroes, making the commonplace virtues as attractive as ordinarily the vices were:

> The reader's sympathy would be maintained by the continuity and variety of the efforts of one or both of the characters, by their indomitable renewal of the struggle with ever fresh invention.

What is to be made of this? Many who offer a theory of literature cannot write: many who write have no critique. Katherine who certainly could write had arrived at a bold – and a very Gurdjieffian – conception. But for a proof of the matter, time was necessary, and it was not towards the publishers that fate was hurrying Katherine Mansfield.

Deep down she knew it. Immortality, not stylistic innovation, was her real priority. Precious immortality, neither within easy reach not yet impossibly impossible: 'more than ever I feel that I can build up a life within me which death will not destroy.' It is a big affirmation, saluted in Olgivanna's response, 'There is no death for one like you who perceives the possibility of sweeping death aside when the time comes.' Meanwhile life buzzed, pulsated, throbbed exasperatedly around her as the Study House, quickening stage by stage, calibrated her remaining days.

What was this Study House? It had begun its existence as a hangar (some say a Zeppelin hangar) and was acquired by Gurdjieff from the French army for the inconvenience of dismantling and carting it away. Miss Merston, who sprang forward heroically to assist the men unload, received a violent kick on the shin from Gurdjieff and hopped aside just in time to escape a large iron girder falling on top of her. The daunting ferrous jigsaw made a strange contrast with the weathered stone blocks of the old priory, lying in the tall grass with their inscription *'Ad maiorem gloriam Dei'*. Like a big meccano set the hangar must be assembled; bodied out with laths, walled with mud and straw, glazed with Miss Merston's geranium frames. ('Anyone grow flower with frame,' Gurdjieff assured her. '*You* grow flower without frame.') The floor must be levelled, the roof must be achieved; gallery, stage, boxes, lighting, fountains must be installed. All, all must be accomplished by the Russian New Year on 13 January. 'Throw everyone into the work,' Gurdjieff commanded. Now began a disciplined frenzy of shovelling, barrowing, pounding, rolling, sawing, tarring, nailing, painting. Winter was closing in; it was cold. But work on the Study House went on by lamplight till two or three in the mornings, or even through the night. 'We had no proper tools,' recalls de Hartmann the concert pianist, 'and worked practically with our bare hands.' Katherine's friend Dr James Carruthers Young diagnosed in himself 'the phenomenon which is known surgically as "snap-finger" '. Finally there arrived the moment of truth: the centre stanchion supporting the entire fabric, 40 ft wide and 100 ft long, must be knocked away. 'When the pole is removed,' said Gurdjieff darkly, 'the House will either stand or collapse.'

In the middle of all this furore, Piotr Ouspensky arrived at the Prieuré. Whether he experienced a moment of *déjà vu* as he passed through the gates, we are not told, but the faces around him seemed mysteriously familiar. Why, here was his wife Sophie; here was Lady Rothermere, his former patron; here, digging like moles, were his senior pupils, Orage, Kenney and doctors Young, Nicoll and Bell. And here was Katherine Mansfield. Ouspensky sat with her one evening in the salon and she spoke to him in a voice which, though not unpleasant, seemed to come from the void:

> I know that this is true and that there is no other truth. You know that I have long since looked upon all of us without exception as people who have suffered shipwreck and have been cast upon an uninhabited island, but who do not yet know of it. But these people here know it. The others, there, in life, still think that a steamer will come for them tomorrow and that everything will go on in the old way. These already know that there will be no more of the old way. I am so glad that I can be here.

It was more than a value judgment or a striking metaphor; it was a graceful expression of thanks to Ouspensky. Katherine was never exactly carried away by *Tertium Organum* but she had no doubts about its author. 'He is a very fine man,' she wrote.

Orage, like Katherine, was beginning to sweep his difficulties aside; perhaps she helped him. He started to loosen up, and his mordant humour returned. The work-shy Rachmielevitch no longer exasperated him. 'Poor fellow. I suppose we must forgive him. After all, he has had his centres balanced.' Faced with a future which seemed to consist exclusively of spades and holes, Orage refused to be defeated.

I vowed to make extra effort, and just then something changed in me. Soon, I began to enjoy the hard labour, and a week later Gurdjieff came to me and said, 'Now, Orage, I think you dig enough. Let us go to café and drink coffee.'

Gurdjieff never allowed anyone to get stuck. In the second week of November he instituted a sort of grand musical-chairs with the sleeping accommodation. Katherine Mansfield stoutly resisted the privileged exemption urged on her; she wanted nothing better than to be treated like her friends.[1] So it was she found herself in the kind of bedroom her maid Gertie Small might have had at Portland Villas. 'When Olga Ivanovna and I had arranged it and she hung up her yellow dance stockings to dry before the fire we sat together on the bed and felt like two quite poor young girls.' But the basic pre-Revolutionary amenities remained at least, for Katherine's account is 'written on the arm of a chair, on a cushion, on my bed, as I try to escape from the heat of my fire.'

Katherine was enthusiastic about cows, in a nice Daisy Ashford way. 'I must tell you . . . my love of cows persists. We now have . . . real beauties – immense – with short curly hair? fur? wool? between their horns.' So at the end of November, Gurdjieff made a resting place for her in the cowshed. An elaborate polemic assures it a place in history which perhaps no other cowshed has enjoyed for 2,000 years. Here is Katherine's version:

> I'll tell you . . . about that couch Mr. Gurdjieff has had built in the cowhouse. It's simply too lovely. There is a small steep staircase to a little railed-off gallery above the cows. On the little gallery are divans covered with Persian carpets (only two divans). But the white-washed walls and ceiling have been decorated most exquisitely in what looks like a Persian pattern of yellow, red and blue by Mr. Salzmann. Flowers, little birds, butterflies and a spreading tree with animals on the branches, even a hippopotamus. But . . . all done with the most *real art* – a little masterpiece. And all so gay, so simple, reminding one of summer grasses and the kind of flowers that smell like milk. There I go every day to lie and later I am going to sleep there. It's very warm. One has the most happy feelings listening to the beasts and looking. I know that one day I shall write a long long story about it.'

But there was more to that cowshed than cows, more even than Alexandre de Salzmann's inspired decorations; there was a link with Gurdjieff himself. It had been Gurdjieff's own place before it was hers; it was Gurdjieff who transformed it; Gurdjieff who leant over the gilded balustrade watching the cows Equivoquetecka, Bridget, Mitasha and Baldaofim; Gurdjieff who had snatched there his fugitive hours of rest. Here painted on the ceiling was Gurdjieff's sacred symbol, the enneagram; beside it that strange bestiary of his pupils – Orage as an elephant, de Hartmann as a toucan and Dr James Carruthers Young as an ape. If science did not positively forbid the idea that a place can be magnetised to transmit a special influence, we might perhaps scry something of that sort.

So here in her last days she lay, the cows chewing rhythmically below; the smell of hay sweet and soothing. Gurdjieff still came occasionally to rest or talk or milk the goats for her. 'Now,' he told Katherine, 'you have two doctors you must obey. Doctor Stable and Doctor New Milk. Not to think, not to write. . . . Rest. Rest. Live in your body again.' And Madame Ostrowska came to milk 'Mrs Murry's Cows'.

> She was tall, beautifully proportioned. She wore a black dress of an old German style, tight in the waist and around the breast, with the skirt flowing down in rich folds. Her beautiful head was tied with a black scarf. A gentle smile, sad and lovely, was always on her lips.'

Separated by language, the two women 'conversed' by smiles and gestures; and by glances that passed between the brown and the grey-blue eyes. 'I think she is splendid,' Katherine told Olgivanna. 'I am certain that the cows are in a state of exaltation while she is milking them! They must experience a super-cow-sensation, if they are at all decent cows!'

The therapy of 1922 – strict regimen, absolute rest and pneumothorax – Katherine had explicitly rejected. X-rays did not enter general use as a diagnostic tool until the thirties. Chemotherapy and pulmonary surgery were not in use until the forties. Streptomycin was not discovered until 1944. Add to all this the fact that Katherine arrived at the Prieuré irreparably damaged, and the case against Gurdjieff begins to evaporate. Could he conceivably check a disease which had run its unchallenged course for twelve years?[2] If the winter was cold, could he do more than provide her with a warm room? If the cowshed sounds incongruous, would Katherine Mansfield herself have preferred a hotel or a ward for the terminally ill? If she drew a sort of inner strength from the friendship and the sacred dancing at the Institute, was Gurdjieff to show her the door? If at moments she nourished herself with an impossible hope, was it his role to undeceive her? If he said that fresh milk, sunshine and the breath of cows would do her good, well at least they did her no harm. Can the same be said of Manoukhin's X-rays, or Dr Bouchage's iodine injections, or Dr Poached Eyes's strychnine prescriptions, or indeed the entire paraphernalia of contemporary medicine?

And if Gurdjieff's regime is under judgment it should be weighed *in toto*; but Katherine did not stick to it *in toto*. 'Not to write,' he insisted, yet her correspondence was incessant. It stirred emotions, it wasted her energies, it brought vexatious replies. Murry suggested his wife was hypnotised, or self-hypnotised, and pictured herself as an angel with a sword. He wondered if he would see her 'on the other side'. She, with mock seriousness, invited him to Fontainebleau. 'You could learn the banjo here and if the worst came to the worst always make enough to keep you with playing it.' (Murry demurred: but whether literature's gain outweighed ragtime's loss is one of those questions we must refer to Professor Meyers.) 'It is very difficult', said Gurdjieff, 'to sacrifice one's suffering. A man will renounce any pleasure you like but he will not give up his suffering.' Surely Katherine's unrelinquishable correspondence – as much in its marshmallow endearments as in its acidities – ravaged her. We know she was unable to sleep. 'I tried', confesses Olgivanna, 'to go to bed at the same hour as the others did, but just as the sweet state of falling into sleep would begin to overcome me, I would see Katherine sitting up by the coal of the fire, sleepless. How could I leave her like that?'

The remorseless advance of winter, Katherine faced with aplomb.

> This life proves how terribly wrong and stupid all doctors are. I would have been dead 50 times in the opinion of all the medical men whom I have known. And when I remember last year and that bed in the corner week after week and those *trays*.

Her move to the small room in early November and her restoration to the grand one on 17 December seemed psychologically apt and timed to perfection. 'But how did Mr Gurdjieff know how much I needed that experience? . . . he always acts at precisely the moment one needs it.' Nor was life all austerity; Christmas was coming. On 22 December, seated at a table heaped with flowers, paper chains, bon-bon cases, gold wire and gilded fir-cones, Katherine wrote to LM:

> We are going to *Fêter le Noel* in tremendous style here. Every sort of lavish generous hospitable thing has been done by Mr Gurdjieff. He wants a real old-fashioned *English* Xmas – an extraordinary idea here! And we shall sit down to table 60 persons to turkeys, geese, a whole sheep, a pig, puddings, heavens knows what in the way of dessert and wines by the barrel. There's to be a tree, too and Father Xmas.

And she added this: 'If you'd like me for a friend as from this Xmas I'd like to be your friend. But not too awfully serious *ma chère.*' It was the last letter LM ever received from Katherine Mansfield.

It is Christmas 1922. In the Prieuré drawing-room Katherine watches avidly as the children receive their presents from the shining Christmas tree; then on an impulse she gives an impromptu recitation, in dialect. Frail, thin-shouldered, in a dark purple taffeta dress embroidered with tiny flowers, she mobilises her small reserves of breath to speak 'with sharp changes in her voice, suggesting peasants quarrelling among themselves.' Wide-eyed, the five- and six-year-olds watch her. Major Pinder's little girl Yvonne is baffled by the accent; Madame Ouspensky's grandson Lonya, and Boussique de Salzmann, Tolik Merkouroff and Nikolai Stjoernval, cannot even understand English. But all smile shyly at Katherine's animation and characterisation, at this final, gala performance of a born actress.

When she returns to her room she finds the fire burning sweetly, and a little Christmas tree of her own brought from the wood, and three candles burning. 'Adèle, why three?' she cries. One each, she is told: for Katherine, Adèle – and Murry. Katherine smiles sadly at the notion and subsides into the armchair; Adèle covers her shoulders with a fluffy blue and white scarf. Now one of the candles flickers obdurately and begins to go out. 'That's me,' whispers Katherine. 'No!' protests young Adèle, jumping up and snuffing out the other candles first, in a gesture at once magical, impassioned and ineffectual.

Though Katherine's vital candle was flickering, she still hoped it might illumine her true nature: 'the question is always: *"Who am*

I?" ' she wrote on Boxing Day. 'You see . . . if I were allowed one single cry to God, that cry would be: *I want to be REAL.*' Against all experience, all intuition, she longed to share her search with Murry, and on New Year's Eve she sent him a decisive letter. 'Would you care to come here on January 8 or 9 and stay until 14–15? Mr Gurdjieff approves my plan and says will you come as his guest? On the 13th our new theatre is to be opened. It will be a wonderful experience.' She wrote a second letter that day: to her favourite cousin Elizabeth. It is significant both for its final judgment on the Institute and her unmistakable presentiment of death:

> But I cannot tell you what a joy it is to me to be in contact with living people who are strange and quick and not ashamed to be themselves. . . . Goodbye, my dearest cousin. I shall never know anyone like you; I shall remember every little thing about you for ever.

She made her peace with Sir Harold Beauchamp: 'The New Year is already here. I must leave the fire and go to bed. God bless you darling Father. May we meet again.' Now one last time Katherine Mansfield put pen to paper; the unposted letter was found in her blotter after she had gone. 'My thoughts are full of carpets and Persia and Samarkand and the little rugs of Beluchistan. . . . I am looking for signs of Spring already. . . . Write and tell me how you are will you? Dear Ida?' At last it was over. One after one the extraordinary caravan of letters had vanished across the rim; the galled and refractory specimens of Ospedaletti and the pure white racers of Isola Bella; conveying from the biographical hinterland their imponderable literary cargo of gold, frankincense, vinegar and marzipan. As the year 1923 came in, an unusual silence descended.

The formal cause of Katherine's death was human mortality; the material cause the tuberculosis bacillus; and the final cause has not transpired. Surely we possess a clue to the efficient cause: she died when Murry came. The brief winter day was already dwindling down as he entered the Prieuré gates on 9 January. Immediately he set eyes on Katherine he felt that something decisive had happened: 'she seemed a being transformed by love, absolutely secure in love.' From her room she led him, via the cowshed, to the crowded Study House, now a scene of intense concentration and activity: costumes were being sewn; fountains installed; aphorisms painted in special script; carpets, cushions, goat-skins arranged; and Asiatic musical instruments hung. Above the deep stage stood the sign of the enneagram. Awkwardly Katherine, Murry and Olgivanna took tea together; he was introduced to Adèle, the de Hartmanns, the de Salzmanns and someone destined to play an enormous role in his own life – Dr James Young. He met Orage again 'a changed man, much gentler and sweeter than I remembered him.' For a moment Murry's ingrained scepticism and hostility wavered: 'there was a blend of simplicity and seriousness in most of the people I met there, and in the company as a whole, which impressed me deeply.' After tea, maladroit and preoccupied, he even took a hand in painting coloured designs on the Study House windows, struck through by the last rays of the dying sun. Just before the supper bell it began to rain down on the tarred felt roof, but Katherine refused the umbrella offered by Olgivanna. 'Oh, no, I love the rain tonight, I want the feeling of it on my face.' After a meal served to Murry and Katherine in her room they came to the salon to watch the sacred dancing. Katherine arrived, chalk-faced, alien, strange, to sit in her accustomed niche by the fire. 'I want music. Why don't they begin? It is quite late.' She wanted above all The Initiation of the Priestess, and for Katherine it was indeed quite late.

For the last time the dance began, which she had longed to enter. 'If only I could have just a little place in that group. . . . How grateful I could be for it.' As Gurdjieff's music rose and vibrated, her eyes, seemingly directed beyond and through the dancers, registered her final impressions. At ten o'clock the class went back to the Study House to begin the night's work; and Katherine to her room. Climbing the stairs with Murry, she suffered a haemorrhage and, having received the benefit of prompt and assiduous attention from three doctors, passed rapidly from this world.

Even now the Gurdjieff–Mansfield contact remains a mystery, which as our clumsy fingers reach out to grasp, passes like smoke between them. Time, said Gurdjieff, is the Arch-Subjective. 'Did you know,' Olgivanna asked Katherine in mid-December, 'that you have been here more than two months already?'

'Two months?' said Katherine. 'Two thousand years you mean.' From the isolated, embittered authoress of *In a German Pension* to a being transformed by love, absolutely secure in love, is a metamorphosis worth reflection. Katherine had not come to the Prieuré by accident; her quality, her aim, her question, bore with them a predisposition to understanding. It was not in a formal sense that

Gurdjieff became Katherine's teacher; but how telling if at the last she found in him a 'man without quotation marks'; from a distance and at the very last.

Orage came running, and Olgivanna; Adèle, who was with her to the end, wept inconsolably in her room; telegrams went out to LM and Brett and Katherine's sisters. The following day Murry settled his negotiations with the *entrepreneurs de pompes funèbres*: sadly, since he forgot to pay the bill, Katherine Mansfield would soon be removed to a *fosse commune*, a plot reserved for those unable to pay for an individual tomb. Meanwhile she lay in the starved Protestant *temple*; on her cold finger the wedding-ring of Frieda Lawrence. First to reach Fontainebleau was LM, who, in a movement both protective and proprietary, covered Katherine in her 'brilliantly embroidered black silk Spanish shawl'. On the day before the funeral, various literary entities and nonentities from London convened in Fontainebleau at the long dinner-table of the hotel Chalet de la Forêt. When pity and *vin ordinaire* had elasticated their tongues, they began to criticise Katherine. 'Why had she come here? What had led to Ouspensky? How? When?' Suddenly the awkward, inarticulate LM found herself on her feet squarely confronting them. Why were they speaking like this, she demanded fiercely, when Katherine was not here to defend herself. The party broke up.

Katherine Mansfield was buried on 12 January 1923, and Murry provided the pastor with notes for his uneasy eulogy in the chapel. Then came the cortège: first the big hearse drawn by black horses sagely nodding their black plumes; then the attenuated crocodile of carriages and cars, twisting in and out of the narrow streets, winding by the longest route and the most grudging pace to the municipal cemetery. 'I began in the car,' recalls LM, 'then could not bear it and got out and walked, miles and miles very slowly.' From their windows the French looked out at the *'groupe de théosophes absurdes et agités'*. Strangely, the embankment bounding Avon cemetery carried the trains which ran between Paris and the Côte; again and again in her brief life Katherine had transited her final resting place. Now Murry and LM, painfully, tensely juxtaposed like siblings, watched her coffin lowered. ('It is not my coffin which is the shell, it is my body which is the shell,' Katherine had written.) LM stepped forward and dropped a bunch of marigolds, her final gauge of allegiance, into the quiet earth; and Gurdjieff handed to the mourners little screws of paper containing *kootia* – that mixture of raisins and corn and honey which is a symbol of decay, germination and re-growth.

On 13 January, the day after Katherine's burial, Gurdjieff brought his Study House to life.

Notes

1. This was the clear and unequivocal recollection of Mrs C. S. Nott who at this time was herself a friend and helper to 'Mrs Murry'.
2. Those asserting that Gurdjieff was responsible for Katherine's death in 1923 neglect this extended pathological history. It is outlined in 'Katherine Mansfield's Illness', *Proceedings of the Royal Society of Medicine*, vol. 48, April 1955, pp. 1029–32, where the author, Dr Brice Clark MD, concludes *inter alia* that pulmonary tuberculosis, then virtually incurable, was already present in 1911.
3. The Initiation of the Priestess is a fragment of a mystery called The Truth Seekers. Is it extant? The question is a natural one, if only because of the dance's place in Katherine Mansfield's estimation and final hours.

    Certainly it has not been included in the extensive film archive of Gurdjieff's sacred dances created by Mme de Salzmann since 1950. However on 16–19 April 1958, when a festival of music and dance was held in the pavilion at Taliesin West, Phoenix, Arizona, the programme included an item entitled 'Initiation of the Priestess'. The music was credited to Olgivanna, and – even more inexplicably – the creation of the dance was credited to her second daughter Iovanna, who was not in fact born when Gurdjieff first gave the Movement in Constantinople in the summer of 1920. (See *Our House* by Olgivanna Lloyd Wright – Horizon Press, New York 1959, page 100.)

    A somewhat nondescript photo of the dance appears opposite p. 51 of C. S. Nott's *Teachings of Gurdjieff* (Routledge & Kegan Paul 1961). Interviewed by the author in 1978, Mrs C. S. Nott (*née* Rose Mary Lillard) indicated that, although the Gurdjieff/de Hartmann musical score was extant, she and Jesmin Howarth had struggled unsuccessfully to reconstruct the authentic choreography. It would be rash, without directly consulting Mme de Salzmann, to pronounce any of Gurdjieff's sacred dances as irretrievably lost, but the auguries are not good.

Chapter 12

The Harrowing of John Middleton Murry

Through an unfortunate fate or a natural predilection, John Middleton Murry had conducted his marriage largely by correspondence, but with his young wife committed to a dubious grave, his pen ran on by its own momentum. A professional training assisted him to express the feelings he supposed people felt at such disagreeable moments. 'The woman I had loved, and whose death worked so upon me, I had loved even to anguish: she was verily all I had – my very life of very life.' He was conspicuously agonised and volubly inconsolable. Let someone try to console him, and he would show them; never, never could another woman replace Katherine in his affections. 'And my loved one was gone. It was the memory of that love that forbade me to seek refuge in the love of a creature. The only creature I could love was she.'

Some men are born consoled, some achieve consolation and some have consolation thrust upon them. LM chaperoned Murry back from Fontainebleau and deposited him at Ditchling, where his reception by his friends the Dunnings developed in a wholly unexpected way. Mrs Dunning hugged him to her bosom in a warm-hearted, matronly fashion, and Murry, in the extremity of his grief, hugged her back. 'But she took it', explains Murry, 'in a different sense. I will not say a wrong one.' It was left to Mr Dunning to articulate, within the more recognisable modalities of family life, his straightforward and natural reaction: 'Take her,' he said. At this point Murry, confessing himself out of his depth, returned hastily to

Pond Street. The Dunning experience had unsettled the bereaved man; he went immediately to Brett and, speaking slowly and distinctly into her ear-trumpet, asked her to marry him 'if he were really cornered'. Without waiting for this tedious eventuality, the Hon. Dorothy Brett, sister of the Ranee of Sarawak, gave him a sufficient and tangible proof of her willingness. Afterwards, as Murry was walking the streets deep in thought, he was accosted by a poor courtesan and, from a concern not to disappoint her and out of deference to her age, he did not refuse the simple transaction she proposed.

Days passed, and nights. Gradually Murry began to experience a spiritual fatigue and an urgent wish for solitude and retrenchment. On the edge of Ashdown Forest, untenanted and remote, stood the Old Farm, Twyford; and here he came, through the February dusk bolt upright on his Levis two-stroke. He sat alone in the dark in the dead still house, facing the fire. Was it some quality in the silence; some strange druidical current in the wood; or simply a glimmering of remorse? All we know is that he started to work.

> Prompted by some instinct, I tried to force . . . consciousness into every part of my body. . . . At last I had the sensation that I *was* in my hands and feet. . . . I was I, as I had never been before – and never should be again.

It is Murry's moment and it cannot be subtracted from him, but he did not make that effort once a day, or once a week, or even once a year. He made it once. It is known as 'Murry's mystical experience' and, thanks to all he wrote on the subject, an elaborate literature now surrounds it. From a particular event he drew a general conclusion: 'some sort of endorsement by the Universe was guaranteed to all my doings and . . . I could do no wrong.'

On 20 February 1923 the initiate was moved to write to the *Daily News*. Gurdjieff's Institute, reported Murry, with the authority of a man who had accidentally spent four days there, was a drug which did not solve the problem it professed to solve. And in any case, Katherine Mansfield had not been concerned with Gurdjieff's theory. His dear wife had been happy at the Prieuré certainly, but 'she died there, with her work barely begun. Whether she would willingly have paid that price for her happiness, who can say?' Even readers of the *Daily News* could grasp the key idea: Katherine Mansfield brought unwillingly to her death.

When his mystical retreat began, Murry had only God for his companion, but they were shortly joined by Mimi Bartrick-Baker from Chobham. Murry heard in her 'the voice of a captive princess whom I longed to set free.' Assured of the necessary physical and metaphysical endorsements, Mr Middleton Murry, for a second time in the two months since Katherine's death, offered his hand in marriage. At this critical moment, a first edition of Lawrence's masterpiece *Fantasia of the Unconscious* dropped through the letter box of the Old Farm, and Murry read it at one sitting on 10 March. He was lost in wonder, love and praise, more particularly since it almost seemed to him that he could have written the thing himself. 'This book contains all my deep beliefs – all.' If Murry sensed a personal difficulty, it was simply this: the *Fantasia* summoned him towards the mountain-tops, where, in an atmosphere altogether more rarefied than that prevailing at Chobham, lay the glittering prizes. The next day he felt reluctantly obliged to write Bartrick-Baker a disappointing letter. 'You see, my dear, I don't want you to marry me because I may appear charming.' Nor, upon a more mature reflection, did he especially wish her to marry him for any other reason.

A series of intoxicating speculations beckoned Murry to the giddy summit, where, armed with the editorship of a new and unique magazine, he would fling defiance at the Bloomsbury clique and Tom Eliot's *Criterion*. Might not his inexpressible mystical vision be somehow set in type? Might not his friendship with Lawrence be coaxed into a literary collaboration? Might not something be made of Katherine's death so talented, so young, so pure – not of course as a cult but as a true *cultus*? He had an awful lot of letters and suchlike. Might not. . . ? But no! Katherine's will had expressly forbidden it:

> All manuscripts, papers, letters, I leave to John Middleton Murry likewise I should like him to publish as little as possible and to tear up and burn as much as possible. He will understand that I wish to leave as few traces of my camping ground as possible.

And yet. And yet. What sensible man construed a legal document legalistically? The Court of Probate was a high authority no doubt, but in those silent hours at the Old Farm was he not referred to One higher than the Court of Probate? To the Great Editor of all things? Ah, what right had he John Middleton Murry to deny the world his wife's laundry bills and medical reports and love letters? She had only left him £232 and that was not going to go very far. No, it was clear: Katherine would have wanted him to publish, she would have begged him to publish – he felt it on his pulses. (And who is to say he was not right?) Yes, it was all settled – he would call his magazine the *New English Weekly*.

Immediately, Murry pressed LM into service to decipher and type Katherine's manuscripts, and bestowed her at his cottage in Ditchling. Thus LM's tireless allegiance blended with Murry's editorial ambition to establish, on firmer ground than ever, Miss Mansfield's claim to literary immortality. It is, incidentally, another question if Katherine achieved the kind of immortality for which she strove at Fontainebleau, but she did appear to LM at Ditchling and saluted her for the last time: 'I saw her face', writes LM, 'radiant with light as she smiled and passed through the room, telling me that all was well.'

It is a strange sighting, but no stranger perhaps than the subterranean connections between men's lives; the *New English Weekly* transpired to be a title already owned by Alfred Richard Orage. Thus Mr Murry's unexpected return to the Prieuré in April 1923 had the character neither of a pilgrimage nor a sentimental journey – it was a business trip. Orage too had his exhilarating vision, not of a new magazine but of a new life with Gurdjieff, and he almost converted the mystic from Twyford. 'He had burned his boats,' reports Murry, moistening his lips, 'and he came near to persuading me to burn mine, such was the contagion of his new condition. I did not.' Avoiding contamination and even quarantine, Murry re-crossed the Channel and laboured long and lovingly over the prospectus of his magazine. On reconsideration it was not to be the *New English Weekly* but a monthly, the *Adelphi*. Brevity was not a fault in this prospectus. 'You forgot to mention,' wrote Shaw acidly, 'that it will be printed on paper in black ink, and will be dependent either on advertisements or charity.' He was wrong. When the *Adelphi* was launched in June, with its yellow cover and its purple editorial, its prefixed photograph of Katherine and its first instalment of *Fantasia*, sales just took off; in four successive printings 15,240 copies were unloaded. Murry was perhaps the least surprised man in England; had not the Universe itself guaranteed endorsement to his doings? He joined the PEN Club, and began to study ballroom dancing.

In September Frieda arrived in England. 'I wish you'd look after her a bit,' Lawrence wrote to Murry. 'Would it be a nuisance?' It was less of a nuisance than Lawrence supposed. History does not record if Murry took Frieda to the *Palais de Danse* but he certainly rushed her to see Fred Carno's Mumming Birds, and shortly afterwards, inflamed by her Wagnerian beauty, he accompanied her to Freiburg. 'The idea of our sleeping together, waking in each other's arms, seemed like heaven on earth.... I said to F. "No, my darling, I mustn't let Lorenzo down – I can't." ' A partial record of this singular journey appears in Murry's article 'On Tolstoi and Other Things', with perhaps an understandable reticence concerning the Other Things.

For John Middleton Murry, 1923 had been a year of helter-skelter: Katherine had finally died; Gurdjieff had offered him a twist of *kootia*; Mrs Dunning had flung herself at his feet and he had flung her back; the Hon. Dorothy Brett had consoled him; the Universe and Mimi Bartrick-Baker had endorsed him; the *Adelphi* had blossomed wonderfully, then withered, under his hands; Frieda Lawrence had gone with him, if not all the way, at least to Freiburg and Fred Carno. Oh yes, and Violet le Maistre had written him a letter.

Like Orage, Miss Violet le Maistre claimed Huguenot descent, but there the resemblance ended. She was twenty-three; a vivacious, sultry-voiced, well-bred, abundantly educated, chestnut-haired slip of a girl. Murry had published one of her stories in the *Adelphi* and, in spring 1924, editor and contributor effected the ritual meeting: 'I took her out to tea in the Strand. We talked about Tchekov ... and I expounded my view of his exquisite and heroic morality.... While I was talking to her, the thought came to me that she was the very girl for my brother.' But Murry's altruism, itself exquisite and heroic, was soon confounded. 'Mr Murry,' said Miss le Maistre in a husky, contained voice, 'I like your brother very much but I can't love him, because you see I love *you*.' Murry's shy acquiescence was implemented with preternatural speed: urgently he retrieved from his brother Katherine's little pearl ring and posted it off to Violet to mark their engagement; adroitly he winkled LM out of the cottage at Ditchling, offering her as a parting inducement £40 'to get a cow or something'; by Easter he had snapped up 'the house of his dreams – the long, squat, white-timbered, grey-slated Old Coastguard Station' in Dorset. (£925 it set him back, but he had now £1,000 royalties from Katherine's books. The cheque, he reflected with modest satisfaction, was 'ten times as big as Katherine had received for her own work.') So John Middleton took Violet for his wedded wife, for better or worse, for richer or poorer, till death did them part. It was 24 April 1924, some fifteen months after Katherine's burial.

Now indeed fate seemed to smile on Murry: he had a brand-new wife and a house by the seaside; he had a magazine and all Katherine's royalties; he even received an invitation to deliver the Clark Lectures at Cambridge. And somehow in those golden honeymoon months he snatched time to fire off a salvo at Fontainebleau. On 17 May 1924 a certain Mr Alan Porter whom time has forgot (but then the literary editor of the *Spectator*) suggested that 'Gourdjiev' be numbered among those who might contribute to a future orthodoxy. Like a bolt from high Olympus came Murry's response: 'I do not like the smell of this "future orthodoxy",' he thundered in the *Adelphi*, 'it smells too perceptively of charlatanry and abracadabra and initiation at a guinea a head.' Yes, these were exhilarating times for Murry. 'Truly,' he wrote, 'we stood on top of happy hours.'

Often Murry and Katherine had wished for a daughter and a son. Now in 1925 Violet bore him an infant girl (christened Katherine and nicknamed Weg). 'I always felt', said Murry, 'quite simply that Violet's daughter was Katherine's daughter.' Then in 1926 Violet duly produced a son (christened John Middleton and nicknamed Col). It seemed like a dream come true; at last all the ingredients of happiness were marshalled. Perhaps best of all, Violet was educable. Her handwriting now looked exactly like Katherine's, so did all her dresses, and her mannerisms and her hair style. Seen from behind, she was Katherine. She could not quite get her short stories to come out like Miss Mansfield's yet, but that was only a matter of time, and she always used serviettes embroidered 'K.M.'. Here was a girl who was trying her damnedest, and yet at the periphery of Murry's satisfaction there stirred the smallest ripple of unease – vague, incalculable and fugitive. It was funny how Violet had proposed to him, funny how she liked Tchekov, funny how washed-out she was looking these days. She really was a *deutero* Katherine. No! Surely fate would not be so cruel to him! The services of Dr James Carruthers Young were secured to confirm Murry's presentiment: James Young, in whose arms Katherine had died. Tuberculosis was suspected, and Violet's sputum analysis proved positive. Once the blow fell, Murry accepted it with the philosophic stoicism of a non-combatant. 'It was the most meaningful thing that could have happened,' he wrote. And Violet's response, although superficially surprising to her husband, was surely in the script. 'O I'm so *glad*!' she exclaimed with shining eyes. 'You see . . . I wanted you to love me as much as you loved Katherine – and how could you without this?' Here was a fearful symmetry; here was parallelism *à l'outrance*.

By July 1927 the hospital superintendent at Midhurst discharged Violet as incurable, and the unfortunate Murry took her home for a Chalet des Sapins re-run. It would have been a nice touch to secure LM's services as a companion; unfortunately LM had withdrawn her labour and goodwill – indeed she had withdrawn altogether – when she realised Murry was publishing Katherine's private and personal papers. One can scarcely imagine a spot more bleak, more exposed, more grossly unsuitable for a delicate consumptive patient than the Old Coastguard Station. But Violet had to make do with it until October 1928, when Murry finally sold up and brought her inland to a handsome, timbered, architect-designed bungalow at Yately. Here he devoted himself to an impassioned contemplation of the Cross, and to reducing his handicap at the East Berks Golf Glub.

His pen meanwhile continued to cover page after page in tight, obsessive handwriting. Some psychiatrists might see a significance in the fact that his book *God* published in 1929 began with forty-odd pages of autobiography. He recollected how 'it would have been easier for me to enter the Catholic Church than the Gurdjieff Institute. They both belonged to the same order. . . . The difference was that Catholicism gave you something in return.' Murry's imagination rambled on in lofty speculation; the mystic of Twyford saw a grand 'correlation between my personal condition and that of the world'. Some occult connection was to be suspected between Katherine and the Great War and between Violet and the stock-market crash. But Murry's private journal spoke of themes less sublime: 'How *tired* I am of listening to that cough of Violet's.' 'Her cough seems to vibrate on my spine.' And, hesitant though one is to mention it, there was naturally a more intimate dimension to his troubles. It was certainly not that Middleton Murry wanted sex: simply that he was 'travailed by a longing for physical love.' He wrote to Mrs Dunning; he toyed with the idea of advertising for Marguéritte in a French newspaper; then on 2 March 1930 D. H. Lawrence unexpectedly solved this problem by dying. Without hesitation Murry sped to the South of France to pay his last respects; to comfort and embrace the grieving Frieda. 'With her,' he mused, 'and with her for the first time in my life, I knew what fulfilment in love really meant.' As for Violet, well he had, after all, dedicated *God* to her and bought her a pair of Woolworth's ear-rings.

Some distinction may perhaps be drawn between a partnership and a coalition; a confederate is not necessarily an ally. Max Plowman and Elizabeth Ada Cockbayne enter our scene more or less simultaneously; both cast a beady gaze on Murry; both wish Violet well. We should not, however, load the notion of their congruity with a weight it will not safely bear. Plowman's blue eyes were wide apart: Betty's were close together. He was saintly, intellectual, wise and foolish: she was primitive, instinctual, sudden. Plowman's modest triumphs lay in the field of letters: Betty's in the field of her dad's farm at Stoneleigh. Plowman's most fervid exclamations of enthusiasm were reserved for the symbolism of William Blake: Betty's for unrestrained and vigorous sexual congress. Plowman placed his final trust in the purifying and redemptive power of faith; Betty in her lemon meringue pie.

It was Betty who was engaged to nurse Violet, but it was Max Plowman who felt 'an active power to drive back the onset of the disease'. What moved Plowman was nothing less than *caritas*, a dangerous feeling which did not go unreciprocated. 'But I must tell you', protested Violet to Murry, 'because I love you. I don't love you any more. I am in love with Max.' It all sounded perfectly logical to Murry and not in the least surprising; evidently Plowman was cast for the Orage–Ouspensky role. But Murry, now a connoisseur in parallelism, registered one irritating discrepancy, 'that whereas I mistrusted Orage and Ouspensky, I trust Max implicitly.' And what precisely did Murry trust Max to do? 'Of this I am certain,' he wrote, 'he is hurrying V. to physical death – to spiritual beatitude and physical death. I accept it, I am even glad of it.' So, just as Katherine had removed to the Prieuré, Violet removed to Plowman's house at Golders Green, and here at half past three in the morning of Sunday 30 March 1931, with an almost excessive regard to the precedent case, she expired. Before the cremation, Murry coaxed Katherine's little pearl ring for a second time from a dead finger. He was sorry to lose Violet of course; it stood to reason. 'Essentially,' he wrote, 'I laid down my life for her,' but here Murry is speaking figuratively. In a more practical sense, things had not turned out so badly: he had acquired two fine children; and two interesting friends in Young and Plowman; and his golf handicap was down to twelve. As for his love of the creature, that had been providentially catered for, as even his children perceived. 'Col!' cried Weg, 'Dadda is cuddling Miss Cockbayne!'

Mr Murry's intentions towards Betty were honourable but perhaps in the final analysis ill-advised: he proposed to marry her. Farmer Cockbayne regarded his future son-in-law with a rheumy and speculative eye. 'Well,' he said, sighing deeply, 'I would not like any man to think I hadn't given him fair warning of what he was letting himself in for.' At this formula, so full of Lawrentian promise, Murry smiled conspiratorially. Violet's funeral was in April 1931, and Murry, not letting a blade of grass grow under his feet, married Betty in May at Odiham registry office. James Young was the witness. An idyllic future promised, as the happy couple set up house at the Old Rectory, Larling, an enchanting, isolated, tree-girt, Georgian building, standing in nine green acres on the edge of the Norfolk brecklands. Murry enjoyed country life and by the end of the summer could actually distinguish a thrush. It must not be thought that he had a heart of stone; Betty would often find him weeping; but his was not the grief which common folk feel at bereavement. No, his thoughts were elsewhere bent. 'I do not suppose that many men of today', he explained, 'know the experience of being consumed even to tears by the reading of *Das Kapital*.' And in this, at least, he may not have been mistaken. But Murry was not destined to live by Marx and lemon meringue pie alone. Before they had been three months at Larling, the pregnant Betty astonished by asking him to let her go away for ever. 'If I would give her twenty pounds, that would be enough. . . . She stood before me like a slave before her master, and pleaded.' As things turned out, this would have been twenty pounds well spent, but Murry, heavily preoccupied in writing his book *The Necessity of Communism*, chose to retain his capital. The next day, when Betty made a bolt for it, Murry actually rushed off and brought her back from the railway station. As Monsieur Léaud so pertinently comments, '*Il a manqué à Murry de concevoir la pensée comme quelque chose qui hésite.*' In the dark years which lay ahead, it would not be Mrs Murry who would do the running.

The superbly named Betty Cockbayne came into her husband's

focus in three distinct stages: at the end of the first, Murry began to wonder if he had not been the teeniest little bit hasty; at the end of the second, he felt on his pulses that this one was not going to die of TB; at the end of the third, he apprehended with horror the true import of Farmer Cockbayne's warning. Murry's son Col remembers how his stepmother 'exuded a sort of black, demonic force of pure annihilation like a psychic miasma. Confronted with it the strongest men became mere straws.' Sir Richard Rees summed it up another way: 'I am a connoisseur in domestic infelicity . . . but . . . I have never seen anything to equal the misery of the life at the Old Rectory.' It was not that Murry had no proper exemplar in dealing with the situation. He had. In June 1932 James Carruthers Young and his new American wife Helen set up house seven miles from Larling. To what extent Dr Young's psychological procedures with Betty relied on his clinical training and to what extent on his studies with Gurdjieff, must be conjectural. He spoke to her in a voice which was modest and low: 'if you don't shut your foul mouth woman – and *keep it shut*! – I swear to God that I'll break this log over your bloody, stupid, ignorant head.'

But John Middleton Murry had not the *dasein* for this approach. Long, long ago his magazine *Rhythm* had been committed to brutality, but now that it actually entered his life, he found himself on the receiving end. Pursued, harried, savaged by his terrible wife, he flapped about in a truly wonderful replica of activity. He converted to pacifism; he joined the Independent Labour Party; he embraced Marxism and would persuade Oswald Mosley to do the same – 'You may think me over-confident but we'll see.' Books gushed like hot lava from his Corona portable: books on Keats, on Lawrence, on William Blake. 'How he has understood so much of Blake in the time at his disposal I simply can't imagine,' said Plowman. It was indeed to be wondered at, but Blake was much on Murry's mind. 'Let the men do their duty,' he quoted nervously, 'and the women will be such wonders.' The trouble was, Betty was such a wonder she would not let him do his duty.

Throughout his hideous difficulties Murry remained industrious, and nowhere more so than in puffing his own literary image; in 1934 he prevailed on young Rayner Heppenstall to write his strange work *John Middleton Murry: A Study in Excellent Normality*. 'I would like', protested Heppenstall grandiloquently, 'to convince most people that my equation (*Jesus* + *Shakespeare* + *Blake* + *Marx*) ×

Murry = Good Modernity is a true one.' But in the privacy of his study, Heppenstall confessed to a different, though equally unrealisable, ambition. 'On the left-hand page I would put what I really thought. Facing it should stand what I needed to say to fulfil my contract.' To other writers Murry was rather less than indulgent. In November 1934 Orage died; the old rival, who had known Katherine at her beginning and her end. Murry's contribution to the commemorative issue of the *New English Weekly* bordered dangerously on sarcasm:

> in Orage there was an obstinate substratum of belief that there was some secret of control of the universe: a key by which one could unlock all the doors, and be a master of Power. There were veritable Masters in Tibet for instance.

Murry was surely right in adding that he belonged to 'the other side'.

On 1 January 1935 an astonished New York audience, gathered to hear Liam O'Flaherty on 'The Art of Enjoying Life', were fobbed off with a sea-sick Murry on 'The Agony of John Keats'. But foreign lecture tours give temporary respite only, and in mid-August, as Murry winds up the *Adelphi* summer school at Caerleon, we discern his pliant mind reaching for a more stable solution to the Betty problem. He had, he said, long felt the need for a permanent centre, where a dedicated nucleus could receive an education in non-sectarian and practical socialism. And someone, who could doubt it, must lead these egalitarian studies. Was this perhaps a call to him? Did the stern imperatives of a revolutionary dialectic require him to sacrifice the pleasures of his domestic life? The more he considered the matter, the more it seemed so. But let his audience be perfectly clear: he was not thinking so much of a community as a *communitas*; he had in mind less a university than a *universitas*. Money was needed.

It wants no labouring that Murry's 'Adelphi Centre' owed somewhat less to idealism than to stark terror; was conceived more as a sanctuary from Betty than an incubator for socialists. But may we not entertain a subsidiary notion, audacious yet strangely persuasive – the Adelphi Centre was a surrogate Prieuré, and Murry a cardboard cut-out of Gurdjieff. If Murry could not pull down the temple he could at least parody it:

It will be located in a large house, with accommodation for sixty to seventy people living under the simplest conditions . . . . there will be simple workshops of various kinds in the Centre – a carpenter's shop, a smith's shop, a printing press, a bindery: likewise in the house there will be a sewing-room and a still-room.

What Gurdjieffian[1] can read these lines from Murry's prospectus without a *frisson* of recognition?

By September 1935, the skeleton of Murry's idea had been clothed with flesh: the Oaks at Langham, big and square, had been bought; the Adelphi School Company Ltd held the deeds; and Murry's children saw less and less of him at Larling. Betty engaged to wreck the entire Langham project within a fortnight, and seemingly tried to poison Heppenstall with an overdose of calomel. But Rayner survived to apply for admission to the Centre, and was surprised by a reply on a red letterhead saying he should be welcome as cook. Confided to his care were the digestions of Murry, a colloidal chemist with bobbed black hair and an operatic tenor voice, an elephantine Canadian girl, a ginger-bearded artist, an ex-paraffin-man, a doctor from Norwich who 'sneered down his thin pink nose into his moustache and made sly observations indicative of a belief in Original Sin,' together with 'an excitable Scotswoman, very thin and bright-eyed and with orange hair'. Murry himself received Heppenstall with a warmth which was almost more than fraternal: 'He ducked his head sideways, rushed at me, folded me in his arms and started going all over me with little nibbling kisses, saying: "Dear old boy, dear old boy, dear old boy, dear old boy."' But these transports were not to last. Soon Heppenstall came in exhilarated from the Shepherd and Dog and made an unfortunate remark during Plowman's lecture on 'The Necessity of God'. Worse than this, his performance in the kitchen consistently disappointed.

Early in 1936, Murry contracted a powerful attachment to James Young's estranged wife Helen, then in New York. Repelled by Betty, enraptured by Helen, but now with three children to consider, Murry feverishly debated if he should cut and run. Whether he finally seized his moment or his moment seized him is a matter of legitimate debate: when Betty went on holiday Murry went absent without leave. 'LEFT LARLING' is his ecstatic journal entry for 28 May 1936. 'My baby, my sweetheart! Oh Christ, Christ. *Jésus sera en agonie jusqu'à la fin du monde.*' (Murry's allusion is to his new baby daughter Mary whom he is sorry to leave.) So he came alone to the Adelphi Centre, where a socialist could forget the cares and stern duties of a vexatious world. The cellar was excellent, the 1929 Côtes de Bourg particularly memorable and, whatever doctrinal nuances and nice distinctions of principle demarked one pupil from the next, they all agreed on this much – that the epoch of the celibate community had withered away. These were strange days at Langham. The rude elders of the hamlet heard the unfamiliar strains of *Porgy and Bess*, and, approaching the Centre like ruminants, perceived through the dusk unlikely silhouettes in galvanic and unmistakable engagement. Gloomily supping their mild and bitter in the public bar of the Shepherd and Dog, the gaffers would recall how the Oaks had been 'built of bad bricks'. As for Murry, despite the consolations of Cupid and Bacchus, a mystical pessimism quickly seized upon him: 'My personal destiny fits absolutely with the abominable horrors of the Fascist counter-revolution in Spain, sanctified by the Catholic Church – the mass-murder at Badajoz.' And there was another thing – Heppenstall's cooking.

Into this strange milieu stepped Helen Young, newly arrived from America on the *Bremen* for her 'honeymoon'. She came on 28 September 1936, and lasted precisely four days; in a gesture of uncharacteristic generosity Murry paid for her return trip. By 14 October he was back at the Old Rectory with Betty. 'Wonderful (isn't it)', he wrote to Plowman, 'that the day I go back to Larling is Katherine's birthday.'

Murry's first action here – in which some might see the expression of a domestic hope rather than a global aspiration – was to join the Peace Pledge Union. Unfortunately Betty was not a signatory. As Murry's son Colin puts it:

> The fury which was eventually to be unleashed at The Old Rectory was something so dark and elemental it is beyond my powers to describe. I find that I lack any scale of normal human experience upon which to draw for reference.

Meanwhile strange questions perplexed Murry's fevered brain: why *par exemple* had his architect written to him from 24 Adamson Road? 'Adamson. Son of Adam. Sons of Adam. Sons of God. 24.

2-4-8. 2-4-8-16. 2-4-8-16-32. 64. 128. 512. 1024. Adelphi. 2 Brothers. Who knows? Who knows anything?' Sometimes he got away again to visit the Centre briefly, but nothing he found there was calculated to buttress his sanity. 'Langham on Friday; faced by a domestic crisis over Rayner's cooking.' To say nothing of the orange-haired Scotswoman now convinced she was about to give birth to the Lord. By May 1937 the Centre had become peripheral; Murry unloaded it onto the PPU, who packed it wall to wall with refugee Basque children. And so ended Murry's first essay in community leadership, which, as he cryptically put it, had 'justified, in ways totally unforeseen, the effort we had undertaken.'

Larling was quite a different story. Except for the real presence of our Lord, Murry could not have stuck Betty two minutes. Before long he discerned his sufferings to be in the pattern and imitation of Christ, and decided to seek ordination. The canon of Westminster could perceive no insuperable objection to his taking holy orders. Had not Her Majesty the Queen herself expressed a wish to read some of Middleton Murry's work? (Although whether her desire had ever been satisfied was not extant in clerical circles.) Neither could the bishop of Chichester apprehend a difficulty. Nor could Canon Raven, though it might perhaps be argued that Canon Raven could apprehend very little. Murry's commonsense we may query, but it is impossible not to salute his pertinacity: he proposed to interest his terrible spouse in saying her prayers and improving her spelling. At breakfast he would slip a marker from the Good Book, clear his throat weightily, and read a few psalms, before spooning his porridge and golden syrup. At night by his bedside he would murmur aloud the Lord's Prayer. Well might the unfortunate man petition to be delivered from evil. His children, tense in their beds, heard through the walls the nightly wailings of a darker, obscener litany; catechisms and burnt offerings which might have rejoiced the devil himself.

Almost immediately Murry submitted himself to Canterbury, he contracted Burger's disease, a rare arterial condition found principally among Jewish immigrants to New York. He knew this for a sure sign he should not enter the Church. Readers who subscribe to the Thirty-Nine Articles will perhaps find Murry's explanation the most likely one: on the other hand he did more or less light his Gold Flake cigarettes one from another for a period of thirty years. Smoking can damage your health. Whatever the cause, the effect was a rotten cramp and numbness in the right leg, *endoteritis obliterans* with intermittent claudication. Colin noticed that,

> my father looked a lot older. The lines on his face seemed to have deepened and his forehead resembled a lump of cobbler's wax so criss-crossed was it with wrinkles. He moved more slowly too, and, if he had been a clockwork motor I should have felt it was high time to wind him up again.

In churlish disregard of the Peace Pledge Union, Europe was sliding towards war; and again Murry read in political and economic events the reflection of his atrocious personal situation. In 1938 he advertised in *The Times* that he would no longer be responsible for his wife's debts; by 25 May, when his second son David was born, he himself was in hospital for observation. By New Year 1939 strange ornamental hermits had descended on Larling: a gentleman with a snow-white beard who announced the end of the world, and an aged convict who spent every interval between his custodial sentences drinking meths in the outhouse. By April 1939 Murry was back in hospital again, for a wickedly botched operation. He went to Cresselly in Wales to convalesce. 'I'm feeling queer,' he said, 'Hellishly queer.' And so he was. For three days John Middleton Murry endured a living cliché: he teetered on the brink of a profound spiritual abyss; his teeth chattered like castanets; he was stalked by Stark Terror and Unspeakable Fear. He longed for a fast car to Larling, but 'it would be in vain. I should be mad before I got there.' Almost miraculously he encountered Dr James Young, who diagnosed 'a classical example of Nervous Breakdown', and put him to bed with a mammoth shot of adrenalin and a cup of tea so strong you could stand a teaspoon in it. So at this further crisis in Murry's life, rescue was effected by Katherine's friend, the former pupil of Gurdjieff.

We do not know how long the fortifying effect of the adrenalin lasted, but when Murry returned to Larling he said pluckily to Betty, 'Please take this seriously. I don't love you any more.' It was not simply insults Betty hurled at Murry now; she threw any object to hand, animal, vegetable or mineral, including on one occasion the baby. She was immensely strong physically, and put herself to some trouble to elaborate her point of view. Colin Murry remembers:

The screaming came again and there was the sound of muffled blows. . . . I found my father half-crouched, half-kneeling in the hallway trying to shield his bowed head from the blows which Betty was raining down on him. She was wholly demented.

Mr and Mrs Murry had been married ten years, and it was increasingly evident that they were not going to make a go of it. The terms of a separation began to be heard even on Betty's lips. 'You take your two children, an' I'll take mine. An' I'll keep Larlin' darlin'.' Murry paced the corridors in sombre reverie: 'Every room has its own particular memory of horror.' He left on 1 October 1941.

Murry was strengthened in his decision by having formed a new attachment. 'If my relation with Mary is not as good, as true and sound, and lovely as is possible for the relation between a man and a woman to be I'm a Dutchman.' Certainly Mary Gamble was an improvement on Betty. Ten years younger than Murry (now fifty-two), she had the distinction of having once been a prospective Labour candidate and having published two or three small volumes of verse. When Murry met her in PPU circles he told her that Katherine had sowed the seed of true love in his heart: 'put into the fingers of his soul the ball of golden thread that, if he unwound it faithfully, would lead to the magic of true love.' He had unwound it, and unexpectedly it had led to Mary Gamble. 'You are a spiritual caveman,' she responded.

A spiritual caveman? Such had long been Murry's own picture, and his next exercise seems, at least in part, another unconscious parody of Gurdjieff. He proposed to establish a very special farm, 'nothing less than the Monte Cassino of a new Christian civilisation. With the same great motto as S. Benedict – *laborare est orare*: to work is to pray.' Indeed, as he scoured up and down for a suitable property we nearly catch him echoing Ouspensky's theme of eternal recurrence. 'Suddenly I was overwhelmed by the strange feeling: "I have been here before". The vehemence with which it swept over me was almost dizzying.'

Finally he settled on Lodge Farm, Thelnetham, near Diss, and acquired it for £3,325. It was a socialist enterprise, but the deeds were in Murry's own name, and each community worker should receive board, lodgings, and an allowance of seven and sixpence per week, rising to ten shillings. The young men would further receive immunity from call-up. Murry, Mary and their entourage took possession on 5 October 1942, and 'not a mangel on the field was bigger than an orange.' From the beginning Murry claimed a natural ascendancy: 'I have the advantage over you that I have had the experience of living an ordered life in the country for the last twenty-five years.' He could indeed spot a thrush, but he quickly felt the lack of his old friend Bodge the gardener, who knew about planting things. His mind clambered rapidly up and down the ladder of abstraction. His farm was certainly 'the social embodiment . . . of what Keats again called Negative Capability.' It was also, paradoxically, the direct consequence of his effort in literary criticism. 'Or, to put it differently, my mysticism is the mysticism of descent.' But concerning the pigs he stood on more debatable ground. 'All things considered they may show a small profit when their muck is taken into account.' He struggled to bear a hand himself but as Katherine had said, he dug 'as though he were exhuming a dead body or making a hole for a loved one.' Colin Murry remembers him trying to harvest beet, and sitting down abruptly in the ooze:

> That night there was a sharp frost, and when I reached the field next morning, it was to discover the perfect imprint of my father's corduroyed backside frozen solid into the mud. You could have taken a plaster cast from it. It remained there for days and one by one the members of the Group made their solemn pilgrimage to the spot and stood, peering down in mingled awe and astonishment at this most remarkable sight.

As year succeeded year, Murry found himself thrown back on a purely social role: he subscribed to *Farmer & Stockbreeder*; he bought a pedigree bull called Gresham Romeo; garden parties and village fêtes were held on his lawn, and tea was served from a silver teapot. The one discordant note was struck by Betty. Her postcards in large childish capitals – ARE YOU STILL LIVING WITH THAT OLD WHORE? – did not escape the attention of the postman and postmistress. There was talk in the local that even Mr Murry had his problems.

The men from the ministry thought surprisingly well of Lodge Farm, but it is not always easy to follow the bureaucratic train of thought. By 1949 Murry's root harvest had failed; his pigs had succumbed to paratyphoid; and his cows to bloat on the leys. In any case, farming was no longer Murry's chief preoccupation. The writer of *The Necessity of Communism* was suddenly found preaching die-hard opposition to Soviet Russia, while the author of *The Necessity of Pacifism* was now prepared if needs be to blow the world up. Yes, yes, he knew all about the apocalyptic splendours of atomic warfare, but the important thing was to stop the Russians. 'I will accept', he said, 'that the annihilation of the entire human species is possible.' And no one could say fairer than that.

On 6 February 1954 Betty died of malignant hypertension, and a month later, in Bury St Edmunds registry office, Mary Gamble became Mrs Murry. Incongruously her husband took her on holiday to Bandol, to the Hôtel Beau Rivage; they stumped hand in hand along the coast to 'Cape Sixpenny'; they made a sentimental journey to the Villa Pauline. Murry was sixty-five now, eking out a posthumous existence; defeat was imperishably etched in every line on his tortoise-like face. Thirty years on and three marriages later, did he even remember Katherine? He sometimes wrote of her: of their idyllic marriage and the discomforts she had endured at Fontainebleau. Yes, he reflected, Gurdjieff's Institute had lent itself to Katherine's purpose of self-annihilation. More he dare not, and less he must not, say. It was not for him, he concluded gravely, to pass judgment on the Institute, but how tragic that Katherine had 'reacted into the spiritual quackery of Gurdjieff – and death.'

Long years have passed like a dream, and the actors, every one, have vanished from our stage. Is it conceivable that Katherine Mansfield had, after all, a truer vision of Gurdjieff than Middleton Murry? In theory it is. Yet Murry held himself out as an arbiter of very special qualities. 'Our strength is not in our mysticism and our fanaticism: it is in our lucidity. We look upon the great world, we look upon ourselves, with serene impartiality. We have no illusions.' Perhaps his life affords the best commentary upon his general claim and his special judgment. It is certainly a piquant one.

Note

1 My adoption of the label 'Gurdjieffian' evokes Gurdjieff's own words in Essentuki: 'In any case they will not understand but it is necessary for them to be able to give us some sort of name.'

Chapter 13

Beelzebub

With Katherine dead just a week, Gurdjieff gave his first lecture in the Study House. Did they sit there – Olgivanna, James Young, Adèle, Orage – spines erect on goatskin rugs; holding their lost friend in the field of their mobilised attention? No eulogy was spoken and only one allusion, uncompromising and oblique, may be deciphered from Gurdjieff's words. 'There is a thousand times more value', he said, 'even in polishing the floor as it should be done than in writing twenty-five books.' Katherine had come to the Prieuré not as a fashionable authoress but as a suffering, questioning human being. And Gurdjieff himself, assailed on all sides by other problems, barely acclimatised linguistically and culturally, and not caring tuppence for popular values, received the woman, not the personage.

And then she died.

Within a week it had begun: reporters settled on the Prieuré like a misfortune of ravens; articles – misinformed, trivialising, sensational – peppered the newspapers. It was precisely the debut Gurdjieff would not have wished for his Institute. As the gentlemen of the Fourth Estate made free of his hospitality, he scathingly recalled the proceedings of the 'New Society of Literati and Journalists' in Baku:

> After these learned sessions, suppers were always served, with two bottles of cheap wine; and many hid in their pockets some

bit of hors-d'oeuvre, either a piece of sausage or a herring with a piece of bread, and if by chance anyone else noticed this they would usually say: 'This is for my dog – the rascal already has the habit – always expects something when I return home late.'

It is evident that the Prieuré was a *pons asinorum* which few, if any, journalists were qualified to cross, and Denis Saurat has left us an amusing account of the *Daily Mail* man's fear and consternation at seeing the sacred dances.

> To reassure the journalist I told him that I was a professor in Bordeaux University and that all these people were mad. He thought about it for a moment, and then seemed much relieved; his confidence in himself came back.

As the Katherine Mansfield avalanche gathered momentum, Gurdjieff himself kept a dignified silence: no boasts, no hints, no excuses – nothing. The young writer's influence had survived her and, like a burning-glass, suddenly focused the attention of literary Europe on the Prieuré. Gurdjieff studied the phenomenon with interest, which although sardonic was purposeful.

On 5 July 1924, shortly after Gurdjieff's first trip to America, occurred a shock which deflected his work. To suggest that he foresaw it raises as many questions as it answers, but the facts are certainly extraordinary. From his Paris apartment on the Boulevard Pereira, he went to the garage and insisted that the mechanic triple-check his small Citroen – lights, nuts, bolts and especially the steering. Then he made over certain papers to Olga de Hartmann, gave her power of attorney, and, refusing to drive her back to Fontainebleau, brusquely told her to get the five o'clock train. Gurdjieff lunched quietly at an Armenian restaurant and set out for the Prieuré alone. Some say he leaned out through the window of his hurtling car to pick an apple *en passant*. He himself merely chronicles the dénoument: 'as a final chord, this battered physical body of mine . . . together with an automobile going at a speed of 90 kilometres per hour crashed into a very thick tree.' The axle was buckled, radiator crushed, engine torn off its seating, steering-column snapped. Gurdjieff was found unconscious on the grass verge, his injured head inexplicably resting on a cushion from the car. The doctors could not understand why he had not been killed outright, and offered little hope to his family. Next day, heavily bandaged, he was brought from Fontainebleau hospital to the Prieuré and carried upstairs to his room on a stretcher. 'Many people, many people,' he murmured.

For five days Gurdjieff lay unconscious, nursed only by his mother, his sister and Madame Ostrowska. On the sixth day he woke, 'a piece of live meat in a clean bed', blind, amnesic and in intense pain. Yet in no more than a month Gurdjieff was struggling to walk in the garden, his purple face masked by dark glasses and his astrakhan hat heraldic on his bandaged head. By slow degrees he recovered his strength and sight and memory. He directed that trees be cut down for great bonfires, and stood hours on end, in his thick black coat, staring into the flames and the blue smoke rising. In the long nights every omen told the fragility of human existence: Katherine Mansfield had died in the very next room; his old mother was now mortally ill with liver disease; his wife Madame Ostrowska had contracted cancer; and he himself had escaped violent death by the slenderest grace. It was a moment of suffering and a moment to take stock. 'How many men and women, roubles and rupees, have passed through his hands? In vain – he is alone. He is the bearer of a radical and overwhelming message, ambitious, urgent and unrealisable?' Before the accident he had counted on the support of his family; on his own formidable energies; on the possibility of 'magnetising' certain pupils who would carry his work into the future. He had counted on a sufficient quantity of time. In the Prieuré garden he gathered his pupils together and dismissed them: 'Everything now stop – dances, music, work. You all must go in two days.' Some of his stunned audience interpreted him literally, but even those who had the wit to stay would not see him so often. The lesson of Katherine's literary influence could not have been lost on Gurdjieff. Fifty years old or thereabouts, he had taken a remarkable decision: 'I, who have lately been considered by very many people as a rather good teacher of temple dances, have now become today a professional writer.'

Gurdjieff was a polyglot, and began his career as an author with a problem which embarrasses few of his critics: which language to use. He could write with facility in Greek or Turkish but had no one he could trust to translate. In fact his pupils in London and New York were the ones most hungry for his writing, but he himself had no feeling for English, admirably suited though it might be for discussing 'the topic of Australian frozen meat or, sometimes, the Indian question.' As for Russian, it was more suitable 'for swapping anecdotes and for use in referring to someone's parentage.' Here was certainly a knotty problem, but Gurdjieff did not seem unduly perturbed:

> Ah . . . me! Never mind, esteemed buyer of my wiseacrings. If only there be plenty of French armagnac and 'Khaizarian bastourma', I shall find a way out of even this difficult situation.
> . . . no matter what language I shall use, always and in everything, I shall avoid . . . the 'bon ton literary language'.

Intriguing, to say the least, was Gurdjieff's starting point: his vision of writers and writing. If modesty is proper in a fifty-year-old beginner, Gurdjieff showed no sign of it; he was deliberately, superbly, hyperbolically provocative. Pushkin and Shakespeare had ruined the Russian and English languages; Tolstoi was a mountebank who achieved fame by mistake. We must never forget of course that the studied insult, the iconoclastic assertion, were to Gurdjieff what ECT is to genuine certificated psychiatrists. But this particular conviction seems unfeigned: that European writing is somehow soulless; an empty and abortive interval in the history of literature; 'music . . . built up of an infinitesimal null idea.' His cartoon of the contemporary intellectual scene, although garish, is uncomfortably close to home. Any literate person who had three months' rent paid in advance was busy writing a novel, describing 'how some John Jones and Mary Smith attain the satisfaction of their "love".' Any gentleman eager to engrave the title 'poet' on his visiting card, had merely to dash off a stanza like:

> Green roses
> Purple mimosas
> Divine are her poses
> Like hanging memories.

Bookshops were groaning with titles like *Why the Sirikitsi Made War on the Parnakalpi*, original studies copied entirely from existing books. More popular with the young were educational works like the *Manual of Bon Ton and Love Letter Writing*. As for religious and philosophical material, why, any modern author felt competent to write his own gospel: 'Am I any worse than those ancient barbarians, Matthew, Mark, Luke and Johnnie?'

Certainly modern authors of literary testaments do not submit their own qualifications to quite the same abrasive interrogation they apply to the world at large. On the other hand, not all their ideas and techniques are as simplistic as Gurdjieff pretends. In 1924, when he turned to writing, André Gide was busy on *Les Faux-monnayeurs*, Franz Kafka on *Der Prozess* and Virginia Woolf on *Mrs Dalloway*. Gurdjieff himself intended to produce a gospel in the authentic tradition, a work transmitting initiatic information which had come down from long-past ages. The plenitude and quality of his life bespoke his competence.

Too weak even to hold a pencil, Gurdjieff had to dictate his first literary experiments. They were conceived for the theatre or cinema and, despite his infirmity, he set himself 'to "bake" every other day a fresh and completed scenario.' Instead of hibernating comfortably at Fontainebleau, he hobbled back into life; went to Paris and produced his apprentice works, 'The Three Brothers', 'The Unconscious Murder', 'The Cocainists', 'The Chiromancy of the Stock Exchange' – none of which satisfied him in the least.

Though physically shaken, Gurdjieff's inner work was accelerated, his individuality heightened: 'When I say "I" it is as if I hear something rattle inside.' From the vantage-point of such a state he had a prevision of a gigantic epic, and, working at white heat, constructed in two or three hours a cryptic, virtually unintelligible synopsis. Then late one evening, sipping black coffee at the Prieuré, he began to dictate to Olga de Hartmann: 'It was in the year 223 after the creation of the World. . . . Through the Universe flew the ship *Karnak* of the "trans-space" communication. . . . On the said "trans-space" ship was Beelzebub with his kinsmen and near attendants.' Here sounded the opening lines of Gurdjieff's undoubted masterpiece *Beelzebub's Tales to His Grandson*, a work which in potency resembles a red pepper and in compass a flying cathedral.

Beelzebub and his grandson Hassein are seated on the upper deck of the *Karnak* under a large glass bell; stars, comets, moons, worlds glide past and are gone into the boundless space. Here is a majestic, living universe, involving and evolving on the basis of reciprocal feeding. Here is the intimation of a Supreme Being, endlessly benign yet veiled by a hierarchy of levels, and obliged to manifest through the primordial Law of Three and Law of Seven; a God who cannot jump over his knees or beat the Ace of Trumps with the Two of Hearts; a God who suffers and whose creatures are particles of that suffering. And here, set in the remote Siberia of the cosmos, is our solar system 'Ors', whose sun, arch-preposterously, neither heats nor lights. Here is our dear Earth, a misshapen ugly-duckling of a planet, enveloped by a thin film of organic life. And in this biosphere each individual man is chastened as a fugitive, mortal atom, yet exalted as an embryonic model of the universe. It is a cosmology which Richard Rees has described as 'bizarre and subtle yet at the same time bewilderingly simple and sublimely, or absurdly, complete.'

Beelzebub has just accomplished that most poignant and symbolic of journeys, the return to the source, and is now outward bound again for the solar system Pandetznokh. Sired and born on the planet Karatas, he possesses an appropriate exterior coating, namely hooves and a curly tail; once he boasted horns, but these – because of the indiscretions of his fiery youth – were confiscated by Our Common Father Omni-Being Endlessness. This Beelzebub comes from an unknown pantheon; he is decidedly not the lord of the flies, the vice-regent of Satan. Like Gurdjieff he has been exiled, like Gurdjieff he has come to full maturity, and like Gurdjieff he has painfully acquired a critique. Well, it is perfectly unnecessary to labour the equation:

> as one continues to read, the description of Beelzebub slowly fades, however one struggles to retain it, and the picture of a human being with an immense head, a sweeping moustache and dark observant eyes takes its place. Instead of watching Beelzebub travelling through the geography and history of this earth, one can only see the wanderings of Gurdjieff. It is Gurdjieff whom one espies sitting at 'Chaihanas' sipping tea with some fellow traveller and discussing with him the strange ways of men. It is Gurdjieff who descends on to the earth at the time of the Babylonian civilization to attend the debates between the great scholars of the day as to whether man has or has not a soul.

Addressing the young Hassein, Beelzebub/Gurdjieff unfolds, in all its extravagantly ironic and burlesque detail, the tragic story of men; those biped Tetartocosmoses, those 'three-brained beings' of the planet Earth, who, for compelling reasons of universal equilibrium and in order to sustain the moon, have been obliged to perceive reality upside-down. Here is a creature who lives and moves in a deep hypnotic sleep, without consciousness or free will, until at last the merciless flow of time destroys him forever. A creature who can only wake to conscience and the germ of immortality by conscious labour and intentional suffering; and whose only prompting to such efforts would be the constant realisation 'of the inevitability of his own death as well as the death of everyone upon whom his eyes or attention rests.'

A stark picture? Certainly. If it had merely been drawn with giant compassion (and it is); if it had only been embellished with excruciatingly funny verbal cartoons (and it is) – that would have been scant consolation. Fortunately Gurdjieff is not conducting a post-mortem: he is calling to life. It is this which entitles Henry Finch to write, 'All appearances to the contrary – and this is the strangest thing of all – the words which most properly characterise the Gurdjieff point of view are health, sanity and good sense.' Gurdjieff goes beyond sombre diagnosis: he prescribes subtle and potent remedies; ideas of therapeutic and instrumental value. It is this which prompts Colin Wilson to say, 'His influence has not yet made itself felt: but when it does he will be seen as an innovator of the same rank as Newton, Darwin or Freud.'

Freud wrote his books in his study, and Marx in the British Museum: Gurdjieff wrote *Beelzebub* in the vortex of life. The man who had endured the aridities of the Gobi desert and studied sacred dances in high monasteries, chose for his oasis and 'headquarters' the Grand Hôtel-Café de la Paix, where the boulevard des Capucines joins the rue Aubert. Here on a green velour *banquette* between gilded Corinthian pilasters sat George Ivanovitch Gurdjieff, the smooth rotundities of his massive head curiously mirrored by the naked cherubs which floated across the frescoed ceiling. Packed about him were the café *habitués*, chattering robotically in compliance with 'the four sources of action existing there under the names "mother-in-law", "digestion", "John Thomas" and "cash".' The morning sun brought Gurdjieff out onto the café *terrasse*, shaded by green leaves and fringed parasols. On the striped chair beside him lay his karakul hat, his gold-headed walking stick and neatly-folded black coat; on the little round marble table, a cup of black coffee, into which he would squeeze his lemon, coaxing the last vivifying drops from the yellow rind. He wrote in Armenian, the language of childhood; he wrote steadily, concentratedly, his shaven cranium bowed over the cheap, ruled exercise book and improbable pencil. Deferentially the waiter set down Gurdjieff's

Château de Larresingle Armagnac, discreetly pocketing his tip and the scattering of marzipan, chocolates, caramels or peppermints. On worked 'Monsieur Bonbon', undistracted by the alien rituals and inanities of café society, which he weighed in his brown spatulate fingers and calibrated between the resolute upward twirls of his moustache:

> And that tall man pretending to be an important gentleman, sitting alone in the corner, making eyes at a lady who sits with her husband among the neighbouring company . . . is he not a real 'Veroonk'? And these waiters, exactly like dogs with their tails between their legs, who serve the people sitting there . . . are they not 'Asklay-slaves'? . . . And again it is the same . . . shoutings, uproar, laughter, scoldings . . . the same as in the city Babylon, as in the city Koorkalai, or even in Samlios, their first centre-of-culture.

From 1924 to 1933 Gurdjieff's axis was set between the Prieuré and the Café de la Paix, but whenever he felt a need to *changer les idées* he made eccentric track for the country and the mountains. The literary stature of Mr Gurdjieff has yet to receive critical attention, but there is already a broad consensus that he was the world's worst driver. We are shown the cavernous black sedan on the wrong side of the road; the desperate engine; the fractured gears; the blue-grey jet-stream of the exhaust; the white-faced passengers and, behind the wheel, the enigmatic Teacher of Dancing, his astrakhan hat rakishly tilted, and a Turkish cigarette angled between faintly smiling lips.

> He drove like a wild man, cutting in and out of traffic without hand signals or even space to accommodate his car in the lanes he suddenly switched to . . . until he was in there, safe by a hair. . . . He always got away first on the green light even (so it seemed) when he was one or two cars behind the starting line.'

Before turns or intersections Gurdjieff invariably accelerated and, once clear of Paris or Fontainebleau, screamed along the *route nationale* like a man possessed; in country lanes flocks of cows and sheep and goats mobilised, as if by planetary compulsion, to block his way. 'Gurdjieff would follow such animals along the road, sometimes nudging them with the bumper of his car, and always leaning out of the driver's side and hurling imprecations at them.'

Sometimes he would call an unexpected halt: 'Here we make pause . . . we listen to *grenouilles*.' More often the engine seized up, the tyres punctured, and the petrol, to absolutely no one's surprise but the driver's, ran out. 'These delays were a great annoyance to everyone except Mr Gurdjieff who . . . would settle himself comfortably at the side of the road . . . and write furiously in his notebooks, muttering to himself and licking the point of one of his many pencils.'

And so *Beelzebub* was written.

Some of Gurdjieff's trips were so surrealistic, it is almost tempting to think that 'car' and 'Karnak' equate! In fact the word comes from an Armenian root related to the Greek idea of the body as the tomb of the soul. We are brought, strangely, back to Katherine Mansfield's formulation: 'It is not my coffin which is the shell, it is my body which is the shell.' Religious allegory is scarcely in critical vogue today, when *Pilgrim's Progress* is seen as something naive, mechanical, laboriously didactic. But as Gurdjieff handles the medium, it is infinitely more subtle, plastic and elusive; it is allegory which conceals allegory. Perhaps the very word 'religious' ushers in debatable associations. 'We may take a sceptical view,' says Colin Wilson, 'and say simply that Gurdjieff was a psychologist of singular brilliance and insight, on a level with Nietzsche.' Curiouser and curiouser, that a twentieth-century psychologist should choose as his vehicle an allegory of kabbalistic complexity.

In itself, of course, the Space-Odyssey format is nothing new (the notion of interplanetary flight dates back to the Hellenistic writer Lucian of Samosata), but Gurdjieff uses the device with rare intelligence. Adroitly he conveys an 'extra-terrestrial' impartiality in historical and social diagnosis, and a superb analogical correspondence between the outer space of the starry world and the inner space of man's psyche. In this wide setting, Gurdjieff's most gnomic and seemingly lunatic assertions ('God made an umbrella when he should have made an enema, and now he is idiot and like everyone else sits in galoshes') are afforded an astonishing structural development. Best of all, he employs his prodigious stage for disturbing perspective effects, abrupt shifts in scale and psychological ambuscades. We are constantly buffeted between the sublime and the ridiculous; raised to the heights of 'The Most Holy Sun Absolute', only to have our attention readdressed to a flea which has an abnormal orange-crimson growth on its left paw.

Beelzebub represents a massive and sustained effort. 'My labourability at that time', reflected Gurdjieff wryly, 'was indeed phenomenal, for I wrote and rewrote at least 10,000 kilos of paper.' The result would plug the Grand Canyon; it is impossible to convey *Beelzebub*'s sweep of time and space, its integration of All and Everything; Mars, Saturn, The Most Holy Sun Absolute, The Holy Planet Purgatory; every continent on earth, not forgetting Atlantis; Tikliamish and New York, Babylon and Paris. Onto this stupendous stage throng the cast: secret brotherhoods of dervishes, Essenes, Heechtvori, Olbogmek; the Arch-Vainglorious Greek, Alexander of Macedon, and ignoble groundlings like Mr Bellybutton and Professor Chatterlitz; Angels and Archangels; scientists as improbable and diverse as the Bokharian dervish Hadji-Asvatz-Troov and the raven-like being Gornahoor Harharkh; the demonic rationalist Lentrohamsanin ('Len' for Lenin and 'Tro' for Trotsky). And towering above them all, the wise fool, the incomparable Mullah Nassr Eddin, and the saintly Ashiata Shiemash. Only women are absent. At first sight this seems a very singular omission, particularly since women always held an honourable place among Gurdjieff's pupils and a pre-eminent place in his sacred dances. Or is it perhaps a just reflection of women's role in vanished cultures and their contribution to the history of ideas? Anyway there seems no baulking Gurdjieff's strong patriarchality:

> Nature of woman is very different from that of man. Woman is from ground, and only hope for her to arise to another stage of development – to go to Heaven as you say – is *with* man. Woman already know everything, but such knowledge is of no use to her, in fact can almost be like poison to her, unless have man with her.

Beelzebub is not easy reading. Gurdjieff's meandering digressions make Burton and Sterne and Rabelais seem positively epigrammatic. His laboured argumentation, onomatopoeic conceits, barbarous syntax, parabolic allusions and Greco-Armenian neologisms make *Ulysses*, by comparison, read like a child's primer. His dislocated sequences and improbable laminates are like those of *The Thousand and One Nights* – except they are more artfully hidden. Generally his prose style has the texture of elephant grass; the sturdy explorer must beat his own path through the dense grammatical scrub, tripping in the tangled underbrush of subordinate clauses. And above, scorching down, is the fiery redeeming sun of Gurdjieff's extraordinary insight.

Why the opacity and tautological languors of *Beelzebub*? Instantly we can dismiss the notion of technical incapacity: Gurdjieff wrote cogently and lucidly enough in his second book, *Meetings with Remarkable Men*. Nor was there some obstinate temperamental compulsion to beat about the bush; Gurdjieff could speak to his pupils with aphoristic brevity, and his sacred dances are miracles of economy and discipline. The mystery only deepens when we remember how Gurdjieff worked and re-worked his material like a medieval alchemist, who by 'magistry' – calcination, putrefaction, sublimation, solution, distillation, coagulation and tincture – transmuted base metal into imperishable gold. Why, if each pondered draft was read aloud to his pupils, and their response was the secret catalytic agent which crystallised *Beelzebub* – why has it that particular atomic weight?

Perhaps there are many answers to this riddle, and Henry Finch has suggested one: 'The Gurdjieff ideas are well camouflaged . . . to guard against . . . being hawked around and distorted in the marketplace. We know what happened to the ideas of Marx and Freud and Nietzsche.' This question of bowdlerisation aside, it is evident we are meant to work for the meaning, like a dog sucking marrow from a bone. *Beelzebub* is not for the lazy, the quickly discouraged, the flippant; not for those 'eager to enter Paradise without fail with their boots on'. Gurdjieff's is the way of the sly man who does nothing without purpose; perhaps after all there is method in his stylistic madness. Long before Benjamin Lee Whorf, he had been fascinated by the psychological corollaries of language – how grammatical structure modifies a man's world-view. The Teacher of Dancing was not a man indifferent to tempo. No one can gauge and nurture a mood more subtly than Gurdjieff. Sometimes he leads us in a prepared state to a single pivotal sentence: sometimes he ruptures the spell with a more-than-Brechtian *Verfremdungseffekt*. Never are we permitted to sleep, to return to the torporous, vegetative level where our inner and outer worlds are taken for granted.

To invest such a quantity of time in writing *Beelzebub* was a signal act of literary courage; it is difficult to conceive a bait less likely to tempt that cold fish, the publisher's reader. Through years, through decades, through innumerable translations and revisions, *Beelzebub* circulated in manuscript; a potentised, talismanic writ, jealously hoarded from hand to hand among Gurdjieff's pupils. 'The knowledge that half the literary Paris we knew would give its eyeteeth for a glimpse of those worn typescript pages added a kind of worldly lustre to their content.' Sometimes Gurdjieff expressed baroque hopes for his production: 'One day *Beelzebub* will be read in Pope's Palace. Perhaps I will be there.' But he didn't exactly grease the wheels; Knopf, for example, approached Gurdjieff with a disingenuous offer to handle *Beelzebub* at G.'s own expense. The unpublished author was affability itself, setting only one pre-condition, a small thing.

'And that is?'

'First clean house, your house, then perhaps can have my book.'

Remorselessly the years evaporated, but Gurdjieff never wasted a drop: he composed over a hundred pieces of music; he wrote a second and a third book; at the Salle Pleyel he taught a new series of Movements based on the enneagram; he visited America; he cast his subtle net over thousands. In 1939 came the war – that involuting stream in which so many governments and cities and dispensations, so many tribes of humanity, were rolled away. For the author of *Beelzebub* there was no escape from Paris by spaceship, but nor have we evidence that Gurdjieff would have cared to embark. On the contrary, he sabotaged an attempt to get him away to the country and returned to the city only hours ahead of the Germans. Though conditions were rigorous they presented an opportunity for intensified work with a new cadre of French students. Gurdjieff commanded his pupils of all allegiances to help one another. Not only did he, by sly manipulation, solve the material question for himself and his relatives; not only was he a staff to his pupils: but he literally kept alive scores of his poor neighbours, quite unconnected with his work. 'Ask self why old lady, with very little money, every day feed birds in park. These people – this family – my birds.'

Dimly from the foyer of 6 Rue des Colonels Rénards, the moth-eaten stair-carpet crept upwards past the aged concierge and the rustling lift, into another world. If symbolically Gurdjieff's flat had become the planet Mars, where Beelzebub set up his observatory and recorded the terrifying process of man's reciprocal destruction, the concrete reality was hardly less bewildering. Strewn with knick-knacks, *bibelots*, dolls, figurines, gilt mirrors, oleographs and abominable paintings bought in the Café des Acacias from hard-up refugees; sealed night and day, winter and summer, by shutters and by curtains closely drawn across the falsely exotic window-panes; lit by naked light bulbs; encumbered by a large Russian Christmas tree, hung upside-down by its roots from the ceiling – Gurdjieff's residence was in a category of its own. From his inner sanctum wafted the all-pervading smell of tarragon, rosemary, mint and saffron. Ranked shelf on shelf were the bottles of calvados, armagnac, vodka; boxes of Turkish delight; white rice and black caviare from Persia; scarlet peppers and tins of guava jelly; rococo garlands of dried eels and sausages of camel's meat. 'By what grocers miracle, with what cash and for what esoteric-culinary fantasy are they gathered here?'

On 25 August 1944, when Charles de Gaulle re-entered Paris, Gurdjieff's financial concerns were classically diversified: he was in a big way of business in carpets; a modest speculator in foreign currency; a therapist for psychosomatic illnesses; and proprietor of a company manufacturing false eyelashes. The war had come and the war had gone; at 6 Rue des Colonels Rénards a transcendent chocolate fish, masked in silvery-blue tinfoil, swung from the store-room ceiling, and beneath it, inextinguishable, sat the Black Greek, The Tiger of Turkestan.

But implacable Time, 'Merciless Heropass', had flowed over Gurdjieff. The magisterial moustache, lofted and smoothed so often, had abated and turned white. The sagacious hands were mottled with age; the tidy feet which had walked to Lhasa and back were grounded now in carpet slippers. Through the flabbergasted waistcoat and jacket butted the triumphal belly. '*Le Patron* is demanding instant attention and *le Patron* is *une personne très importante.*' Migrating pupils flocked and wheeled and settled in the tiny flat. 'These poor herons, balanced precariously on one leg, searched in vain for a resting place.' Half host, half apothecary, half ornithologist, Gurdjieff dispensed peppered vodka and insight; pilaf and caviare and wild strawberries. 'He would seat a Nobel prize winner next to a street cleaner, a countess next to a prostitute.' Ironic and compassionate, sad and mirthful, the embodied reconciler of large opposites. Gurdjieff had finally become Grandfather Beelzebub, with all the lawful infirmities of age. He moved more slowly now, yet still 'with a grace and an economy of gesture that were in themselves enough to induce in those near him a sense of relaxation and well-being.' Beneath the kingly magenta fez, the antique olive face was strangely smooth and serene, and, for those who had eyes to see, some indefinable quality in the old man hinted at his undismayed and unimaginable attention.

Beelzebub is a seminal work. Just as Gurdjieff once predicted Ouspensky's India while Ouspensky was still on his way there, so we might catalogue a dubious library which Grandfather Beelzebub, to his own sorrow, will infallibly generate. Here for example – the fruit of over-generous research grants – are some scientific papers, gingerly relating Gurdjieff's Law of Seven to Mendeleev's table, his typology to Sheldon's, his psychology to John B. Watson's. On this shelf is found a subtle Christian exegesis of Gurdjieff, achieved *non sine divino auxilio*. Here is a little philological work, with suggested Armenian, Greek, Turkish and Tibetan roots of Gurdjieff's neologisms. This other shelf sags ponderously beneath the philosophical critiques: *Beelzebub: Some Syntactical and Conceptual Implications in the Use of Language as Hieroglyph*. Below, bound in mauve and set in Caslon Old Face, is an essay in literary criticism, evidently some PhD thesis served up hot: *Gurdjieff, Stein and Joyce: Three Types of Obscurity*. It remains merely to write all these books, to cut down the necessary forests and pulp them into paper. What a mass of knowledge; but will these commentaries bring a granule of understanding? The catch of the ichthyologist depends on the gauge of his net, to use Eddington's metaphor. Understanding, says Gurdjieff, is a function of being, and knowledge is merely a passing presence in it.

Round Gurdjieff's patriarchal table his pupils sat like sons and daughters, as Katherine Mansfield did; and to those special days and special conditions there is no returning. But surely through *Beelzebub* his voice, in all its full Toulousite-wholly-manifested-intonation, carries to his 'Grandsons' – pupils of the New Age, generations who could not know him, but who bear the seed of his ideas into the unknown future. We cannot see the whole plot and say which tree will fail and which will grow. But already lively voices are raised. 'Gurdjieff', says Peter Brook, 'is the most immediate, the most valid, and the most totally representative figure of our time.'

Which will be crushed like a louse? Always there were two possibilities. 'Either the old world will make me "Tchik"', said Gurdjieff, 'or I will make the old world "Tchik". Then the new world can begin.' The siftings of the years will establish or confound the author of *Beelzebub*; either the chapters on Ashiata Shiemash, the Law of Heptaparaparshinokh and The Holy Planet Purgatory are specious, or they are vehicles of ideas it would be an impertinence to praise. Perhaps *Beelzebub* is trumpery: perhaps it is a piece of objective art. It resembles the Sphinx, whose vision is directed far off, as if piercing the very depths of space. Where is the new Oedipus who will stand between these paws and travail to unlock this riddle?

Chapter 14

Cultural Bon Ton

In the realm of cultural bon ton, Katherine Mansfield is an inalienable citizen, with all the rights and privileges pertaining thereto. Reverend professors break their teeth over the body of her work and its critical reception. Her relationship with Virginia Woolf is loaded with an awe-inspiring significance. A discarded garter from Mansfield emerges from the bon ton salt-mines, a glittering diamanté fantasy. Ten new letters from Katherine Mansfield discovered at the bottom of a laundry basket might subvert our entire conception of the Georgian literary scene. Miss Mansfield is sombrely present in the examination room: 'Retell the first part of "The Fly" as it might be recounted by old Woodifield talking to one of his friends.' Miss Mansfield is eminently collectable. (What bibliophile has not stalked Charing Cross Road in foot-weary search for the rare Hogarth Press edition of *Prelude*, in its blue paper cover? What schoolboy does not know how many first editions of *In a German Pension* went down in the *Titanic*?) Streets, parks, literary prizes, bus-shelters and little children are named after Katherine Mansfield. Like all good citizens of the realm of cultural bon ton, she is to be taken very, very seriously. And, indeed, why not?

Gurdjieff had no bon ton. In her life he made shift with a Nansen passport issued to stateless persons, and in the critical aftermath he seemed obliged to do much the same. For thirty years no one troubled even to stigmatise his music, his dances, his books; for to stigmatise was to recognise, and in some mysterious way Gurdjieff simply did not count. He was a non-person. It was not Gurdjieff's name inscribed on the Prieuré wall at Fontainebleau: it was Mansfield's. Then in 1979 something astounding happened. World-famous director Peter Brook, walking, breathing embodiment of bon ton, released *Meetings with Remarkable Men*, premièred in the Bloomsbury which Katherine had never quite penetrated. This production, made without the least indulgence, the least artifice, the least concession, had the rough-hewn virtues of folk art. Almost it seemed designed to set on edge the teeth of the critics and sophisticates. Quite without cultural chic, it yields more, much more, at a second viewing.

In historical retrospect it is astounding how many bon ton names may be uneasily linked with Gurdjieff. Not that a tedious exercise in name-dropping adds one cubit to his stature. Gurdjieff is not important because Lawrence of Arabia[1] read him, Gertrude Stein met him or Simone Weil visited him. Gurdjieff is important, if at all, because he is Gurdjieff, *sui generis*, a messenger from the planet Karatas, richly deserving his thirty years' cultural quarantine. And yet it is somehow impossible to resist peopling that glittering cultural stage and setting Gurdjieff (Yes, and Ouspensky too) in fine and improbable juxtaposition with the contemporary intelligentsia – or 'tramps' as Gurdjieff scathingly called them. Surely we have lost the full folio of the play, and what remains seems lumpy and episodic; but down with the house lights, and raise the curtain on the Theatre of Bon Ton. Very much this is a drama with trans-atlantic backcloths and accents; not for nothing was 'Beelzebub in America' the longest chapter in Gurdjieff's book. Some of our actors demand no programme notes: from St Louis, Missouri, Thomas Stearns Eliot; from Hailey, Idaho, Ezra Loomis Pound. But Mr Jean Toomer, the Black Renaissance poet, or the cultural mutant Margaret Anderson are perhaps more slenderly known. And nonetheless they are justly cast: Toomer was a considerable writer; Anderson – convicted and fingerprinted for publishing Joyce's *Ulysses* – has her modest niche in the literary Valhalla.

While Mr Joyce and Mr Eliot were experimenting with new modalities of allusion; while Miss Anderson and her colleague Miss Heap (it would certainly have been Ms Anderson and Ms Heap in our times), were touching off their *avant-garde* fireworks in the *Little Review*, the Great European War staggered bloodily to a halt and the whole of Tsarist Russia began to be destroyed. In August

1921, the author of *Tertium Organum* suddenly appeared in London, wielding a new critique and very palpable influence. Eliot and Ouspensky met almost immediately, and 'eyed each other with cautious curiosity' over Lady Rothermere's golden plates. Was her ladyship's patronage all the two men had in common? Certainly that is the received view; and the notion that Eliot attended Ouspensky's groups (as Aldous Huxley did) and manoeuvred to meet Gurdjieff, fails for lack of extant evidence. But surely commonsense argues a fair affinity and connection between Eliot and Ouspensky. Both men knew Sanskrit and had immersed themselves in the Vedas, the Upanishads and the *Gita*. Both, in their own media, were experimental mystics, exercised by the same questions: the relation of time and eternity; echo and recurrence; redemption and eschatology. Eliot's encounter with Ouspensky completes a literary triad; it was Katherine Mansfield who first read 'Prufrock' to the company at Garsington.

In September 1922, one week before Katherine Mansfield attended her first Ouspensky group at 38 Warwick Gardens, D. H. Lawrence met a lady incongruously destined to be his link with Gurdjieff. The place was Taos, 7,000 feet up in New Mexico, where the painted mountains rose above the line of the cottontrees – the lady in question was Mabel Evans Dodge Sterne. Middle-aged and masterful, an accomplished horsewoman, three times married, disgracefully *nouveau-riche*, her head congested with Navaho rug patterns and Apache tribal dances, her squat, powerful body sheathed in turquoise blue and weighed down with chunky ethnic jewellery, Mrs Sterne was a cross between rogue anthropologist and literary hostess – a sort of Lady Ottoline Morrell gone native.

If Lawrence ever wondered why he stood before this extraordinary creature, the explanation was quite simple: Mrs Sterne had done it all by long-distance hypnosis:

> Before I went to sleep at night, I drew myself all in to the core of my being where there is a live, plangent force lying passive –
> waiting for direction. Becoming entirely that, moving with it, speaking with it, I leaped through space, joining myself to the central core of Lawrence. . . . 'Come, Lawrence! Come to Taos!' became, in me, Lawrence in Taos. This is not prayer, but command.

Mabel gave Frieda a ranch in the Sangre de Cristo mountains, and Lawrence a copy of *Tertium Organum*. Today the ranch holds Lawrence's mortal remains, while the book is in Taos public library, covered with his hostile annotations. *Tertium Organum*, written by Ouspensky before he met Gurdjieff, has twenty-three chapters; shrewdly Lawrence chose as his battleground chapters VIII and IX, which deal with the perception and conceptualisation of animals:

Ouspensky: The syllogism in the psychic sphere is literally the same thing as the lever in the physical sphere.
Lawrence: Bah, the syllogism is derived from the sensual experience of a lever. . . . A syllogism is a distilled bit of experience.
Ouspensky: The animal lives *in a world of two dimensions*. Its universe has for it the properties and appearance of a surface.
Lawrence: On the contrary, the animal sees the world as a kind of *deeps* from which things emerge, or start or sink: it sees *flux* not surface.

Perhaps, after page and page of this extended refutation, we have learned less about animals than about men: how the intellectual and emotional types construe the world differently. Ouspensky is prepared to follow his reason humbly yet quite ruthlessly, wherever it leads; but it is Lawrence who has a real animistic feel for the subject, who seems closer to Castaneda's don Juan or Laurens van der Post's Kalahari Bushman. It is perhaps churlish and bathetic to add that Lawrence, for all his empathy, was a grand kicker of dogs and shooter of porcupines, while Ouspensky, despite his glacial-seeming abstraction, was warmly devoted to his cat and his old horse 'Jingles'.

In the game of cultural bon ton, Mrs Sterne is a card of the lowest value; one leads her shamefacedly merely to draw the trump of Lawrence. Already by 1922 far higher denominations in the pack were being exposed. Freud *ipsissimus* remarked Gurdjieff's unexpected conversion of Dr Nicoll and Dr Young. 'Ah,' he said, clearly nettled, 'you see what happens to Jung's disciples.' And then there was Diaghilev. Consider. No one on the planet had more bon ton: he worked with composers like Stravinsky, Prokofiev and Moussorgsky; and with designers like Braque, Utrillo and

Matisse. Nijinsky danced for him, Cocteau wrote for him and Picasso designed his curtain for *Le Train Bleu*. Yet this same Sergei Diaghilev sat, time and again, in a converted Zeppelin hangar at Fontainebleau and peered through his monocle at Gurdjieff's sacred dancing.

When Katherine Mansfield died on 9 January 1923, a hostile critique sprang into fashion. Wyndham Lewis wrote contemptuously of 'the famous New Zealand Mag. – story writer, in the grip of the Levantine psychic shark.' François Mauriac saw a two-dimensional Gurdjieff, significant merely as the instrument of Mansfield's loss to Catholicism: 'In the end it was to Gurdjieff, the *mage*, that she gave her faith, at the phalanstery of Fontainebleau, where she went to die in misery.' Beatrice Hastings expressed her high disdain of 'that mystical fish-shop at Fontainebleau'. The poet Yeats, who no longer commanded the energy to set a bad example, was prompt with good advice. 'Don't join that community at Fontainebleau,' pleaded Frater Demon est Deus Inversus. 'I have had a lot of experience of that sort of thing in my time, and my advice to you is – leave it alone.' Notables like Sinclair Lewis who actually reached the Prieuré wrote accounts which, in one way or another, leave us in their debt. Discounting Lewis's slight command of English (so excusable in a future Nobel Prizewinner), it might nevertheless be mentioned that his particular vision was as simple as pumpkin pie:

> Goudjieff is a Russian, and his chief apostle Ouspensky is a Russian, and between them they run the latest thing in phony High Thought colonies. . . . some of the dances are imitations of Oriental sacred temple rights [*sic*], some of them stunts requiring a high degree of muscle control. . . . But it must be a hell of a place to live. . . . they have built their own 'gymnasium' . . . a cross between a cabaret and a harem.

In the golden summer of 1923, Pound met Gurdjieff more intimately in Paris. Superficially some common ground existed: each man was an accomplished cook, a musician, a polyglot; each was the friend of Orage. But Ezra Loomis Pound was humping too much intellectual luggage to board Gurdjieff's express. By now he was a 37-year-old exquisite, who knew everyone and whose Montparnasse apartment rivalled the salon of Gertrude Stein; he went to Gurdjieff not to listen but to speak, and there is something almost frightening in the clever, dismissive sophistication of his account:

> Gurdjieff made Persian soup, bright yellow in colour, far more delicate – you might say Pier della Francesca in tone, as compared with a bortch (tinted Rembrandt). If he had had more of that sort of thing in his repertoire he could had he suspected it, or desired it, have worked on toward at least one further conversion.

But Gurdjieff did not desire the conversion of tramps, and Ezra Pound had soon left for Rapallo on his long, tragic and ambiguous journey. Perhaps Pound's repudiation was inevitable. Yet strange that his editors should have such a different valuation: Orage already stood at Gurdjieff's right hand, and in that same summer of 1923, under the blue locust trees in Brookhaven, Long Island, Margaret Anderson and Jane Heap began to read *Tertium Organum.*

In December 1923, D. H. Lawrence appeared unexpectedly in London, a truant from Mabel Sterne. Guests at his celebrated Café Royal function were nonplussed to find they had been cast as recruits for a Mexican adventure. They had come out for a quiet drink and found themselves menaced by a new life-style. It is one of the great literary set pieces, this Café Royal 'Last Supper', a grand continuum of claret and sycophancy and splintered glasses; of golden ornaments, caryatids, prophetic mirrors and potted plants; of fluttered eyelids and switched allegiances; eternal making and unmaking – reaching at last its apogee when John Middleton Murry draws to Lawrence, kisses him, and, in a voice choked with sincerity and crusty port, murmurs, 'I love you Lorenzo, but I won't promise not to betray you,' upon which the inscrutable Lawrence, 'without uttering a sound fell forward with his head on the table, was deadly sick, and became at once unconscious.'

It is a much-told tale and only its sequel commands our special interest, for it concerns Katherine's friend, Dr James Carruthers Young. Young had severed his connection with the Prieuré, he was accessible and affable, he knew all about communes and snake-bite remedies, and Murry was desperate to enlist him. Fortunately or unfortunately, the obligatory Lawrence–Young confrontation proved a complete fiasco. Young simply sat silent, while others talked their heads off; worse still, he took a robust dislike to Lawrence. So it transpired that D. H. Lawrence never set out for the New World with one of Gurdjieff's most intelligent and energetic pupils. The novelist's picture of Gurdjieff, the man, would now perforce rely on Murry's self-justifying innuendo and on the well-meant vapourings of Mabel.

Mrs Mabel Evans Dodge Sterne Luhan (her nomenclature changing by a too-frequent accretion of husbands) now wrote to Lawrence, asking him to find out about Gurdjieff. Pat came Lawrence's famous reply of 9 January 1924, that the Prieuré was a 'rotten, false, self-conscious place of people playing a sickly stunt.' There is none of Murry's nice equivocation here; Lawrence gives a wholesome, full-throated answer, all the more remarkable since he had never been to the Prieuré. Verdict first – evidence afterwards! Ironically enough, just three weeks later, on or about 1 February 1924, while staying at the Hôtel Versailles, 60 boulevard Montparnasse, D. H. Lawrence did indeed make a flying visit to the Prieuré. Off went another letter to Mabel Luhan: 'we called at that Fontainebleau place. The Russian there believes entirely in going against the grain. He would make you wash windows and scrub floors eight hours a day, and the viler your temper the better.' This graphic eye-witness account of 'The Russian' clearly satisfied some impulse in Lawrence: how much it will satisfy posterity is more debatable. Worth remembering, perhaps, that 'The Russian', with all his principal pupils of dance, had sailed for America on the *Paris* in the first week of January 1924, and that D. H. Lawrence never had and never did set eyes on him.

In December 1923, Orage had crossed the Atlantic before Gurdjieff, to prepare the way for him. Whatever Orage's capacity for digging holes and milking goats, there was never the least doubt about his skill as a public speaker. His lectures in the Sunwise Turn bookshop on East 44th Street drew an interesting and disparate New York audience, including, strangely enough, that good grey goose, Katherine's first husband George Bowden. Effortlessly Orage magnetised and entangled Margaret Anderson and Jane Heap. In certain circles there began to mount the liveliest anticipation of Gurdjieff's arrival. And then in January 1924 he came, walking down the gangplank with forty pupils and no money. As soon as Gurdjieff lectured it became evident that his platform manner was different from Orage's, and less in conformity with the expectations of New York's intelligentsia. 'He came in from another room, wearing a grey suit and an old pair of carpet slippers and holding a large baked potato. Everyone became frigidly silent. He sat on the edge of the low platform facing us and began to eat.'

Barely had his audience recovered from this shock, when on 23 January the first demonstration of the sacred dances was given at Leslie's Ballroom, 260 West 83rd Street. Gurdjieff – without funds, without orchestra, without any of the impressario's massive apparatus – somehow contrived an audacious tour covering New York, Boston, Philadelphia and Chicago, in venues which ranged the bon ton spectrum from the Church of St Martin's-in-the-Bowery to Carnegie Hall. Astonished Americans watched the Obligatories, the Ho Yah Dervish, the Big Seven, the Camel Dervish, the Sacred Goose, the Great Prayer and 'Katherine's Movement', The Initiation of the Priestess. No one knew what to make of it; for absolute discipline the dancers seemed 'like the soldiers of Christophe who marched without breaking step off the parapet of the citadel on that sheer mountainside in Haiti.' Margaret Anderson first glimpsed Gurdjieff in the wings of the Neighbourhood Playhouse in New York City. As editor of the *Little Review*, she knew positively everything and everyone in the world of *avant-garde* culture, but here was a phenomenon of a new order. 'He had a presence impossible to describe because I never encountered another with which to compare it.' In June 1924 she left New York for Fontainebleau to become Gurdjieff's pupil.

Orage electrified with a new idea and given licence to propagate it, was Orage at his most magnetic. Now comfortably installed in an apartment in Gramercy Park, he stayed on in New York, more or less as Gurdjieff's ambassador. His groups were an improbable amalgam of the intelligentsia and 'the 100 neediest cases'. By far the strangest figure to sit before the chain-smoking lecturer was Mabel's new husband, Tony Luhan, a full-blooded Pueblo Indian; 'a massive man who wore his greasy black hair in long pigtails, wrapped himself in a striped blanket and never spoke.' Scarcely less picturesque was Jean Toomer. But Toomer did speak, and quickly proved so serious a pupil that Orage empowered him to hold preparatory groups, first in Harlem and then in Chicago.

Orage was not the only one impressed with Toomer; by January 1926 Mabel Luhan, a lady never chicken-hearted in her enthusiasms, was completely infatuated with him. It seemed to her that the arrangement best answering her affectional and spiritual needs would be if Gurdjieff opened a full-scale branch of his Institute at Taos, with Toomer in charge. Immediately Mabel conceived this notion she gave Toomer $15,000 as Gurdjieff's representative, and offered to throw in her ranch. This flamboyant largesse sent Toomer on the long haul down to New Mexico. Considering his all-too-human wish to have an institute of his own, Toomer's inspection report, made directly to Gurdjieff, was commendably balanced. Mabel's ranch was certainly ideal for hard physical work, but too remote from the necessary commerce of life. As for the splendid Mabel herself: 'I can hope for her', wrote Toomer sententiously, 'just in so far as she will persist in her present idea of following your method – but I could not persuade myself to certainty in regard to her constancy.' And if Toomer could not persuade himself, certainly no one else could. So on 1 February 1926 Gurdjieff wrote to Mabel Evans Dodge Sterne Luhan a letter of profuse thanks but regretting that he was now in a phase of liquidating his Institutes, not creating them; a phase of writing, not teaching. With extreme reluctance he was therefore obliged to decline her kind offer. It was certainly a historic decision. Taos was rapidly becoming a transatlantic Hellerau, a focal point of cultural influence. In effect it was offered to Gurdjieff for the trouble of picking it up – and he refused it.

It is strange how contrariwise we are: how the fiercest salvos merely send us scuttling deeper into our prepared philosophical redoubts. Gurdjieff's disengagement seems to have increased, not diminished, Mabel's ardour for his teaching. And Mabel's ardour seems merely to have stiffened Lawrence's resistance. The novelist – now pursuing his 'Savage Pilgrimage' in such desolate outposts as Monte Carlo, Capri, Ravello, Spotorno and Florence – was remorselessly bombarded with Mrs Luhan's potted version of the system, lobbed across the Atlantic from Finney Farm, Croton-on-Hudson.

> Gurdjieff says quite calmly, here's a way. Sounds crazy, sounds awful. Try it. Observer Mabel. Stand back a bit and see her.... This Mabel has three modes or centres – instinctive, mental, and emotional. They have eaten up the universe. She *must* create a fourth one herself – the I.

Was the author of *Fantasia of the Unconscious* quite indifferent to the notion of an occult and evolutionary psychology? Was the sponsor of Rananim so closed to the ideals of Fontainebleau? Perhaps not. But Lawrence was essentially in the market to sell ideas, not to buy them – and least of all from a well-meaning huckster like Mabel Luhan. Back went his counterblast:

> My I, my fourth centre, will look after me better than I should ever look after it. . . . In the end, if you Gurdjieff yourself to the very end, a dog that barks at you will be a dynamo sufficient to explode your universe. When you are final master of yourself, you are nothing, you can't even wag your tail or bark. . . . when the *I* finally emerges, that way, it will be half demon and half imbecile. . . . Don't you see Gourdjieff's ultimate I is the ultimate self important?

The baffled Mabel urged Lawrence at least to meet Gurdjieff; it seemed to her a necessary apotheosis. So had it seemed to Katherine Mansfield. But Lawrence resolutely would not. 'You don't imagine how little interest I have in these modes of salvation.' This may be true: it may be not. Katherine at least had offered a different explanation: 'Lawrence's pride would keep him back.'

Just how envenomed that pride could be, we see in 'Mother and Daughter', D. H. Lawrence's short story of 1929. Here is a merciless encryptment of our principals: Murry is represented by 'Henry Lubbock'; Mabel Luhan by 'Mrs Bodoin'; Katherine Mansfield by 'Virginia Bodoin' and Gurdjieff by 'Arnault'. One thing is immediately evident: whatever the developmental and artistic considerations which drew Lawrence to the short-story format, it was a splendid vehicle for the character-assassination of his friends. Virginia is odd, elvish, sluttish, 'thin as a rail. Her nerves . . . frayed to bits. . . . Virginia would appear with black lines under her eyes . . . the *stigma* upon her: badly dressed . . . acid in humour.' Monsieur Arnault the ruined Armenian millionaire is presented not as Virginia's teacher, but as her suitor and fiancé, a creature at once attractive and repellent.

> The Turkish Delight was sixty, grey-haired and fat. He had numerous grandchildren . . . a grey moustache . . . and glazed brown eyes over which hung heavy lids with white lashes. . . . There was a strange potency in his fat immobile sitting, as if his posterior were connected with the very centre of the earth. . . . he sat, with short thighs, like a toad, as if seated for a toad's

eternity. His colour was of a dirty sort of paste . . . he never spoke until spoken to, waiting in his toad's silence, like a slave.

Virginia is Arnault's natural prey.

He saw, first and foremost, the child in her. . . . A fatherless waif! And he was the tribal father, father through all the ages. . . . 'But you are so thin, dear little thin thing, you need repose, for the blossom to open . . . she needs repose, she needs to be caressed. . . . Dear little thing! Arnault loves her so dearly!'

Those, like Katherine Mansfield, who veritably encountered Gurdjieff, encountered an enigma, but Lawrence resolves the Gurdjieff riddle with all the magisterial authority of one who never met him. Yet surely with an animus impossible to a man not struck in the citadel of his own feelings.

Some celebrities on the other hand had shells so thick, so encrusted with success, they felt nothing but a supercilious condescension. John Broadus Watson the behaviourist is a case in point. What is so fascinating about this particular sighting in January 1931 is how close and yet how far apart were their positions; Gurdjieff would unquestionably have endorsed Watson's indictment of modern writers (perhaps even writers like D. H. Lawrence) for their 'laziness in observation and scornfulness about the need of observed human material.' Man as a stimulus–response mechanism was the very chockstone of Watson's psychology: it was also a key idea in Gurdjieff's uncompromising system. 'Man is of the order of the moon: he eats impressions and excretes behaviour.'

Professor Watson – from humble apprenticeship 'investigating the market for rubber boots on each side of the Mississippi river from Cairo to New Orleans' – had merited to become vice president of the J. Walter Thomson Company. Then let us now try to differentiate: Watson employed his awesome academic standing and his dangerously practical knowledge to modify, then reinforce, the conditioning of the masses, while Gurdjieff struggled to de-condition his pupils; Watson never paused for a second to consider the fundamental question of his own conditioning, while Gurdjieff had set out from the painful interrogation, 'Know Thyself'.

Their encounter took place in apartment Q at 204 West 59th

Street, at the instigation of the inebriate writer William Seabrook. Seabrook conceived the idea of confronting Gurdjieff with the very vanguard of American culture: journalists, painters, musicians, philanthropists, writers, 'individuals whose intelligence was strictly in the nine-minute-egg category.' This company, arriving at midnight – the gentlemen in evening dress, the ladies in evening gowns under mink coats – were astonished to find themselves shown to wobbly, steel-framed folding chairs with hard seats. Seabrook himself had come 'somewhat fortified for the evening ahead', and John B. Watson took his place in the front row. At last Gurdjieff came in and, with a heavy sigh, sat on the shabby liver-coloured couch toying with his ponderous gold watch-chain. 'I write book,' he said abruptly, *Beelzebub's Tales to His Grandson.* But who here can read?' After one hour listening to chapter 42, 'Beelzebub in America', Watson could contain himself no longer: 'Either this is an elaborate and subtle joke whose point is completely over our heads, or it is piffle.' And Gurdjieff said kindly, 'Enough, enough. We rest.' During the ensuing meal ('superb Algerian melons, stuffed eggplant, stuffed grape leaves, great cook pots of stewed goat') Watson moved alongside Gurdjieff on the couch and offered to send him a copy of his own book *Behaviorism.* 'Mr Gurdjieff smiled and nodded pleasantly: Then he waved a hand toward the grand piano. The top was closed and spread out on it was a formidable array of glasses and liquor in a variety of bottles.' During this dizzy, non-musical interlude, Gurdjieff proved so brilliant, witty, agreeable, keen, affable, that Watson and the rest took him completely into their confidence, tactfully explaining that his future did not lie in the field of *belles lettres.* Eventually Gurdjieff spoke: 'Now we read some more.' Till three in the morning the distinguished assembly were read at; till one old gentleman with a red ribbon across his starched shirt-front actually burst into tears. When finally all had left Gurdjieff said softly, 'You see what called "intelligentsia" in America. Can you imagine? Such empty thing. Intelligentsia they are called. Such non-entities.'

Non-entities? It seems a harsh judgment. Yet if we look beyond Gurdjieff's committed circle, we find only one figure with whom he built a substantial relationship – the master architect Frank Lloyd Wright. The two men first met in June 1931 but their encounter had really been programmed seven years before. That happened on the afternoon of 30 November 1924 at the Chicago Opera, where

Karsavina was dancing with the Petrograd Ballet. High in a balcony box sat Wright. Small, immaculate, dapper as a mole; with white hair and light-grey eyes – Wright had already two unfortunate marriages and six children to show for his fifty-seven years; he also had a string of revolutionary architectural triumphs, including the Imperial Hotel, Tokyo, which had just emerged vibrating from the earthquake of 1923. Now as the house lights dimmed, the usher showed into the next seat a beautiful stranger aged about twenty-five. 'French I thought – very French . . . or was she a Russian princess?' She was not a Russian princess: she was one of Gurdjieff's front-row dancers, the companion of Katherine Mansfield's last days, Olgivanna. Immediately Wright lost interest in the stage. 'Karsavina won't do,' he murmured. 'She's dead. They are all dead: the dead is dancing to the dead.' Olgivanna's quick comprehending glance reassured Wright. 'Fate the dealer dealt her to me at that particular moment.' They were free to marry on 28 August 1928.

Immediately Wright had met and sounded Gurdjieff, he acknowledged him to be: 'the stuff . . . of which our genuine prophets have been made. And when the prejudice against him has cleared away, his vision of truth will be recognised as fundamental.' Just a year later in 1932, Wright threw open the doors of the Taliesin fellowship at Spring Green, Wisconsin. Despite Olgivanna's potent influence here, it cannot be claimed that Taliesin was a school of architecture in the very special sense that the Prieuré was a school of dancing. To go further and suggest that Wright became Gurdjieff's pupil would be absurd. Spiky and independent, a man whose prolific genius in his own field has been compared to Michelangelo's, Frank Lloyd Wright accepted no man's tutelage. But when all the caveats have been issued, certain cameos will not be denied their historicity and their significance. Here is Gurdjieff cooking for the company at Taliesin:

> he asked them to bring him the oldest and toughest fowls they had. While cooking them he took out of his pockets a number of little paper bags of spices and peppers and herbs and put pinches now and again in the pot, and produced a superb meal.

Now here is Wright seated beside Gurdjieff at 6 Rue des Colonels Rénards, reading aloud from *Meetings with Remarkable Men*. And here is Gurdjieff insisting on a scandalous diet for Wright's ailing gall bladder (mutton, avocado with sour cream and armagnac laced with black pepper). Here again is Gurdjieff sending Wright a special album of the prehistoric paintings at Lascaux, with the urgent message, 'tell him that such place exist.' Then here is Wright in his blue beret and flowing blue cloak, arranging a public demonstration of Gurdjieff's sacred dancing in his own superb Unitarian Meeting House at Madison, Wisconsin.

This story of Gurdjieff and the world of bon ton arrives at no grand finale. All our actors pass to their several fates: Freud perishes of cancer; Huxley goes blind; Pound, deranged and disgraced, languishes twelve years in Chestnut Ward; Eliot receives the Order of Merit, the Hanseatic Goethe Prize and the Nobel Prize for Literature; Frank Lloyd Wright fades away full of years and honours. The war maroons Gurdjieff in Paris, and we do not find him any more transiting the *beau monde*. His music, his dancing, his writing are all realised but marvellously contained. According to the cosmic law, 'the soup of the soup of the soup', a tincture of his ideas passes into the cultural broth. He captures the attention of J. B. Priestley, and his bowdlerised words appear on 'Mr Propter's' lips in Huxley's *After Many a Summer*.

Perhaps the diaspora of this special influence will always be a sensitive even a contentious issue, but the basic chronology is not in dispute. In 1913, George Ivanovitch Gurdjieff suddenly appeared in Moscow bearing a revolutionary and fundamental idea: the idea of man's hypnotic sleep. By the twenties and thirties it was a theme on many lips. Here is D. H. Lawrence in *Aaron's Rod*:

> 'But the war did happen right enough,' smiled Aaron palely.
> 'No, it didn't. Not to me or to any man, in his own self. It took place in the automatic sphere, like dreams do. But the *actual man* in every man was just absent – asleep – or drugged – inert – dream-logged.'

And here T. S. Eliot in *The Family Reunion:*

> You are all people
> To whom nothing has happened, at most a continual impact
> Of external events. You have gone through life in sleep,
> Never woken to the nightmare. I tell you, life would be
>   unendurable,
> If you were wide awake.

Enough! To drag on, cataloguing Gurdjieffian echoes in

Lawrence's novels, Spender's poetry, Isherwood's essays and Eliot's verse-plays were burdensome indeed. And finally proving what? Simply to echo an idea is not to breathe it, to be transfixed by it, to live by it and die by it. We should not confuse literary parallelism with psychological stature. It is a terrible thing to rise into the hands of a living idea, as Gurdjieff rose into the idea of our sleep and awakening. And it is not given to every man.

In the last years of his life, Frank Lloyd Wright set down his final judgment on Gurdjieff:

> He will one day be of great value to our West if with persistent intelligence we strive to understand his work. . . . we have for the first time a philosopher distinguished from all others; a man searching. . . . Georgevanitch was not only an original philosopher: he was a great artist. . . . I often hear his music . . . It is from another world.

It is a nice tribute, but if we fix the slightest trust in it, we perceive reality upside-down. The choreographer of the Great Prayer, the composer of 'Holy Affirming, Holy Denying, Holy Reconciling', the author of *Beelzebub*, needs no commendation. We each have scope to make our own reconnaissance, proper to ourselves alone. Some of us Gurdjieff will attract: some repel. That is legitimate and in the order of things – but who is to weigh him and in what scales?

Note

1 A letter from David Garnett deprecating 'Russian yogis at Fontainebleau' – see *Letters to T. E. Lawrence* (Jonathan Cape 1962) – clearly implies that Lawrence was giving attention to Gurdjieff as early as January 1928. Writing on 12 April 1934 to Lincoln Kirstein, the promoter of the American School of Ballet, Lawrence indicated that he had long ago read Gurdjieff's work in French; liked it and found it real and close-knit as prose and argument. See *The Letters of T. E. Lawrence* (Jonathan Cape 1938) 797, letter No. 516. Gurdjieff's *Herald of Coming Good* was in Lawrence's library at Clouds Hill and listed in *T. E. Lawrence by His Friends* (Jonathan Cape 1937) 490.

Chapter 15

Rites of Passage

The biographer (unable, as it happens, to sense the inevitability of his own death), calmly discovers in the extirpation of his subjects a rich, artistic significance.[1] Whether they go to oblivion, consummation or renewal he cannot know, but he clutches desperately at their death for some last insight which may unlock the meaning of their lives. Again and again Katherine Mansfield returns to this theme of last things, and in the round of Gurdjieffian toasts, drunk in calvados, armagnac and peppered vodka, there is also this: 'Addition: By the way, it is necessary to add that only those can die honourably who have worked on themselves in life. Those who do not work on themselves will inevitably, early-lately, perish like dirty dogs.'

When it became evident that Madame Ostrowska's cancer was beyond treatment, Gurdjieff told the boy Fritz Peters, 'you can help by making strong wish for her, not for long life, but for proper death at right time.' A piano was moved into her room in the Ritz corridor, and Thomas de Hartmann played her favourite pieces. Gurdjieff, with all his redoubtable force, entered her struggle, spending the better part of each day with her and supervising the preparation of all her food. A Polish priest was sent for from Paris, and in the spring of 1927 Madame Ostrowska fell into a coma, passing away at four o'clock on a Friday morning just as the birds began to sing. At his wife's funeral Gurdjieff 'remained silent and withdrawn . . . as if only his body were actually present among the mourners.' Afterwards he and all the company went to pay homage at the graves of his 'unforgettable old mother' and of Katherine Mansfield.

'I suppose Gurdjieff is . . . an imaginary incarnation of Lucifer,' wrote D. H. Lawrence on 11 February 1929, 'but I doubt he'll never strike much of a light.' It is neatly expressed, but surely there is in life itself a larger, grander irony, surpassing literary artifice. Lawrence was staying at that very Hôtel Beau Rivage in Bandol where Katherine had had her first haemorrhage, and now he was eaten by the same insidious disease.

On 1 October 1929, Lawrence and Frieda took the Villa Beau Soleil, and here Earl Brewster came to massage the sick man with coconut oil. At dawn, while fishermen in the bay moved against the rising sun like dark hieroglyphs, Lawrence coughed out his malediction: 'I can't die, I can't die, I hate them too much. I have given too much and what did I get in return?' On 6 February 1930, he surrendered himself to the Ad Astra sanatorium in the Alpes-Maritimes. They weighed him and found he weighed very little; they X-rayed him but did not know how to proceed. 'I have had bronchitis', said Lawrence, 'since I was a fortnight old.' H. G. Wells came to visit him and told him his illness was mainly hysterical, but the superintendent of the Institute was of a different opinion. 'Monsieur Lawrence is a lamp that is slowly failing,' he said. The Ad Astra sanatorium was a place of profitless coughing, 'old coughing and young coughing'. After three weeks Frieda resolved, 'It is enough, it is enough, nobody should have to stand this.'

On Saturday 1 March, she brought Lawrence to the Villa Robermond to die. In his moments of remission, he sat up reading a book about Columbus, which presaged his own longer voyage. After lunch on 2 March he began to suffer and cried, 'I ought to have some morphine now.' Frieda sat at his feet. 'I held his left ankle from time to time, it felt so full of life, all my days I shall hold his ankle in my hand.' He died at ten in the evening.

> Let me guide myself with the blue, forked torch of this flower down the dark and darker stairs, where blue is darkened on
> blueness.

There is a postscript to his death. Early in 1935 Lawrence was exhumed, cremated in Marseilles, confided to an urn, shipped aboard the *Conte de Savoia*, passed – not without technical difficulty – through United States customs, and inadvertently left at the railway station in Lamy, New Mexico. The distraught Frieda recouped him from the platform, again inadvertently mislaid him, and eventually, more by luck than judgment, got him back to the ranch at Del Monte; here Mabel Luhan insisted that he be peppered over the landscape. In order to circumvent this, Frieda mixed D. H. Lawrence with three parts of sand and one part of cement, and made him into a 1-ton concrete block, which constitutes the altar of his memorial chapel.

In New York, early in December of 1930, Gurdjieff issued a provocative and liberating ultimatum: Orage's pupils must all sever their relations with Mr Orage. Each must sign to this effect – and so must Orage himself! The thing had the character of an initiatory ordeal. Gurdjieff was cooking when he heard that Orage had actually complied. He was so overcome that, instead of a piece of ginger, he 'dumped into the casserole with the left hand the whole supply in the kitchen of powdered cayenne pepper.' As for Orage, he left his groups, he left New York, he took passage for London and he never saw Gurdjieff again.

Orage had acquired at least some insulation against the shock. In 1927 he had married Jessie Dwight, co-proprietor of the Sunwise Turn bookshop, and in 1928, aged fifty-five, had become a fond and indulgent father. Now comfortably based at 6 Keats Close, Hampstead, Orage lifted his head and sniffed the air. His easy option was to teach the ideas of Gurdjieff in England; this was precisely what Ouspensky had done. For Orage it was the more feasible because he still held his teacher in awe. ('Gurdjieff is a kind of walking god – a planetary or even solar god.') What Orage in fact did is positively enigmatic: he resumed his place on 'the old hebdomadal treadmill', giving in his final years the curious impression of a man imitating himself. In April 1932 he brought out the first number of the *New English Weekly*. Again Orage's editorial office was at 38 Cursitor Street, where he had first set eyes on Katherine; again he held court in the Kardomah in the Strand; again he ordered his 'large black coffee and a dish of prunes' in the ABC in Chancery Lane; again he badgered his long-suffering readership with the dubious benefits of Social Credit. It seemed he had never walked through the Prieuré gates, encountered Gurdjieff, sensed the sacred dances. Yet here and there we catch hints of a distinctly

Gurdjieffian play-acting. Orage holds George Russell (AE) with a gaze of magisterial and 'deferential intentness' and, with the other eye, winks conspiratorially at a bystander; he describes Social Credit as an important 'pseudo interest'.

In April 1934, Orage – still at sixty-one arguably the most charismatic orator in London – received and accepted his first invitation to broadcast. In the *New Age* and the *New English Weekly* he had spoken to the dedicated few: suddenly he could address tens of thousands. Specifically the BBC producer commissioned a talk on Social Credit to be given on 5 November in the series 'Poverty in Plenty'. It is a paradox that Orage's vision, Orage's plans, no longer centred on Major Douglas: they centred on Gurdjieff. Once the broadcast was done, he would transform the editorial policy of the *New English Weekly*, Social Credit being phased out and Gurdjieffian ideas being phased in. Such, unquestionably, was the intention but, meanwhile, Orage was more and more troubled by an excruciating pain below his heart. 'You know,' he told C. S. Nott, 'I thank God every day of my life that I met Gurdjieff.' A week before his broadcast, during a night of unrelieved suffering, he wrote his weekly editorial, revised his speech and read the whole of *Hamlet*. 'I did not know before', he told a friend, 'how clearly the mind can work with the body in severe pain.' It hit him even at the microphone but somehow, by extending intervals between sentences, he finished his speech. Orage went up to Hampstead as the last rockets broke and starred in the night sky. In the morning he was dead.

Orage was buried under the sign of the enneagram in Old Hampstead churchyard. The dean of Canterbury conducted the service, and the intellectual elite of England congregated to mourn him. The fat Bechhofer-Roberts voiced what surprisingly many felt: the loss of Orage 'was like the death of a father.' There is not in modern letters any fellow to the commemorative edition of the *New English Weekly*, where fifty major tributes jostled for space. Gurdjieff was writing at Child's Café on Columbus Circle when the news came through on the telephone. Some report he said, 'I loved Orage like a brother,' but others remember the words, 'Only an Englishman need have died.' There is no question he was deeply struck, and immediately began to write his perplexing paper, 'The Outer and the Inner World of Man'.

Decades have passed. No one today remembers the *New Age*;

and Orage the editor who 'wrote writers' is submitted to our cold, horizontal critique:

> In thirty years of public life he never supported a winning cause, or profited from a losing one; the movements that consumed his energies are dead, and so are the journals that he edited, and the books that he wrote.

It may be so. But Orage aspired, he was a brother to hundreds, and from Fenstanton to Fontainebleau is a fair distance for any man to travel.

When Modigliani died of tubercular meningitis on 24 January 1920, Orage's old mistress Beatrice Hastings passed down the line. She drank, she took drugs. She had, or said she had, forty different affairs, reaching crescendo pitch with the writer Raymond Radiguet, a lad of eighteen. She stood in ambiguous intercourse with George Letterin, a lover from the spirit world, who guided her *surnormalist* painting and struck her typewriter keys with his insubstantial fingers. She instituted a Christo-Buddhist Union of Non-Ritualists with one member – herself. She invented songs and conceits to be accompanied by drums, bugles, whistles and hornpipes.

But sadly her writing took no effect. Today we salute, too late, a major talent: her salty insights, her scalding invective, her ferocious cohabitation with the English language. 'Yet, in twenty years,' she complained, 'I have never had a book published in England and my total literary earnings have been twelve and sixpence.' Subsisting chiefly on porridge, jam and condensed milk, fortified by a rich if indigestible sense of grievance, and by spirituous liquors, Beatrice Hastings haunted the Sir Richard Steele Tavern, where, stopping one in three, she hinted darkly at a 'social cabal and literary boycott', and swore her five swears in every permutation and combination.

Orage was at fault. Yes, it was all Orage's doing. He had ruined the *New Age* and now he was out to ruin her. 'I should have sentenced him', wrote Beatrice, 'to Talk to Katherine Mansfield to the end of the Kalpa.' She had come back to England about the same time as her former lover, and set herself up ten minutes' walk from him. If ever they met in the quiet dusk, strolling down Fellows Road, it has escaped the attention of historians. Nor can we answer for her feelings when Orage died on 5 November 1934, but the funeral eulogies maddened her. No one had mentioned her connection, her contribution or even her name. To Mrs Hastings' sense of injured merit we owe *The Old 'New Age'*. *Orage – and Others* published by the Blue Moon Press, surely one of the most invigorating character-assassinations in our language.

Her barbarous good looks ravaged by age and drink, studiously ignored by the literary establishment, alone and impoverished, always ill and often haemorrhaging, Beatrice energetically launched a series of her own magazines. The *Straight Thinker*, the *Straight Thinker Bulletin*, the *Democrat*: Editor Beatrice Hastings, printed and published by Beatrice Hastings, price two pence. She would expose St Thérèse of Lisieux, she would rehabilitate Madame Blavatsky, she would guarantee the Soviet Union. Curious vertical marginalia attacked the Jews, the government and the Vatican. Mrs Hastings was dying of cancer. She offered her Psychic Diary to the Society for Psychical Research, who respectfully declined it. She sent all her letters (surely some marvellously compromising stuff from Orage and Katherine), to the British Museum, who instantly returned them in a re-used buff envelope.

On Saturday 30 October 1943, Beatrice burned her papers, stuffed a towel under the door, cradled her little white mouse in her hand, and turned the gas on: 'if Miss Green will kindly throw the ashes down a hill or in a field, I shall be obliged.' Thus Beatrice Tina, J. Wilson, Robert à Field, Alice Morning, Ninon de Longclothes, D. Triformis, Edward Stafford, Cynicus, S. Robert West, Gorged Laynsberrie and G. Whiz came to their final rest. It had been a life drunk to the very dregs; not successful, certainly not judicious, but lived with a desperate, stylish bravery.

> Though, after all, there may be another life beyond, and whatever may be the rules and regulations of it I am ready to risk the chance of carving it pretty much to my own fashion. A person like me will never come to grief.

Piotr Ouspensky, cast up on English shores by the First World War, was washed to America by the Second. And there, alighting on a hilltop, at Franklin Farms in Mendham, New Jersey, he devoted himself to teaching Gurdjieff's ideas, and to some heroic drinking. 'It is the only thing', he admitted, 'that relieves the boredom and depression that comes over me at times.' Ouspensky's vision of Gurdjieff seemed irreversibly crystallised: G. had been the bearer of the miraculous System, but he was also, unfortunately, a man who had lost touch with the source and gone dangerously wrong. A very, very long spoon was wanted to sup with the author of *Beelzebub*. Such at least were the accents of the sober Ouspensky, but in his cups he sang a different song: 'Doesn't he understand how much I love him? Why does he not let me go back to him? He knows that I need him and I know that he needs me.'

At the end of the war, the London groups, with an almost messianic expectation, prepared for Ouspensky's return. Their town facilities at Colet Gardens they recaptured from the Admiralty. At Lyne Place, their country house of work, they dismantled the paraphernalia of the auxiliary fire station. They polished – metaphorically at least – the brass door-plate of their Historico-Psychological Society, and trooped to Southampton to meet the ship. 'There stepped onto English soil a man whom we hardly recognised, a man who had aged by twenty years since we had last seen him, a man on whom Death had already set his mark.' So in January 1947 Piotr Ouspensky, suffering from kidney failure, was hastened along icy roads to Lyne Place.

Immediately he called his lieutenants to him and said:

'Collect three hundred people.'
'How long have we got?'
'Say three weeks.'
'What shall we say to them?'
'Why say anything? Ask them what they want.'

When his 300 Ironsides were forgathered, Ouspensky held six momentous meetings at Colet Gardens; the first took place on 24 February and the last on 18 June. Hobbling with a stick, his every movement a painful effort, Piotr Ouspensky accomplished the two steps up the platform. From 1919 in Essentuki he had nicely discriminated between Gurdjieff and his ideas, repudiating the man but embracing 'The System'. Now as he stood there, shabby, ill and incorruptible, his theme was revolutionary: his sometime pupils must start again from what they knew themselves, reconstructing *everything* from the very beginning. It was Dr Kenneth Walker who summoned the courage to put the critical question.

'Does that mean Mr Ouspensky, that you have abandoned The System?'

'There is no System,' came the devastating reply.

There is no System. Yet Ouspensky had been teaching it for twenty-five years! His disavowal is not unlike Orage's commitment to have no more relations with Mr Orage. Quixotic and puzzling, heroic yet absurd, it invites us to deepen our understanding of sacrifice and new beginnings. After the last meeting, on 18 June, Ouspensky had to be helped from the platform and given an injection.

In his last months at Lyne, Ouspensky fell silent, scarcely speaking even to the intimates who shared his bread. Yet the silence was not oppressive and 'nothing negative ever touched the idea of death.' Long ago he had trotted the bridleways here, a ponderous, myopic, unlikely figure, glued to his horse Jingles (that gentle creature which, guided by the principles of *Tertium Organum*, could only see surfaces). Now, as the dying Ouspensky sat in the Green drawing-room 'like a dejected bird huddling up in a rainstorm', it seemed to his anxious pupils that a powerful presence hovered about him. It was a strange period. 'I will always be with you,' Ouspensky said lightly, smoking a cigarette. Yet suddenly, disconcertingly, he announced he would sail for America on 4 September. When passage had been booked, when his pupils had frantically restructured their own lives, when his luggage had been put aboard, when he had been driven to Southampton and the dock gates actually opened so that his car could address the gang-plank, then Ouspensky said quietly. 'I am not going to America this time.'

What exactly did he mean by 'this time'? Pitifully weak and sick, his days numbered, unwilling to surrender or even to sleep, Ouspensky had himself driven to the places he had known: to Hayes, to Sevenoaks, to West Wickham, to Sidlesham. On these painful, exhausting journeys the old man took no food, and only his cats shared his company and perhaps his feelings. So, making more and more demands on himself, Ouspensky 'seemed to rise in a crescendo of effort to meet the moment of death.' And yet to the vital crossroads, to the real terrain of decision, there was no returning: to the Second Moscow Gymnasium; to Essentuki and the country villa on the Panteleimon Road; to Moscow and the 'small café in a noisy though not central street'. Perhaps, for the man who had rejected his teacher and abandoned the System, nothing finally could – or need – be guaranteed.

Piotr Demianovich Ouspensky died at dawn on 2 October 1947. His book *Strange Life of Ivan Osokin* was being printed and pupils tried to bring him the first impression, but it arrived just too late. Unaccountably it was discovered in the glove compartment of his car, at the funeral. Ouspensky lies buried in the consecrated earth of Holy Trinity Church in the parish of Botley's and Lyne.

> P. D. Ouspensky
> Born Moscow
> 5th March 1878
> Died Lyne Place
> 2nd October 1947

It is a quiet and private place, befitting a man who prayed, 'Please God, protect me from becoming famous during my lifetime.' By a supreme irony Ouspensky's best memorial is *In Search of the Miraculous*,[2] that masterpiece of clarity and psychological juxtaposition. 'No system of gnostic soteriological philosophy that has been published to the modern world', says Philip Mairet, 'is comparable to it in power and intellectual articulation.' Ironic nevertheless. For here *par excellence* is the book of the abandoned System, comprising, for two parts in three, the direct and reported speech of the repudiated Gurdjieff.

The solemn requiem service for Ouspensky was held in the Russian church in Pimlico. As the incense rose before the icons, as his pupils gathered themselves silently, candles in hand, they could not weigh the past or discern the future. Absent through illness was Madame Sophie Grigorevna Ouspensky, and from her, in Mendham, the council of the Historico-Psychological Society eagerly sought the advice which, when it came, split them in two. 'Get in touch', she directed, 'with Mr Gurdjieff in Paris.'

Gurdjieff himself was now in his late seventies. On the night of 9 August 1948 in the town of Montargis, a drunken lorry-driver accelerated out of a side-road and hit his car. The old man's ribs were broken, his skull fractured, his sternum crushed. The subsequent return to Rue des Colonels Rénards was observed by John Godolphin Bennett:

> The door of one car opened, and Gurdjieff came slowly out. His clothes were covered with blood. His face was black with bruises. But there was something more, that made me realize that I was looking at a dying man. Even this is not enough to express it. It was a dead man, a corpse, that came out of the car;

and yet it walked ... into his room and sat down. He said: 'Now all organs are destroyed. Must make new.' He saw me and smiled saying: 'Tonight you come to dinner. I must make body work.'

Gurdjieff's recovery was swift and astonishing, and his reception of Ouspensky's pupils at this time was especially magnanimous. Every day he poured out his strength; he journeyed to America and back; still he gave 'a massive impression of contained energy – leonine, alert, watching and capable of springing up.' But all his organs could certainly not be made new. It was now he told his pupils he would 'disappear' once *Beelzebub* was published. They said they would follow him wherever he went, but he replied, 'You will not easily find me.' On his last long trip he drove to see the palaeolithic cave-paintings at Lascaux, but the journey taxed him. The doctors noted 'a spasmodic cough, a deep, gurgling, tracheal rumble.' His ankles were swollen, his breathing laboured, his lips tinged with blue. He struggled to the Salle Pleyel to give his demonstration class the last Movement – one concentrated entirely on inner work. Already he had given thirty-eight Movements, and had promised forty in all. 'Number 40!' he announced throatily. 'No Mr Gurdjieff, number 39.' But he insisted, smiling, 'No, 40.'

Early in October 1949, Gurdjieff drove to the rue Daru, pulled over to the curb and sat for an hour in massive silence before the Russian cathedral. On Saturday 22, he walked out of his flat for the last time; he had no strength left in his legs to brake his car, and crossing the avenue Carnot escaped collision by a hair's breadth. He was helped back to the flat, where ominously the proofs of *Beelzebub* had now arrived. To 'physic the king' was a thankless task, and technically perplexing; there was urgent need to reduce fluid in the abdomen, but because of high blood pressure serum albumin could not be administered. The eminent cardiologist Dr Welch, himself a pupil of Gurdjieff, was flown at twenty-four hours' notice from New York, but his prognosis was a black one: 'The mark of death was on his face.' Dr Welch proposed that Gurdjieff would never rise from his bed, but 'as I was speaking I looked up and saw him walking toward me, slowly in a kind of caricature of his old vital stride.' He said, 'Bravo, America! Bravo, *docteur!*' But he was not to walk any more. A room had been taken at the American hospital at Neuilly, and here Dr Welch desperately performed a puncture to drain off 12 litres of fluid. It was like a scene from some strange surrealist court. Gurdjieff, crowned with a tasselled magenta fez, his rich camel's-hair coat cast with imperial negligence about his shoulders, manoeuvred his cup of black coffee and his harsh Gaulois Bleu like a miniature orb and sceptre. Down below, the American physician and the prim Scottish nurse addressed themselves to an abdominal presence, which recalled Rodin's Balzac. 'Only if you not tired Doctor,' said Gurdjieff with indulgent irony. But the treatment gave merely temporary respite, and pain increased. On the afternoon of Thursday 27 October he summoned Jeanne de Salzmann to his bedside and gave indications for the future. On the Friday she spoke to him in Russian but he could only hold out his hand for her to take. At eleven o'clock on the morning of Saturday 29 October 1949 George Ivanovitch Gurdjieff was dead. His life requires no superstitious embellishment, and concerning the actual moment of death, the clinician Dr Welch has written, 'I was present, and the events that occurred were unique in my experience.'

In the chapel of the American hospital, Gurdjieff's embalmed body lay four days on an open bier. On Saturday night, the French came straight from the Movements class to kneel beside the Teacher of Dancing. In their economy of movement, in their mobilised attention, in the dignity of their grief, some have construed the last – the missing – Movement. The cramped space between the chapel walls and the low mortuary table was soon braced with mourners. While Americans were airborne over the Atlantic, the English arrived on the Golden Arrow and came to the bier with suitcases heavy in their hands. Night and day, Gurdjieff was never left alone; the sweet, green gardens of the hospital were thick with his followers, and each afternoon a little black-bearded priest chanted the office.

As a boy Gurdjieff had not owned a pair of shoes. Now he lay resplendent in his best suit, with prodigious bunches of tuberoses and violets on either side of his profound, enigmatic head. Wednesday 2 November. *Un froid de loup.* While their teacher was committed to his coffin at Neuilly, a massed congregation waited at that same Russian cathedral in the rue Daru. But Gurdjieff had one last trick in reserve. His body proved altogether too big, and another coffin was frantically obtained. 'He would laugh,' ventured Thomas de Hartmann. Meanwhile, so wholly contained was the cathedral congregation, that the priests became moved by a 'remarkable quality of silence which is so rare as to be noted as unique.' At last he came. As they carried him in, there sounded from high choir-stalls a sudden, deep, anguished salute. At the end of the low mass, just as the priest closed the *ikonostasis*, the electricity failed and all light was obliterated, except for the small candles of each individual follower, which had to serve.

Thursday 3 November, the day of the funeral, dawned cold but bright. At eleven in the morning, high requiem mass was sung in the cathedral. Five priests, weaving in the incense before the catafalque, told the ancient liturgy: 'O Holy God, Holy Firm, Holy Immortal, have mercy upon us. Give rest eternal in blessed falling asleep, O Lord, to the soul of thy servant George, departed this life, and make his memory eternal.' In blessed falling asleep! What were they saying? George Ivanovitch Gurdjieff, translated to whatever sphere, was surely struggling to awake. Thomas de Hartmann had written the eulogy, and the priest never knew that the closing words he spoke came from *The Struggle of the Magicians*. 'God and all his angels keep us from doing evil by helping us always and everywhere to remember our Selves.' For fully an hour, from right to left, the long line of pupils moved to kiss the little icon at the foot of the coffin. It was St George, Gurdjieff's 'very expensive saint', whose aid was not negotiable for candles or money but only for intentional suffering.

The streets for blocks around the cathedral were closed to traffic; a great concourse of pupils mingled with humble people of the quartier des Ternes. Mr Gurdjieff's final journey by motor car strangely recalled his own distinctive and adventitious driving procedures. The four fat coaches quickly came unstuck in the narrow canyon of the Rue des Colonels Rénards; the hearse itself, cocooned in a jolly superfluity of flowers, bounded away at a Gurdjieffian pace. It shot past the Étoile, whizzed down a long street full of booths, merry-go-rounds and coconut shies, out, out through a countryside of hoar-frost, white bullocks and black rooks; and so at last inescapably to the grave at Avon deep in the rocky, watery ground.

The same sympathetic little priest with the black beard sang the funeral service almost like a lullaby, his tender voice carrying away on the 'cruel, icy, sunny wind'. When the coffin was lowered a great sigh rose from the people. But who exactly were they burying? The son of John Georgiades the carpenter? Ushe Narzunoff? Prince Ozay? The man who killed Katherine Mansfield? Surely here was confided to the earth one who throughout his long transit had sounded a deep call and touched corresponding lives. This much one may assert without being a Gurdjieffian, or troubling to deny his undeniable transgressions against conventional morality, or even guessing his provenance. He enters as a question and remains a question. Scholars and critics will delve like blind moles; dogs will bark; metaphysicians will beat their gossamer wings. But who, finally, was George Ivanovitch Gurdjieff?

John Middleton Murry, in his final years, was betrayed by a sort of peace settling on him like golden pollen. He would never be much good with people or sugar-beet; as a political influence he was a nullity; as a literary critic he was 'a quaint old veteran, long ago superseded by the stream-lined Richards, the mass-distributed Leavis.' And somehow in the posthumous, bumblebee atmosphere of Lodge Farm, Thelnetham, it hardly seemed to matter. He pottered happily about in his ancient tweed jacket, bound with leather at the cuffs. 'I have taken in the season's honey: about 1 cwt. in all. And I have gone on reading Shakespeare.'

Angina pectoris was diagnosed after three minutes' agony on the night of 23 February 1957. Morphia was first administered on the night of Tuesday 5 March. The ambulance arrived in the small hours of Wednesday morning, and Middleton Murry was conveyed through the fog with harrowing slowness to Bury St Edmunds hospital. 'My precious,' he murmured, 'my precious!' It was his wife Mary who was kneeling beside him at the time, and presumably he referred to her. The hospital authorities first put their patient in a room he disliked, but they were afterwards good enough to move him. By Tuesday 12 March this matter of a congenial room had become redundant; the family were gathered at the bedside and Murry was *in articulo mortis*. Already his memory was failing him: 'I should not have asked Katherine to go on,' he said. 'I should not have asked Lawrence to go on.' The author of *God* was not fortified in his last hours by any belief in personal immortality. And if it was sorrow he would never see Katherine again, there was good consolation he would not be meeting Betty. He had not been a lucky man, and he had no relish to re-enter life. 'I can't go back there,' he said candidly. But his daughter Weg supposed him to allude to the unsatisfactory room. 'Dadda, there's no *question* of your going back,' she assured him. 'No, I don't suppose there is really,' he said.

John Middleton Murry died of coronary thrombosis in the early hours of Wednesday 13 March 1957. At Lodge Farm the sweet, musty smell of his home-grown yellow tobacco had already begun to fade, and in a few more days it was gone. This was not a death which created a great stir. *The Times* obituary desk rang Heppenstall, requiring some credible computation of Murry's wives, but on 16 March, when the hearse emerged from the drive in the drifting rain, only half-a-dozen cars fell in to make up the sad convoy. Soon the mourners were astonished to observe a large notice lofted over a draggled hedge:

THE ADELPHI HERO

Was this conceivably some spontaneous popular recognition of Murry, come ironically too late? But no, a closer inspection disclosed merely a dozen melancholy cows, ruminating beneath the legend 'The Adelphi Herd'.[3] At the lychgate the coffin was placed on 'something resembling a hospital trolley', and worked along the path to the little flint church. The handsome face, cross-hatched by time and trouble, had settled now in confident waxen repose. The elderly lady at the harmonium was the only one who could sing to any effect. 'God be in my head', she bawled. And that, certainly, was where Murry had always situated him. The parson climbed the pulpit steps and crossed himself ambitiously in the Anglo-Catholic way. Might he perhaps invite visitors' attention to the cost of maintaining this agreeable small church and to the collection box located directly behind them? As to his late, lamented parishioner Mr John Middleton Murry, he had been one who, like our Lord, had preached a gospel of love. Doubtless the vicar was right but, just the same, Larling lay twelve miles to the north-west.

At last, as the harmonium-lady played Handel's *Largo*, the mourners paddled their way circumspectly to the graveside; the coffin was slackened down; and sufficient dollops of ponderous Suffolk clay were ladled onto the unfortunate little man. There in that narrow trench so many singular agitations, so many crackpot notions came to their final rest. At least he had never been apathetic, and certainly not lazy; he had written forty, or was it fifty? strangely forgettable books; he was the friend of T. S. Eliot, the intimate of D. H. Lawrence, the husband of Katherine Mansfield, the critic of Gurdjieff. And he had to his credit a verse-play about condiments. Farewell Prince Cinnamon, prince of the Cloves, duke of Bombardon, praetor of Nectarine, legate of Pomegranada. Farewell! A stone was erected over his grave, inscribed:

> In Loving Memory of
> *JOHN MIDDLETON MURRY*
> AUTHOR AND FARMER
> 1889–1957
> 'Ripeness is All'

The death of Katherine Mansfield altered the content, not the form, of LM's life. So sharp a necessity for service and dominance demanded new subjects. Other mistresses, other houses, as if summoned by LM's imperious need, swam compliantly into view. And with them a dense asteroid belt of kittens and puppy dogs, goats and horses and hens, babies and godchildren and old dears. All took the imprint of the sturdy figure 'beset and breathless', the well-stacked khaki shirt and matching khaki hair, the orange headscarf and 'sensible' brogues.

In her little cottage at Woodgreen in the New Forest, LM lived always for today. Her carved Burmese figure, a last remembrancer of Colonel Baker, was given to the children and fell into the woods in bluebell time. Whole schools of babies, established in LM's lap, reached with questing hands for Katherine Mansfield's gold watch on its slender gold chain. Nothing delighted the good lady more than to teach the infants astronomy with the help of an orange and a ping-pong ball, and if she departed somewhat from the strictest orthodoxy, it must be remembered that she lacked the necessary scientific training. LM survived into the space age, a Victorian relic surprised by time. The hundredth anniversary of Orage's birth came and went – and Gurdjieff's and Ouspensky's. Still LM soldiered on, but no one's term is infinitely extensible: she was not told when she contracted leukaemia. She sank gradually and decently; she felt a bit seedy but, then, her own health had never really interested her. Perhaps in her bones she knew at the last where she was going: she was going to Katherine.

Ida Constance Baker died on 4 July 1978 at the age of ninety.

There is a great passage from Corinthians in the service for the burial of the dead, which she would particularly have liked:

> There are also celestial bodies, and bodies terrestrial; but the glory of the celestial is one, and the glory of the terrestrial is another. There is one glory of the sun, and another glory of the moon, and another glory of the stars: for one star differeth from another star in glory.

Admittedly, in the authorised ephemeris of bon ton, LM is more a ping-pong ball than an orange, but who will deny her a small corona of glory?

Notes

1. The minor actors in our drama, being human, also fell away. In 1933 Alexandre de Salzmann died of tuberculosis. Dmitri Ivanovitch Gurdjieff died from cancer in 1937 at his Paris flat 6 Rue des Colonels Rénards in the Russian quarter. Carl Bechhofer-Roberts was killed in a motoring accident in London on 14 December 1949. Dr James Carruthers Young died at Edgbaston, Birmingham, in 1950. Thomas Alexandrovitch de Hartmann died at Princeton, New Jersey, on 26 March 1956, just before an important concert of his music. At the age of eighty-eight, Katherine's first husband George Bowden wrote a book *F. Matthias Alexander and the Creative Advance of the Individual*. Ten unlikely years later, in September 1975, he died in Palma de Majorca. Dorothy Brett went with Lawrence to New Mexico in 1924 and died in Taos in August 1977. Madame Olga Arcadievna de Hartmann, whose closing years were spent in a desert community of musicians and friends in the American Southwest, died in September 1979. The fate of Dr Lewis Alexander Richard Wallace has defied my scholarship, as I suspected it would.
2. This book's earliest MS. dates from 1925 and Ouspensky laboured ten years to perfect its form. It was not published during his life and debatable if he actually desired publication. In January 1949 when Gurdjieff was at the Wellington Hotel, New York, Mme Ouspensky sought his agreement to its publication as *Man and the World in which he lives: Fragments of an Unknown Teaching*. Gurdjieff agreed: 'This very exact, he tell what I say.' The book first appeared in NY later in 1949 as *In Search of the Miraculous: Fragments of an Unknown Teaching*, a title probably influenced by Harcourt Brace the publishers. 'In Search of the Miraculous' was originally the title of a lecture given by Ouspensky in Petrograd in February 1915; those who study his book refer to it colloquially as 'Fragments'.
3. My account of Murry's funeral relies on Rayner Heppenstall's amusing and poignant memoir in *Four Absentees*.

Abbreviations

1 *Writers frequently quoted*
- ARO   Alfred Richard Orage
- BH   Beatrice Hastings
- BR   Carl Bechhofer-Roberts
- DHL   David Herbert Lawrence
- G   George Ivanovitch Gurdjieff
- JMM   John Middleton Murry
- KM   Katherine Mansfield
- LM   Ida Constance Baker
- O   Piotr Demianovich Ouspensky
- TH   Thomas de Hartmann

2 *Sources frequently quoted*
- B   *Beelzebub's Tales to His Grandson* (G)
- BTW   *Between Two Worlds* (JMM)
- F   *In Search of the Miraculous* (O)
- KMJ   *The Journal of Katherine Mansfield* (1927) (KM)
- KMJD   *The Journal of Katherine Mansfield* ('Definitive edition', 1954) (KM)
- KML   *The Letters of Katherine Mansfield* (1928) (KM)
- KMLM   *Katherine Mansfield: The Memories of LM* (LM)
- KMMM   *Katherine Mansfield's Letters to John Middleton Murry 1913–1922* (1951) (KM)
- NA   *New Age* (ARO)
- NM   *New Model of the Universe* (O)
- OLWG   *Our Life with Mr Gurdjieff* (TH)
- RM   *Meetings with Remarkable Men* (G)
- TONA   *The Old 'New Age': Orage – and Others* (BH)

3 *Standard abbreviations*

f.	and on the following page
Ibid.	in the same work (book or article) as that cited immediately above
Idem.	in the same work (book or article) *and on the same page* as that cited immediately above
loc. cit.	in the *article* by this author, cited previously in this chapter's references
op. cit.	in the *book* by this author, cited previously in this chapter's references
q.	quoted in the ensuing reference

References

These references will yield to a little study and a glance at the Abbreviations and Select Bibliography.
Each *quotation* is identified by a 'tag-phrase' based on the quotation proper. Common *sources* appear thus:

> G *RM* 37   meaning G. I. Gurdjieff. *Meetings with Remarkable Men*, Routledge & Kegan Paul 1963, page 37.

Quotations identified simply by author are from the *one and only* book by that author in the Select Bibliography. Thus:

> Glenavy 103   means Glenavy, Lady Beatrice. *Today We Will Only Gossip*, Constable 1964, page 103.

Where the author is listed twice or more in the Select Bibliography, a clue is given to the quotation source. Thus:

Nott *Teachings* 29   means Nott C. S. *Teachings of Gurdjieff*, Routledge & Kegan Paul 1961, page 29.

Alpers (1954) 128   means Alpers, Antony. *Katherine Mansfield*, Jonathan Cape 1954, page 128.

Chapter 1   Beauty and the Beast

'KM was perfect'   JMM q. Nott *Teachings* 47.
'A princess manifest'   JMM 'In Memory of Katherine Mansfield' *Adelphi* 1 (January 1924) 664–5.

'among the saintliest of women'   Thomas Moult 'Katherine Mansfield' *Bookman* LXIII: 377 (February 1923) 228.
'the most exquisite prose'   Aiken 13.
'doll-like seriousness of face'   Ibid. 19.
'Could one have'   Ibid. 13.
'Death had preserved her'   Roland Merlin 'Le drame de Katherine Mansfield' *L'Illustration* 16 (19 January 1946).
'raise the lid'   Idem.
'his violent temper, greed for money'   Meyers 247.
'50 per cent charlatan'   Philip French *Observer* (16 September 1979).
'one particularly weird'   Blanche 63.
'rotten, false, self-conscious place'   DHL to Mabel Dodge Luhan (9 January 1924) q. Luhan 128.
'dancing round the pig-sties'   Miron Grindea, editorial *Adam International Review* 300 (1965) 14.
'torture, even with whips'   Seabrook 184.
'His shaved Tartar's skull'   Merlin loc. cit.
'an invisible bull-whip'   Seabrook 181.
'You all dirt'   Kenneth Cavander 'To awake. To die. To be born.' *Horizon* XIV:2 (spring 1972) 60.
'small, chill, fireless room'   Clarke 283.
'rites more voluptuous'   Blanche 64.
'The Forest Lovers'   Nott op. cit, 64.
'an insidious intoxication'   Merlin loc. cit.
'depths of mental anguish'   Eustace 76.
'assumed the hair shirt'   Blanche 69.
'Gurdjieff and his hosts are doomed'   Whitall N. Perry 'Gurdjieff in the Light of Tradition' *Studies in Comparative Religion* (spring 1975) 125 f.
'the *simpleton* like Parsifal' Blanche 69.
'Gurdjieff a mountebank'   White 243.
'the guidance of a crazy Russian'   Gordon 29.

Chapter 2   Katherine Mansfield

'The only true statement'   Koteliansky q. Glenavy 160.
'an altogether happy childhood'   Ian A. Gordon in KM *Undiscovered Country* (Longman 1974) Introduction ix.
'promise of great merit'   editorial note *High School Reporter* (Wellington Girls' High School 1898).
'great effort of Victorian England'   Mantz 171.
'didn't abandon the 'cello'   Miron Grindea, editorial 'Only one K.M.? – notes and footnotes to a biography' *Adam International Review* 370–5 (1972–3) 15.
'the whole octave of sex'   KM *KMJD* 5, emended from Mansfield Notebook 1, Alexander Turnbull Library Acc. 97266.
'To weave the intricate tapestry'   KM *KMJD* 37.'

'sweet Eddie Bendall'   KM, Mansfield Notebook 39, Alexander Turnbull Library.
'completely self-centred'   Jeanne Renshaw (KM's younger sister) interviewed by Owen Leeming 'Katherine Mansfield and her Family' *New Zealand Listener* 1227 (29 March 1963) 4.
'a girl come back'   Willa Cather *Not Under Forty* (Cassell 1936) 157.
'round oval face'   Anne Estelle Rice 'Memories of Katherine Mansfield' *Adam International Review* 300 (1965) 76.
'the beautiful eyes'   Idem.
'almost surrealistic first marriage'   Brigid Brophy 'Katherine Mansfield' *London Magazine* 2 (December 1962) 41.
'candles stuck in a skull'   Orton 270.
'Grandmother would have forbidden'   Mantz 329.
'made love like two wild beasts'   Orton 281.
'no baby and a closed bank account'   LM *KMLM* 65.
'my own revulsion from life'   JMM *BTW* 184.
'Would seven-and-six be too much'   KM q. Ibid. 200f.
'Murry was the editor'   Alpers (1954) 156.
'an angry tigress'   Douglas Jerrold *Georgian Adventure* (William Collins 1937) 194.
'a triangular love affair'   Helen McNeish *Passionate Pilgrimage* (Michael Joseph 1976) Preface 5.
'so DON'T WORRY!' Leslie Beauchamp to his parents (11 February 1915).
'the exalted girl'   Grindea loc. cit. 3.
'Follow me'   Francis Carco q. *KMJD* 75.
'The act of love'   KM *KMJD* 78.
'I believe in immortality'   KM *KMJ* 35.
'O God'   KM 'To God the Father' *Poems* (Constable 1923) 31.
'more than one creator'   KM q. Rice loc. cit, 81.
'snail under the leaf'   KM *KMMM* 344.
'to get down to myself'   KM q. *BTW* 309.
'Sorry. There's no reply'   KM *KMJ* 80.
'looking on, noting all'   LM *KMLM* 65.
'To find Truth'   Ibid. 23.
'In the profoundest Ocean'   KM 'The Secret' (1912) q. *KMLM* 69.
'one of his lungs'   KM letter to Ottoline Morrell (University of Texas).
'this is *not* serious'   KM *KMMM* 173 (19 February 1918).
'You never once held me'   Ibid. 265 (27 May 1918).
'like a china figure'   Sylvia Lynd q. Alpers (1954) 267.
'eat the little bear's porridge'   KM q. *KMLM* 114 (18 April 1918).
'balimanate of zinc'   KM *KMMM* 401 (21 November 1919).
'inevitability of his own death'   G B 1183.

Chapter 3 George Ivanovitch Gurdjieff

'Immediately interesting questions arise'   Peter Brook interviewed by James Moore *Guardian* (20 July 1976).

'Eldest of my grandsons'   G B 27f.
'not a single book'   G RM 70.
'hysteria is hysteria'   Idem.
'sacred aims and intentions'   G Herald 17
'Mme. Vitvitskaia'   G RM 254.
'all kinds of specialists'   G q. F 15f.
'holy-of-holies'   G Herald 17.
'freely moving "Guinea Pigs" '   Ibid. 22.
'liquidated all my affairs'   G RM 270.
'Call him Prince Ozay'   (and all the immediately following Ozay quotes) Dukes 101–7.
Russia . . . peaceful, rich and quiet'   G Herald 24.
'an oppositional flash'   L. D. Trotsky History of the Russian Revolution vol. 1 (Gollancz 1932) 95.
'the Empress's "mauve boudoir" '   Douglas Brown Doomsday 1917 (Sidgwick & Jackson 1975) 30.
'exquisitely polite cadet sentries'   N. N. Sukhanov The Russian Revolution (Oxford University Press 1955) 518.
'sincerely beloved wife'   G Life is Real 36.
'apartment in the Bolshaia Dmitrovka'   O F 271.
'to tunnel under a wall'   G q. F 30.
'an extremely mixed crowd'   TH OLWG 5.
'usually more whores here'   Ibid. 6.
'the theory of music'   BR Denikin 67.
'He was different!'   O F 324f.
'My fellow traveller'   Unknown journalist q. (with minor excisions) O F 325f.
'a Sealed Train'   Winston Churchill The World Crisis 1916–1918 (Thornton Butterworth 1927).
'It would be difficult'   O F 346.
'days endlessly long'   Ibid. 356.
'G. superintended the kitchen'   Ibid. 346.
'the plan of the whole work'   Idem.
'we began rhythmic exercises'   Ibid. 372.
'something like Sodroojestvo'   G q. F 373.
'Sometimes on getting up'   G RM 271.
'skeletons of people'   Ibid. 278.

Chapter 4   Ida Constance Baker

'calm, deeply dark eyes'   LM KMLM 22.
'Her body was obedient'   KM KMJD 54.
'my nom-de-plume'   KM q. Mantz 185.
'a kind of walking shadow'   Jeanne Renshaw (KM's younger sister) interviewed by Owen Leeming 'Katherine Mansfield's Rebellion' New Zealand Listener (5 April 1963) 6.

'savagely crude'   KM, Mansfield Notebook 39, Alexander Turnbull Library Acc. 97273.
'raspberry seeds'   LM *KMLM* 25.
'only person who believes in me'   KM q. *KMLM* 31.
'The ghost of L.M.'   KM q. Mantz 186.
'always a fine adventure'   LM *KMLM* 39.
'sweet-tempered, quiet Garnet'   Ibid. 42.
'the way that Garnet ate his egg'   Ibid. 44.
'shiny black straw hat'   Ibid. 46.
'tied a label on him'   Ibid. 52.
'unprofessional interest'   Ibid. 54.
'Bowden snatched off his bowler'   Ibid. 57.
'Penelope nor Scheherazade'   Alpers (1954) 137.
'I wanted to kill'   KM q. Orton 281.
'little red elephants'   LM *KMLM* 66.
'Have you brought any money?'   KM q. Ibid. 66.
'fill his cupboard with good things'   LM Ibid. 68
'Lesley Moore and Rebecca Rinsberry'   Alpers (1954) 178.
'a personal extravagance'   LM *KMLM* 77.
'had a broom somewhere'   Ibid. 83
'tear up English money'   Ibid. 88.
'Almighty Spirit of Love'   Ibid. 96.
'munition worker called Leslie Moor'   Virginia Wolf, Diary (11 October 1917) q. Quentin Bell *Virginia Wolf: A Biography* (Hogarth Press 1972) 45.
'My dear, send me away!'   KM 'Psychology' *Bliss and Other Stories* (Constable 1920).
'unseen third person'   LM *KMLM* 102.
'a touch of pleurisy'   KM q. Ibid. 105.
'her hour of need'   LM Ibid. 105.
'swaying with weakness as she walked'   Ibid. 106.
'she will be furious'   JMM q. Ibid. 107.
'meal times and walk times'   KM *KMMM* 169.
'a dreadful little man'   LM Ibid. 108.
'ever so gay'   KM q. Ibid. 114 (18 April 1918).
'pock-marked or an ampute'   Ibid. 119 (22 June 1918).
'For the sake of all that has been'   KM q. Ibid. 122 (1 July 1918).
'headway with my machinists'   LM Ibid. 121.
'none in Hampstead'   Ibid. 129.
'tough strip of leather'   Idem.
'Hate is the *other* passion'   KM *KMMM* 399 (20 November 1919).
'Oh, what heaven!'   Idem.
'never stare at me again'   Ibid. 365.

Chapter 5   Piotr Demianovitch Ouspensky

'Why did he say that?'   G q. *F* 262.
'I went into the forest'   O Idem.

'From the age of three'   O   *A Further Record Chiefly of Extracts from Meetings held by P. D. Ouspensky between 1928 and 1945* (Stourton Press, Capetown 1952) q. Taylor 9–13.
'I remember the river'   O q. Taylor 9.
'They looked exactly'   O *F* 3.
'A stick pushed under a stone'   O *NM* 2.
'the tall German'   Idem.
'Cupio, desidero'   O *Osokin* 47.
'decision of the Masters' Council'   a nomenclatural transposition from Ibid. 94.
'professors were killing science'   O q. Taylor 10.
'never to take any degrees'   Idem.
'sleeve of my overcoat missing'   O q. BR *Denikin* 91.
'only work on "left" papers'   O q. Taylor 10.
'This means that . . .'   O *NM* 477.
'Pushing aside the papers'   Ibid. 3.
'The paper would be seized'   Idem.
'miracles on Kuznetsky Most'   Ibid. 388.
'*They* were the soul of Constantinople'   Ibid. 385.
'Yellowish-grey sand'   Ibid. 362.
'I did not exist'   Ibid. 364.
'satiated, semi-nocturnal life'   Alexei Tolstoi q. Colin Wilson *Rasputin* (Arthur Barker 1964) 75.
'Better to say "No" once'   O q. Butkovsky 25.
'the gentle, poetic radiance'   Ibid. 23.
'We shall find the Miracle'   O q. Ibid. 21.
'The meaning of life'   O *Tertium* 336.
'They can be seen only'   O *NM* 347.
'whatever the name of the school'   O *F* 5.
'Hindu writers of ballet scenarios'   Ibid. 6.
'My first meeting with him'   Ibid. 7.
'when you went to India'   G q. Ibid. 16.
'the assurance of a specialist'   O *F* 12.
'If you understood everything'   G q. *F* 20.
'Er, er . . . it is difficult'   O q. Butkovsky 79.
'exactly like a cow'   G q. Idem.
'how easy it is to *turn* you'   G q. *F* 251.
'G's chaff did not affect me'   O Idem.
'You want a fourth, eighth dimension'   G q. Butkovsky 81.
'unpainted wooden *crutches*'   O *F* 51
'The marionettes failed to understand'   Ibid. 327.
'Tramways, railways, post'   O 'Letters from Russia III' *NA* (4 December 1919) 71.
'Come here to me'   G q. *F* 340.
'wait five years'   Ibid. 342.
'to see the Nevsky'   O *F* 341.
'You ought to know that'   G q. *F* 178.
'begun to separate G. and the *ideas*'   O *F* 373.

'the most sensitive corn'   G *Life is Real* 51.
'G.'s methods did not suit me'   O *F* 373f.
'I felt very silly'   O *F* 376.

Chapter 6   John Middleton Murry

'I am an unlucky man'   Frieda Lawrence 75.
'I had left my wallet behind'   JMM *BTW* 167.
'heads and tails'   Ibid. 168
'towards the open gutter'   Idem.
'I was a beautiful baby'   Ibid. 9.
'A thin line of mucus'   Ibid. 57.
'He settled *Hoti's* business'   Robert Browning 'The Grammarian's Funeral'.
'the experience of physical love'   JMM *BTW* 133.
'disgraced the regiment'   Ibid. 165.
'I never wrote again'   Ibid. 173.
'I had contracted gonorrhoea'   Ibid. 183.
'I had been the man'   KM *Scrapbook* 125.
'timid girlish soul'   JMM *BTW* 493.
'the torment of physical passion'   Ibid. 206.
'a spiritualised rubber glove'   Huxley 569.
'Christ goes deeper'   Frank Harris q. *Frank Harris* Vincent Brome (Cassell 1959) 6.
'Hamlet's full throated father'   Kingsmill 40.
'Frank Harris is the greatest'   JMM *Rhythm* 2 (July 1912) 39.
'the image of a panther'   Ibid. 224.
'a sort of presentiment'   Ibid. 223.
'a woman who was bodily ill'   H. S. Ede *The Savage Messiah* (Heinemann 1931) 2.
'Sophie will *live* there'   Gaudier q. *BTW* 226.
'a dangerous turning'   Gaudier q. Ede op. cit. 148
'I should like to throttle you'   Gaudier q. *BTW* 246.
'not worth a twopenny damn'   JMM Ibid. 248f.
'four million'   Ibid. 235.
'my code did not allow it'   Ibid. 279.
'a holiday in Cornwall'   Ibid. 296.
'a tenacious catarrh'   Ibid. 297.
'I got so drunk'   Mark Gertler, letter to Lytton Strachey (1 January 1915) *Mark Gertler Selected Letters* ed. Noel Carrington (Rupert Hart-Davis 1965).
'his posture was crumpled'   Kingsmill 75.
'*Order of the Knights of Rananim*'   DHL *The Quest of Rananim* ed. George J. Zytaruk (Queen's University Press 1970).
'communism based on riches'   DHL to Lady Ottoline Morrell (1 February 1915).

'He rubbed every speck'   DHL *Aaron's Rod* 91.
'sick and sensitive fingers'   JMM *BTW* 393.
'Katherine's tower'   DHL q. Ibid. 401.
'If I love you'   JMM q. Lea *Murry* 53.
'pre-Christian blood-rite'   JMM *BTW* 409.
'no impulse to intervene'   Ibid. 409.
'an obscene bug'   DHL q. Ibid. 416.
'A policeman came'   KM letter (16 May 1916) *The Letters and Journals of Katherine Mansfield* ed. C. K. Stead (Allen Lane 1977) 80.
'I pedalled off' JMM *BTW* 417.
'shooting myself as a protest'   JMM *God* 17.
'wrists turned to damp string'   JMM *BTW* 445.
'only part of the nightmare'   Ibid. 479.
'There was no escape'   Ibid. 490.
'homeless and vagrant'   Ibid. 486.
'black, cold stone of unfaith'   JMM *God* 22.
'hopeless illness in a loved one'   JMM *Keats and Shakespeare* (Oxford University Press 1925) 28.

Chapter 7   Alfred Richard Orage

'to make a ploughboy'   Howard Coote *While I Remember* (London 1937) 72.
'best literary critic'   T. S. Eliot *New English Weekly* VI (15 November 1934) 100.
'a cult, with affiliations'   ARO *NA* XXXVIII:20 (18 March 1926) 235.
'iron and brass and silver and gold'   ARO 'Esprit de Corps in Elementary Schools' *Monthly Review* XXV:75 (December 1906) 48.
'To go back is to go forward'   ARO *NA* XVIII:5 (2 December 1915) 110.
'walls covered in brown paper'   Mairet *Orage* 10.
'Leeds Art Club born'   Holbrook Jackson 'A. R. Orage: personal recollections' *Windmill* 3:1 (1948).
'an exciting brew'   Jackson *New English Weekly* VI (15 November 1934)
'Nietzsche or Blavatsky'   Idem. .
'through pretensions like butter'   Harold Massingham *Remembrance* (B. T. Batsford 1942) 31.
'magnetic personality'   Jacob Epstein *An Autobiography* (Hulton Press 1955) 61.
'intellectuality that radiated'   Anthony M. Ludovici *New English Weekly* VI (15 November 1934).
'conscious of his aura'   Jackson *Windmill* loc. cit.
'every one of his gestures'   BR *Let's Begin* 174.
'no mere legend'   Selver *ONAC* 15.
'cat-like in his movements'   Jackson loc. cit.
'Prossy's complaint'   Idem.
'His gospel, always preached'   Gerald Cumberland.
'A coal merchant of Pudsey'   Mairet *Orage* 28.

'We decline into animal'   ARO *Consciousness: Animal, Human and Superhuman* (Theosophical Publishing Co., London and Benares 1907).
'Do what you will'   Mairet *Orage* 17.
'white silky hair'   Selver *ONAC* 27.
'capable of singing'   Miron Grindea *Adam International Review* 300 (1965) 7.
'married to a pugilist'   Alpers (1954) 128.
'the handmaid of the Spirit'   ARO 'Readings and Re-Readings: The Mystic Valuation of Literature' *Theosophical Review* XXXI:185 (15 January 1903) 430.
'Bernard Shaw and Belford Bax'   Kenney 153.
'wouldn't pay cigar bill'   Selver *Schooling* 259.
'did more to feed me'   Ezra Pound *The Letters of Ezra Pound, 1907–1941* ed. D. D. Paige (Faber & Faber 1951) 344.
'During twelve years'   Hobson 141.
'something of a mystery man'   Nott *Journey* 31.
'The graveyards overflow'   Hobson 141.
'appraise a revolution in guineas'   Ibid. 146.
'true to one master – Socrates'   Holbrook Jackson q. Selver *ONAC* 87.
'the "New Age" editorially a rag'   BH *TONA* 4.
'the whole seeming to occupy'   Mairet *Orage* 78.
'it had all been horrible'   LM *KMLM* 65.
'down to valentines'   ARO *NA* IX:22 (28 September 1911) 518.
'There was a piano'   ARO *NA* XI:4 (23 May 1912) 85.
'nothing the matter but "flop" '   BH *TONA* 10.
'kind of a wobbly'   Ibid. 11.
'thievish "literary" pen'   Ibid. 6.
'a rustic, a lout, a snob'   Ibid. 18.
'I had wealthy relatives'   Ibid. 27.
'memories of past lives'   BR *Let's Begin* 248.
'he was Yudisthira'   BH *TONA* 19.
'I was already disillusioned'   O q. Nott *Teaching* 27.
'his skewbald witanagemot'   Selver *ONAC* 28.
'the perilous system'   BH *TONA* 19.
'*scènes avec des revolvers*'   Max Jacob *Correspondance* vol. II, 186.
'*curious* – blonde – passionate'   KM *KMMM* (22 March 1915).
'Orage wants kicking'   Idem.
'tall, dark, bullet-headed Serbian'   Edwin Muir 174.
'squat and bald'   Selver *ONAC* 28.
'ultimate Aryan glory'   Dmitri Mitrinovic *NA* xxvii (6 January 1921) 113.
'prose style so anfractious'   Martin 270.
'I nearly lost consciousness'   Selver *ONAC* 57.
'Word of Mystery'   Willa Muir 41.
'The Great War'   ARO 'An Editor's Progress' *NA* XXXVIII (1 April 1926) 258.
'a secret knowledge'   Edwin Muir 173.

Chapter 8 The Caucasus

'Possibilities for *everything*'   G q. *F* 251.
'The expedition intends'   G q. *OLWG* 49.
'The bearer, Citizen Gurdjieff'   *RM* 275.
'compelled to run about the city'   G *RM* 279.
'nearly two hundred people'   Ibid. 277.
'a former dervish'   René Daumal *Mount Analogue* (Vincent Stuart 1959) 6.
'only for disciples'   G q. *F* 14.
'work in Sacred Gymnastics'   G q. *OLWG* 77.
'What name. . . ?' Ibid. 89.
'squeezing a tube of toothpaste'   TH Idem.
'Bombay, Alexandria, Kabul'   G q. *F* 380.
'general public significance'   *RM* 280.
'Minister for National Education'   G q. *F* 380.
'For me and my family'   O *F* 376.
'God-forsaken place'   O 'Letters from Russia' *NA* (25 December 1919).
'Boots and trousers'   Ibid. (4 September 1919).
'A New French Course'   *Denikin* 219.
'big two-dimensional creatures'   O 'Letters' *NA* (4 September 1919).
'Bolshevism something very old'   Ibid. (27 November 1919).
'the Law of Opposites'   Ibid. (4 September 1919).
'Georgiy Ivanovich Gourjiev'   BR *Denikin* 65.
'instead of talking theosophy'   Ibid. 66.
'muddy waters of the Kura'   Idem.
'mysterious monasteries in Thibet'   Ibid. 68.
'my friend Mr Ouspiensky'   Ibid. 81.
'the clothes he was wearing'   Ibid. 82.
'received me cordially'   Ibid. 81.
'not like the old days'   O q. Ibid. 82.
'turned up my nose'   Ibid. 83.
'when the porter was busy'   Idem.
'a quantity of spirit'   Ibid. 89.
'vodka and salted cucumber'   O q. Idem.
'wonder as much as you like'   O q. Ibid. 92.
'The panic had begun'   Ibid. 125.
'the minarets of Stamboul'   O *NM* 388.
'there was even no Russia'   Idem.
'liquidate everything in Tiflis'   G *RM* 281.

Chapter 9 The Alps

'I loathe you'   DHL q. *KMMM* 469f. (7 February 1920) and Lea 83.
'we are both abnormal'   KM Ibid. 532 (June 1920).
'In a foreign bed'   KM *KMJ* 74 (February 1918).
'The nasturtiums blaze'   KM *KMJ* 153 (12 August 1920).

'I can so imagine'   KM *KMJD* (12 August 1920).
'Menton which killed her'   McNeish 5.
'cutting *re* tuberculosis'   KM *KMMM* 542 (24 September 1920).
'Dead true'   KM *KML* 41 (15 September 1920).
'L.M. fond of bananas'   KM *KMJD* 220 (September 1920).
'What is milk a metre?'   LM q. *KMMM* 581 (1 November 1920).
'What is the *authority*?'   LM q. Ibid. 566 (17 October 1920).
'You have been a perfect friend'   KM *KMLM* 20.
' "mushroom growth" of psycho-analysis'   KM *KML* 53 (13 October 1920).
'You don't take me in'   Ibid. 70 (1 November 1920).
'He wore a green overcoat'   Ibid. 71 (1 November 1920).
'Which self?'   KM *Scrapbook* 136 (July 1920).
'a self continuous and permanent'   Ibid. 137.
'Is it right to resist suffering?'   KM *KML* 57 (18 October 1920).
'I've *acted* my sins'   Ibid. 68 (31 October 1920).
'starving for feminine warmth'   JMM Journal (4 January 1951) q. Lea *Life* 80f.
'The Cocoa-Pacifist'   Ford Madox Ford *Letters* ed. Richard M. Ludwig (Princeton University Press 1965) 128.
'A man is a man'   LM q. *KMMM* 606 (end of November 1920).
'sent me that Corona'   KM *KMMM* 615 (8 December 1920).
'K.M. can't go on'   KM Idem.
'I told you to be free'   KM Ibid. 621 (12 December 1920).
'It is finished'   KM q. *KMLM* 153.
'the pale morning light'   Idem.
'letter blaming Katherine'   Ibid. 154.
'no limit to human suffering'   KM *KMJ* 163 (19 December 1920).
'Let me remember'   Ibid. 170 (27 December 1920).
'The root of the trouble'   JMM *KMMM* 622.
'He went up to her room'   LM *KMLM* 154.
'I explained to Elizabeth'   JMM Journal (4 January 1951) q. Lea *Life* 81.
'the *Athenaeum* lost £5000'   DHL to Koteliansky (2 March 1921).
'a new and interesting experience'   LM *KMLM* 155.
'a 6d glass of salvolatile'   KM q. Ibid. 159.
'withstood her gallantly'   Princess Bibesco q. *KMLM* 162.
'he NEVER tries to help'   KM q. Idem.
'I found him'   LM Ibid. 161.
'Switzerland might be best'   KM q. Ibid. 160 (10 March 1921).
'that man Spahlinger'   KM q. *KMLM* 163.
'if he comes he comes'   KM q. *KMLM* 160 (10 March 1921).
'torture for cats?'   KM q. Ibid. 162.
'v. willing not to come'   KM Ibid. 163.
'country with a bicycle'   Idem.
'from kerridge to door' KM *KML* 102 (May 1921).
'I had to arrange'   LM *KMLM* 165.
'The journey to Geneva'   KM *KMJ* 179.
'mountains glittering with snow'   KM Idem.

237

'Spahlinger costs 14 horses'   KM *KMMM* 638 (23 May 1921).
'lungs of Spanish leather'   KM *KML* 100 (7 May 1921).
'an automatic pistol'   Ibid. 118 (June 1921).
'*grown in* to you'   JMM to KM (19 May 1921) q. Lea *Life* 84.
'especially the young ladies'   Mark Gertler q. Lea *Life* 84.
'The old man was everything'   JMM to KM (26 May 1921) q. Lea *Life* 85.
'Dear Orage'   KM q. Mairet 59 (9 February 1921).
'I am not qualified'   Selver 60.
'introduction of psycho-analysis'   Martin 5.
'London is Looney-bin'   Mitrinovic q. Willa Muir 41.
'Brighter than the sun'   Mantra q. Edwin Muir 173.
'Orage's extraordinary spiritual effort'   Ibid. 174.
'Oh Life! accept me'   KM *KMJD* 229.
're-create one's own inner being'   Kenney 325.
'Prayer to Hermes'   Maurice Nicoll q. Pogson 70.

Chapter 10   Cosmic Anatomy

'large consignment of caviar'   G *RM* 282.
'better understood than I myself'   Bennett *Witness* 65.
'a specialised knowledge'   Ibid. 66.
'G. the artist and poet'   O *F* 383.
'The Initiation of the Priestess'   Bennett *New World* 129.
'wiseacrings of the Young Turks'   G *RM* 283.
'sense of complete assurance'   Bennett *New World* 132.
'matchboxes of solid gold'   David Garnett *The Flowers of the Forest* (Chatto & Windus 1955) 225.
'psychosynthesist had materialised'   J. A. M. Alcock q. Kenney 326.
'I learned more from him'   Kenney 329.
'You must come hear Ouspensky'   Nicoll q. Pogson 71.
'one of the magicians'   Mairet *Orage*.
'Mr Ouspensky is the first teacher'   ARO to Claude Bragdon (30 May 1922) q. Bragdon *Springs* 320.
'Is Buddha the seventh state?'   Landau 228.
'unspeakable rhymesters'   Selver *Orage* 72.
'my mount in the Grand National'   Walker *Venture* 44.
'cobbling old boots'   ARO q. Kenney 328.
'the complete, ideal *Existenzphilosophie*'   Wilson *Outsider* 264.
'Grandmother with her pink knitting'   KM *KML* 134 (September 1921).
'Wingley our gooseberry-eyed-one'   Ibid. 135 (22 September 1921).
'a half-sucked peppermint'   Ibid. 164 (13 December 1921).
'terrific disguises'   Ibid. 152 (12 November 1921).
'Ah, Koteliansky – wish for me'   Ibid. 161 (5 December 1921).
'a book called Cosmic Anatomy'   KM to Violet Schiff (November 1921).
'one must have a miracle'   KM *KML* 165 (19 December 1921).
'strained every nerve'   JMM *KMMM* 643.
'bake me or boil me'   KM *KML* 176f. (January 1922).

'ways had really parted'   JMM *KMM* 643.
'tore up and ruthlessly destroyed'   KM *KMJ* 224.
'cost me *much* money'   KM KML 180.
'My work infinitely more important'   G q. A. S. Neill *'Neill! Neill! Orange Peel!'* (Weidenfeld 1973) 120.
'He who in childhood'   G *B* 50.
'nobody can control his actions'   G *Views* 76.
'choose a teacher'   G q. Nott *Journey* 99.
'Everything more vivid'   G q. Pogson 72.
'Gurdjieff was the teacher'   ARO q. Nott *Teachings* 27.
'Her handsome dark eyes'   Francis Carco, see *Bohème d'artiste* 253–60 and *Montmartre à vingt ans* 204–5.
'leaving Katherine to her fate'   LM *KMLM* 194.
'a bored Home Secretary'   Walker *Study* 13.
'beyond all understanding'   Brett to Koteliansky (June 1922) letter in possession of Mrs Catherine Stoye q. Carswell 183.
'*Gymnastes de Provence*'   KM q. *KMLM* 198 (5 June 1922).
'snow or rain or something'   G *RM* 285.
'deeply sorry for Murry'   KM to Koteliansky (23 August 1922).
'Are the trousers full enough?'   JMM q. *KML* 241.
'rare, white-plumed pigeon'   Llewelyn Powys *The Verdict of Bridlegoose* (Jonathan Cape 1922) 113.
'a river flowing away'   KM *KMJ* 243.
'a typically false life'   Ibid. 244.
'the doctrines of Ouspensky'   JMM q. Lea *Life* 90.
'Christ's Coat'   Ibid. 92.
'speaking Russian using English words'   Landau 214.
'work of general and special interest'   ARO *NA* XXXI:267 (28 September 1922).
'the striving in her'   O *F* 386.
'Consciousness of will'   putatively O q. *KMJ* 244.
'the maddest periods of my life'   G *RM* 285.
'room where one could work'   KM *KMJ* 245.
'Large grave gentlemen'   KM *KML* 248.
'*Don't* feed her'   KM *KMJ* 245.
'Be born again'   KM *KML* 253.
'chief mate on a cargo steamer'   KM Ibid. 258.
'fabulous and other-worldly'   KM *KMMM* 672.
'no belief in medical treatment'   KM *KML* 256.
'candidates for departure'   G *Life is Real* 6.
'*a child of the sun*'   KM *KMJ* 249ff.

Chapter 11   *The Initiation of the Priestess*

'Mrs. Serious Problem'   G *RM* 285.
'twenty-four hours a day'   Ibid. 287.
'to know European languages'   Ibid. 286.

'exactly like a desert chief' KM *KMJD* 335.
'I feel *absolutely confident*' KM *KMMM* 676f.
'Fire is condensed sunlight' LM *KMLM* 214.
'Came away absolutely dazed' Idem.
'animals and simple people' Ibid. 218.
'She *was* me. KM *KMMM* 678.
'eat, walk in the garden' G q. Ibid. 677.
'Gurdjieff serves the dish' KM Idem.
'In all my travels' Nott *Teachings* 56.
'sharp, intense, dark eyes' Olgivanna (Mrs Frank Lloyd Wright) 'The Last Days of Katherine Mansfield' *Bookman* LXXIII (March 1931) 6.
'You take care of her' G q. Idem.
'Why had she to die?' Ibid. 7.
'I wish I could have been' KM q. Idem.
'Katherine slightly touched my head' Idem.
'abundance of untried strength' Adèle Kafian 'The Last Days of Katherine Mansfield' *Adelphi* XXIII (October–December 1946) 36.
'Dr Young, a real friend' KM *KML* 262.
'Nina, a big girl' KM *KMMM* 680.
'Alice in Wonderland' This *bon mot* is James Webb's.
'Be slave freely' Greek proverb q. Nott *Teachings* 50.
'I was told to dig' ARO q. Ibid. 28.
'This *is* the place' KM *KMMM* 683.
'like a toy gun' Peters 50.
'so delicate, so refined' G q. Idem.
'very mystical pigs' KM *KML* 263.
'avoid identifying' Maurice Nicoll q. Pogson 84.
'My hands are ruined' KM *KMLM* 222.
'Mr Gurdjieff hardly speaks' KM *KMMM* 678.
'It is worth mentioning' G *RM* 289.
'Patience the Mother of Will' G q. Bennett *Witness* 121.
'It is not "my music" ' TH, talk at Colet Gardens (9 March 1950) q. *Flying Saucer: Gurdjieff Revisits Earth* Brynhild Wooldridge Thring (Coombe Springs Press 1979).
'made even Lenin blush' Denis Saurat 'A Visit to Gourdjev.' *Living Age* CCCXLV (January 1934) 427–33.
'She watched so eagerly' Olgivanna loc. cit. 12.
'ancient Assyrian group Dance' KM *KMMM* 684.
'There is one takes 7 minutes' Ibid. 685.
'Do send *Lit Sups.*' Ibid. 679.
'a world of Peeping Toms' KM q. 'Talks with Katherine Mansfield' by ARO *New English Weekly* 111 (19 May 1932).
'The reader's sympathy' KM Idem.
'death will not destroy' KM q. Olgivanna loc. cit. 8.
'There is no death' Idem.
'Anyone grow flower with fràme' G q. Merston.
'no proper tools' TH *OLMG* 107.
'the phenomenon "snap-finger" ' James Young 'An Experiment at

Fontainebleau' *New Adelphi* NS, 1 (September 1927) 36.
'When the pole is removed' G q. *OLWG* 107.
'I know this is true' KM q. *F* 386.
'a very fine man' KM *KMMM* 688.
'Poor fellow' ARO q. Bechhofer 'The Forest Philosophers' *Century Magazine* NS LXXXVI (May 1924) 76.
'I vowed extra effort' ARO q. Nott *Journal* 28.
'two quite poor young girls' KM *KMMM* 695.
'the heat of my fire' Ibid. 686.
'my love of cows' Ibid. 687.
'in the cowhouse' Ibid. 692.
'Doctor Stable and Doctor Milk' G q. Ibid. 695.
'She was tall' Olgivanna loc. cit. 9.
'a super-cow-sensation' KM q. Idem.
'Not to write' G q. *KMMM* 695.
'You could learn the banjo' KM *KMMM* 681.
'sacrifice one's suffering' G q. *F* 274.
'I tried to go to bed' Olgivanna loc. cit. 11.
'dead 50 times' KM *KMLM* 223.
'how did Mr Gurdjieff know?' KM *KMMM* 695.
'We are going to *Fêter le Noel*' KM *KMLM* 224.
'not too awfully serious' Ibid. 225.
'sharp changes in her voice' Kafian loc. cit. 37.
'Adèle, why three?' KM q. Kafian loc. cit. 37.
'*Who am I?*' KM *KML* 266f.
'would you care to come' Ibid. 268.
'Goodbye, my dearest cousin' Ibid. 429.
'God bless you darling Father' KM to H. Beauchamp (31 December 1922) q. Alpers (1980) 379.
'My thoughts full of carpets' KM q. *KMLM* 226.
'transformed by love' JMM *KMMM* 700.
'a changed man' Idem.
'a blend of simplicity' Idem.
'I love the rain tonight' KM q. Olgivanna loc. cit. 13.
'I want music' Idem.
'How grateful I could be' Ibid. 12.
'Two thousand years you mean' Idem.
'embroidered Spanish shawl' LM *KMLM* 229.
'Why had she come here?' Ibid. 230.
'I began in the car' Idem.
'*groupe de théosophes*' Kafian loc. cit. 36.
'It is not my coffin' KM q. Orton 274.

Chapter 12 The Harrowing of John Middleton Murry

'The woman I had loved' JMM *Things To Come* (Jonathan Cape 1928) xiv.
'my loved one was gone' Ibid. xv.

'she took it in a different sense' JMM MS. (1947) q. Lea *Life* 100.
'if he were really cornered' Idem.
'Prompted by some instinct' JMM *God* 35.
'endorsement by the Universe' Ibid. 39.
'she died there' JMM letter to *Daily News* (23 February 1923).
'All manuscripts, papers, letters' KM's will (proved 23 April 1923).
'I saw her face' LM *KMLM* 19.
'He had burned his boats' JMM *New English Weekly* VI (15 November 1934).
'printed on paper' G. B. Shaw to JMM (27 April 1923) q. Lea *Life* 107.
'The idea of our sleeping together' JMM Journal (18 December 1955) q. Lea *Life* 118.
'tea in the Strand' JMM manuscript (1947) q. Lea *Life* 122.
'I like your brother' Violet le Maistre q. Ibid. 123.
'to get a cow or something' JMM q. *KMLM* 207.
'the house of his dreams' Lea *Life* 124.
'ten times as big' JMM manuscript (1947) q. Idem.
'smell of "future orthodoxy"' JMM 'Quo Warranto' *Adelphi* II:3 (August 1924).
'on top of happy hours' JMM manuscript (1947) q. Lea *Life* 126.
'Violet's daughter was Katherine's daughter' JMM Journal (9 October 1950) q. Lea *Life* 329.
'the most meaningful thing' JMM manuscript (1947) q. Lea *Life* 143.
'O I'm so *glad*!' Ibid. 144.
'it would have been easier' JMM *God* 26.
'correlation between my personal condition' JMM to T. S. Eliot (6 January 1945) q. Lea *Life* 163.
'How *tired* I am' JMM q. Colin Murry *Clapping* 24.
'travailed by a longing' JMM to Plowman (27 January 1931) q. Lea *Life* 163.
'fulfilment in love' JMM Journal (12 July 1953) q. Lea *Life* 165.
'an active power' JMM Journal (21 December 1930) q. Lea *Life* 173.
'But I must tell you' Violet le Maistre q. JMM manuscript (1936) q. Lea *Life* 174.
'whereas I mistrusted Orage' JMM Journal (7 March 1931) q. Lea *Life* 174.
'Of this I am certain' JMM q. Colin Murry *Clapping* 31.
'I laid down my life' JMM Journal (12 April 1931) q. Lea *Life* 178.
'Dadda is cuddling Miss Cockbayne' Ibid. 33.
'given him fair warning' Ibid. 36.
'consumed to tears by *Das Kapital*' JMM *Things to Come* (Jonathan Cape 1938) xxvii.
'If I would give her twenty pounds' JMM manuscript (1947) q. Lea *Life* 187.
'*Il a manqué à Murry*' Léaud *Les Langues Modernes* (May–June 1961).
'black, demonic force' Colin Murry *Clapping* 41.
'I am a connoisseur' Richard Rees *A Theory of My Time* (Secker & Warburg 1963) 62.
'and *keep it shut*!' James Young q. Colin Murry *Clapping* 58.

'You may think me over-confident'   JMM to Rees (13 November 1931) q. Lea *Life* 194.
'How he has understood Blake'   Max Plowman (3 March 1933) q. Lea *Life* 213.
'(*Jesus* + *Shakespeare* . . .) × *Murry*'   Heppenstall *Murry* 171.
'On the left-hand page'   Heppenstall *Absentees* 37.
'Masters in Tibet'   JMM *New English Weekly* VI (15 November 1934).
'It will be located'   JMM *The Necessity of Pacifism* (Jonathan Cape 1937) 83f.
'his thin pink nose'   Heppenstall *Absentees* 119.
'an excitable Scotswoman'   Idem.
'little nibbling kisses'   Ibid. 130.
'My baby, my sweetheart'   JMM Journal (28 May 1936) q. Lea *Life* 229.
'built of bad bricks'   JMM manuscript (1936) q. Lea *Life* 237.
'My personal destiny'   JMM q. Lea *Life* 232.
'the day I go back to Larling'   Ibid. 236.
'The fury to be unleashed'   Colin Murry *Clapping* 139.
'Adamson. Son of Adam'   JMM manuscript (1936) q. Lea *Life* 237.
'crisis over Rayner's cooking'   JMM q. Heppenstall *Absentees* 131.
'a clockwork motor'   Colin Murry *Clapping* 161.
'I'm feeling queer'   JMM manuscript (1947) q. Lea *Life* 263.
'it would be in vain'   Idem.
'a classical example of Nervous Breakdown'   James Young q. Lea *Life* 264.
'I don't love you anymore'   JMM q. Lea *Life* 264.
'The screaming came again'   Colin Murry *Clapping* 199.
'I'll keep Larlin' Darlin''   Ibid. 179.
'If my relation with Mary'   JMM q. Mary Murry 96.
'the fingers of his soul'   Mary Murry 37.
'You are a spiritual caveman'   Ibid. 127.
'nothing less than Monte Cassino'   JMM q. Lea *Life* 306.
'Suddenly I was overwhelmed'   JMM *Farm* 31.
'not a mangel on the field'   Ibid. 32.
'I have the advantage over you'   Ibid. 53.
'Keats called Negative Capability'   Ibid. 88.
'All things considered'   Ibid. 64.
'That night there was a sharp frost'   Colin Murry *Shadows* 50.
'I will accept the annihilation'   JMM q. 'Communist Occupation or World War; Which would be Worse?' *Picture Post* 48:5 (5 August 1950).
'spiritual quackery of Gurdjieff'   JMM letter to Beatrice Campbell (1955) q. Carswell 262.
'We have no illusions'   JMM *The Necessity of Communism* (Jonathan Cape 1932) 113.

Chaper 13   Beelzebub

'a thousand times more value'   G *Views* 105.
'After these learned sessions'   G *RM* 27.
'all these people were mad'   Denis Saurat *Nouvelle Revue française* XLI (1 November 1933).
'as a final chord'   G *Life is Real* 30.

'How many men and women'   Pierre Schaeffer q. Pauwells 412.
'Everything now stop'   G q. Nott *Teachings* 83.
'I, who have lately' G B 9.
'Australian frozen meat'   Ibid. 10.
'swapping anecdotes'   Idem.
'Ah . . . me! Never mind'   Ibid. 13.
'Green roses, Purple mimosas'   G *RM* 26.
'Matthew, Mark, Luke and Johnnie'   G B 99.
'to "bake" a scenario'   G *Herald* 42.
'When I say "I" '   G q. Nott *Journey* 23.
'It was in the year 223'   G B 51.
'bizarre and subtle'   Richard Rees 'Monsieur Gurdjieff' *Twentieth Century* (November 1958) 440.
'as one continues to read'   Walker *Venture* 177.
'the inevitability of death'   G B 1183.
'All appearances to the contrary'   Professor Henry LeRoy Finch 'The Gurdjieff Perspective Today' lecture (1 March 1961).
'Newton, Darwin or Freud'   Wilson *Occult* 537.
'the four sources of action'   G B 343.
'And that tall man'   Ibid. 675.
'He drove like a wild man'   Hulme 66.
'we listen to *grenouilles*'   Idem.
'These delays were an annoyance'   Peters *Boyhood* 130.
'It is not my coffin'   KM q. Orton 274.
'We may take a sceptical view'   Wilson op. cit. 519.
'God made an umbrella'   G q. Nott *Journey* 229.
'Nature of woman'   G q. Peters *Boyhood* 114.
'Gurdjieff ideas well camouflaged'   Finch loc. cit.
'half literary Paris'   Hulme op. cit. 86.
'Beelzebub read in Pope's Palace' G q. Bennett *Witness* 271.
'First clean house'   G q. Nott *Journey* 19.
'feed birds in park'   G q. Peters *Remembered* 93.
'By what grocer's miracle?'   Schaeffer q. Pauwells 410.
'*Le Patron* is demanding attention'   G q. Walker *Venture* 145.
'These poor herons'   Schaeffer q. Pauwells 405.
'a Nobel prize winner'   René Zuber *Qui êtes-vous Monsieur Gurdjieff?* (Courrier du Livre, Paris 1977).
'grace and economy of gesture'   Bennett *Witness* 245.
'Gurdjieff is the most immediate'   Peter Brook q. Margaret Croyden 'Filming the Saga Of a Sage with Peter Brook' *New York Times* (26 February 1978).
'Either the old world'   G q. Bennett   *Witness* 278.

Chapter 14 Cultural Bon Ton

'eyed each other with caution'   David Garnet *The Flowers of the Forest* (Chatto & Windus 1955) 225.

'Come, Lawrence! Come to Taos!' Luhan 43.
'The syllogism in the psychic sphere' for this and successive quotations of DHL and O see E. W. Tedlock, 'D. H. Lawrence's Annotations of Ouspensky's *Tertium Organum*' *Texas Studies of Literature and Language* 2 (1960).
'what happens to Jung's disciples' Sigmund Freud q. BR 'The Forest Philosophers' *Century Magazine* NS, LXXXVI (May 1924) 77.
'Levantine psychic shark' Wyndham Lewis to Violet Schiff (20 September 1922) British Library.
'In the end it was to Gurdjieff' François Mauriac q. Anderson 3.
'Don't join that community' William Butler Yeats q. Monk Gibbon *The Masterpiece and the Man* (Rupert Hart-Davis 1959) 88.
'Goudjieff is a Russian' Sinclair Lewis q. Mark Schorer *Sinclair Lewis: An American Life* (New York 1961) 378.
'Gurdjieff made Persian soup' Ezra Loomis Pound q. Noel Stock *The Life of Ezra Pound* (Routledge & Kegan Paul 1970) 253.
'I love you Lorenzo' JMM *Reminiscences of D. H. Lawrence* (Jonathan Cape 1933) 175.
'rotten, false, self-conscious place' DHL letter to Luhan (9 January 1924) q. Luhan 128.
'we called at that Fontainebleau place' DHL letter to Luhan (7 February 1924) q. Ibid. 132.
'He came in from another room' Nott *Teachings* 22.
'like the soldiers of Christophe' Seabrook 180.
'He had a presence' Anderson 78.
'a massive man' T. S. Matthews *Name and Address* (Antony Blond 1961) 205.
'Gurdjieff says quite calmly' Mabel Dodge Luhan letter to DHL (3 April 1926) q. Luhan 263.
'My I, my fourth centre' DHL q. Luhan passim.
'You don't imagine how little interest' DHL letter to Luhan (3 July 1926) q. Ibid. 275.
'Lawrence's pride would keep him back' KM *KMMM* 688.
'thin as a rail' DHL 'Mother and Daughter' *The Collected Short Stories* (Heinemann 1955) 756.
'The Turkish Delight' Ibid. 760.
'Man is of the order of the moon' G, see ARO *On Love* (The Janus Press 1957) 48.
'the nine-minute-egg category' Seabrook 187.
'somewhat fortified for the evening' Edwin Wolfe *Episodes with Gurdjieff* (Guild Press, Bray 1973) 15.
'I write book' Idem.
'elaborate and subtle joke' Watson q. Seabrook 188.
'superb Algerian melons' Idem.
'Mr Gurdjieff smiled and nodded' Wolfe op. cit. 16.
'You see what called "intelligentsia"' G q. Ibid. 18.
'French I thought' Wright 441.
'Karsavina won't do' Idem.

'Fate the dealer'   Ibid. 440.
'the stuff of genuine prophets'   Frank Lloyd Wright q. R. C. Twombly 'Organic Living' *Wisconsin Magazine of History* (winter 1974–5).
'the oldest and toughest fowls'   Nott *Journey* 152.
'But the war did happen'   DHL *Aaron's Rod* 113.
'You are all people'   T. S. Eliot 'The Family Reunion' (1939) *The Collected Plays* (Faber & Faber) 65.
'He will one day'   Frank Lloyd Wright *Wisconsin State Journal* II (3 November 1951) 3.

Chapter 15   Rites of Passage

'Addition: By the way'   G q. Marjorie von Harten *A Way of Living* (Coombe Springs Press) 43.
'proper death at right time'   G q. Peters *Boyhood* 78.
'remained silent and withdrawn'   Ibid. 107.
'an imaginary incarnation of Lucifer'   DHL to Mabel Dodge Luhan (11 February 1929) q. Luhan 309.
'I can't die, I can't die'   DHL q. Frieda Lawrence 270.
'I have had bronchitis'   DHL q. Ibid. 272.
'Monsieur Lawrence is a lamp'   memoir Barbara Weekley Barr.
'old coughing and young coughing'   Frieda Lawrence 274.
'It is enough, it is enough'   Idem.
'I ought to have some morphine now'   DHL q. Ibid. 275.
'I held his left ankle'   Idem.
'dumped into the casserole'   G *Life is Real* 124.
'Gurdjieff a kind of walking god'   ARO q. Nott *Journey* 31.
'I thank God every day'   Ibid. 52
'I did not know before'   ARO q. Mairet *Orage* 120.
'In thirty years of public life'   Hynes 39.
'Yet in twenty years'   BH *TONA* 33.
'I should have sentenced him'   Ibid. 30.
'carving it to my own fashion'   BH *NA* (14 February 1918).
'It is the only thing'   O q. Nott *Journey* 161.
'Doesn't he understand'   O q. Bennett *New World* 235.
'There stepped onto English soil'   Walker *Venture* 128.
'Collect three hundred people'   O q. Yale 40.
'nothing negative ever touched'   Rodney Collin *The Theory of Conscious Harmony* (Vincent Stuart 1958) 178.
'like a dejected bird'   Kenney 326.
'I am not going to America'   O q. Collin op. cit. 179.
'seemed to rise in a crescendo'   Collin op. cit. 180.
'Please God, protect me'   O q. Yale 40.
'No system of gnostic'   Mairet *Orage* (University Books, New York 1966) xxiv.
'The door of one car opened'   Bennett *Witness* 249.
'a massive impression of contained energy'   Welch 134.

'as I was speaking I looked up'   Ibid. 138.
'only if you not tired Doctor'   Ibid. 139.
'I was present'   Ibid. 140.
'remarkable quality of silence'   Solita Solano q. Anderson 201.
'a quaint old veteran'   Lea *Voices* 177.
'taken in the season's honey'   JMM letter to K. de Coninck (15 September 1955) q. Ibid 190.
'I should not have asked Katherine'   JMM q. Mary Murry 189.
'I can't go back there'   et seq Lea *Life* 353.
'something resembling a hospital trolley'   Heppenstall *Absentees* 201.
'There are also celestial bodies'   I Corinthians 15, 20.

Select Bibliography

My select bibliography is dictated solely by the form and content of *Gurdjieff and Mansfield*. Hence Katherine Mansfield's fiction, and critical examination of it, are excluded: so are purely expository books on Gurdjieff's ideas, without biographic relevance. Scholarship moves on; thus readers whose interest is strongly oriented either towards Mansfield or towards Gurdjieff may find that the Alexander Turnbull Library or The Gurdjieff Society, respectively, can advise them further.

1. Aiken, Conrad. *Costumes by Eros*, Jonathan Cape 1929.
2. Alpers, Antony. *Katherine Mansfield*, Jonathan Cape 1954.
3. Alpers, A. *The Life of Katherine Mansfield*, Jonathan Cape 1980.
4. Anderson, Margaret. *The Unknowable Gurdjieff*, Routledge & Kegan Paul 1962.
5. Baker, Ida Constance. *Katherine Mansfield: The Memories of LM*, Michael Joseph 1971.
6. Bechhofer-Roberts, C. E. *In Denikin's Russia and the Caucasus, 1919–1920*, Collins 1921.
7. Bechhofer-Roberts, C. E. *Let's Begin Again*, Jarrolds 1940.
8. Bennett, John Godolphin. *Witness*, Turnstone Books 1962.
9. Bennett, J. G. *Gurdjieff: A Very Great Enigma*, Coombe Springs Press 1963.
10. Bennett, J. G. *Gurdjieff: Making a New World*, Turnstone Books 1973.
11. Berkman, Sylvia. *Katherine Mansfield: A Critical Study*, Oxford University Press 1952.
12. Blanche, Jacques-Émile. *More Portraits of a Lifetime*, Dent 1939.
13. Bland, Rosamund (Rosamund Sharp). *Extracts from Nine Letters Written at the Beginning of P. D. Ouspensky's London Work in 1921*, Stourton Press (Cape Town) 1952.

SELECT BIBLIOGRAPHY

14 Bragdon, Claude. *Merely Players*, Knopf (New York) 1929.
15 Bradgon, C. *The Secret Springs*, Andrew Dakers 1939.
16 Butkovsky-Hewitt, Anna. *With Gurdjieff in St Petersburg and Paris*, Routledge & Kegan Paul 1978.
17 Carswell, Johnathan. *Lives and Letters*, Faber & Faber 1978.
18 Clarke, Isabel, C. *Six Portraits*, Hutchinson 1935.
19 Curnow, Heather. *Katherine Mansfield*, Reed (New Zealand) 1968.
20 Dukes, Sir Paul. *The Unending Quest*, Cassell 1950.
21 Eustace, C. J. *An Infinity of Questions*, Dennis Dobson 1946.
22 Foster, John. *The Influences of Rudolph Laban*. Lepus Books 1977.
23 Gibbons, Tom. *Rooms in the Darwin Hotel*, University of Western Australia Press 1973.
24 Glenavy, Lady Beatrice. *Today We Will Only Gossip*, Constable 1964.
25 Gordon, Ian A. *Katherine Mansfield*, Longman (for the British Council) 1954 (revised 1963, 1971).
26 Gurdjieff, George Ivanovitch. *The Herald of Coming Good* (Paris) 1933.
27 Gurdjieff, G. I. *Beelzebub's Tales to his Grandson*, Routledge & Kegan Paul 1950.
28 Gurdjieff, G. I. *Meetings with Remarkable Men*, Routledge & Kegan Paul 1963.
29 Gurdjieff, G. I. *Views from the Real World*, Routledge & Kegan Paul 1973.
30 Gurdjieff, G. I. *Life is Real Only Then, When 'I Am'* (privately printed by Triangle Editions, New York) 1975.
31 Hartmann, Thomas de. *Our Life with Mr Gurdjieff*, Cooper Square Publishers (New York) 1964.
32 Hastings, Beatrice. *The Old 'New Age': Orage – and Others*, Blue Moon Press 1936.
33 Heppenstall, Rayner. *Middleton Murry: A Study in Excellent Normality*, Jonathan Cape 1934.
34 Heppenstall, R. *Four Absentees*, Barrie & Rockliff 1960.
35 Hobson, S. G. *Pilgrim to the Left*, Edward Arnold 1938.
36 Hormasji, Nariman. *Katherine Mansfield: An Appraisal*, Collins 1967.
37 Hulme, Kathryn C. *Undiscovered Country*, Little, Brown & Co. (Boston) 1966.
38 Huxley, Aldous. *Point Counterpoint*, Chatto & Windus 1928.
39 Hynes, Samuel *Edwardian Occasions*, Routledge & Kegan Paul 1972.
40 Kenney, Rowland. *Westering*, Dent 1939.
41 Kingsmill, Hugh. *The Life of D. H. Lawrence*, Methuen 1938.
42 Land, Myrick. *The Fine Art of Literary Mayhem*, Hamish Hamilton 1963.
43 Landau, Rom. *God is my Adventure*, Nicholson & Watson 1935.
44 Lawrence, D. H. *The Collected Short Stories*, Heinemann 1974.
45 Lawrence, D. H. *The Quest for Rananim* (DHL's letters to S. S. Koteliansky, ed. George J. Zytaruk), Queen's University Press 1970.
46 Lea, F. A. *The Life of John Middleton Murry*, Methuen 1959.
47 Lea, F. A. *Voices in the Wilderness*, Brentham Press 1975.
48 Luhan, Mabel Dodge. *Lorenzo in Taos*, Secker 1933.

SELECT BIBLIOGRAPHY

49 Mairet, Philip. *A. R. Orage: A Memoir*, Dent 1936.
50 Mairet, P. *John Middleton Murry*, Longman 1958.
51 Mansfield, Katherine. *The Journal of Katherine Mansfield* (ed. JMM), Constable 1927.
52 Mansfield, K. *The Letters of Katherine Mansfield* (2 vols ed. JMM), Constable 1928.
53 Mansfield, K. *The Scrapbook of Katherine Mansfield* (ed. JMM), Constable 1939.
54 Mansfield, K. *Katherine Mansfield's Letters to John Middleton Murry 1913–1922* (ed. JMM), Constable 1951.
55 Mansfield, K. *The Journal of Katherine Mansfield* ('definitive edition' with new material ed. JMM), Constable 1954.
56 Mantz, Ruth Elvish and JMM. *The Life of Katherine Mansfield*, Constable 1933.
57 Martin, Wallace. *The New Age under Orage*, Manchester University Press 1967.
58 Merlin, Roland. *Le Drame secret de Katherine Mansfield* (Paris) 1950.
59 Merston, Ethel. 'Journal' (unpublished).
60 Meyers, Jeffrey. *Married to Genius*, London Magazine Editions 1977.
61 Meyers, J. *Katherine Mansfield*, Hamish Hamilton 1978.
62 Moorman, Lewis, J. *Tuberculosis and Genius*, University of Chicago Press 1940.
63 Morrell, Lady Ottoline. *Ottoline at Garsington*, Faber & Faber 1974.
64 Muir, Edwin, *An Autobiography*, Hogarth Press 1940.
65 Muir, Willa. *Belonging*, Hogarth Press 1968.
66 Murry, Colin Middleton. *One Hand Clapping*, Gollancz 1975.
67 Murry, C. M. *Shadows on the Grass*, Gollancz 1977.
68 Murry, John Middleton. *God*, Jonathan Cape 1929.
69 Murry, J. M. *Reminiscences of D. H. Lawrence*, Jonathan Cape 1933.
70 Murry, J. M. *Between Two Worlds*, Jonathan Cape 1935.
71 Murry, J. M. *Community Farm*, Nevill 1952.
72 Murry, Mary Middleton. *To Keep Faith*, Constable 1959.
73 Nott, C. S. *Teachings of Gurdjieff*, Routledge & Kegan Paul 1961.
74 Nott, C. S. *Journey Through This World*, Routledge & Kegan Paul 1969.
75 Orage, A. R. *On Love*, Janus Press 1957.
76 Orton, William. *The Last Romantic*, Cassell 1937.
77 Ouspensky, P. D. *Tertium Organum*, Manas Press (New York) 1920.
78 Ouspensky, P. D. *New Model of the Universe*, Routledge & Kegan Paul 1931.
79 Ouspensky, P. D. *Strange Life of Ivan Osokin*, Faber & Faber 1948.
80 Ouspensky, P. D. *In Search of the Miraculous*, Routledge & Kegan Paul 1950.
81 Pauwells, Louis. *Gurdjieff*, Times Press (Douglas, Isle of Man) 1964.
82 Peters, Fritz. *Boyhood with Gurdjieff*, Gollancz 1964.
83 Peters, F. *Gurdjieff Remembered*, Gollancz 1965.
84 Pogson, Beryl. *Maurice Nicoll: A Portrait*, Stuart 1961.
85 Priestley, J. B. *Man and Time*, Aldus Books 1964.
86 Rees, Richard. *For Love or Money: Studies in Personality and Essence*,

Secker & Warburg 1960.
87 Seabrook, William, *Witchcraft – Its Power in the World Today*, Harrap 1940.
88 Selver, Paul. *Schooling*, Jarrolds 1927.
89 Selver, P. *Orage and the New Age Circle*, Allen & Unwin 1959.
90 Speeth, Kathleen Riordan. *The Gurdjieff Work*, And/Or Press (California) 1976.
91 Taylor, Merrily E. (ed.). *Remembering Pyotr Demianovich Ouspensky*, Yale University Library 1978.
92 Walker, Kenneth. *Venture with Ideas*, Jonathan Cape 1951.
93 Walker, K. *A Study of Gurdjieff's Teaching*, Jonathan Cape 1957.
94 Wallace, Lewis A. R. (Pseud. 'M.B. Oxon.') *Cosmic Anatomy, or the Structure of the Ego*, Watkins 1921.
95 Webb, James. *The Harmonious Circle*, Thames & Hudson 1980.
96 Welch, William J. *What Happened in Between*, George Braziller (New York) 1972.
97 White, Nelia Gardner. *Daughter of Time*, Constable 1942.
98 Wilson, Colin. *The Outsider*, Gollancz 1956.
99 Wilson, C. *The Occult*, Hodder & Stoughton 1971.
100 Wright, Frank Lloyd. *An Autobiography*, Faber & Faber 1945.

Index

Alcock, Dr J. A. M., 123, 128
Alexandra Feodorovna, Tsarina, 28
Anderson, Margaret (Caroline), 195, 199–201
Artzibashev, Mikhail Petrovich, 12, 54
ashokh, 21, 34n.

Baker, Ida Constance, see 'LM'
Baker, May (sister), 35
Baker, Colonel Oswald (father), 35, 40–3, 46, 115
Bartrick-Baker, Vere ('Mimi'), 163, 165
Beauchamp, Sir Harold (father), 6n., 8–9, 157
Beauchamp, Kathleen Mansfield, see MANSFIELD, KATHERINE
Beauchamp, Leslie Heron (brother), 8, 14–15, 75
Bechhofer-Roberts, Carl E. (Roberts, Carl E. Bechhöfer), 83, 90, 105–8, 212, 224n.
Beelzebub (*Beelzebub's Tales to his Grandson*), 183–93
Bendall, Edie, 9
Bennett, Capt. John Godolphin, 126–7, 148, 217

Besant, Annie, 57
Bessaraboff, Nicholas, 125
Bibesco, Princess Elizabeth (*née* Asquith), 116–19
Borsh, Father Dean, 20–21
Bowden, George Charles (KM's 1st husband), 10, 17, 38, 40, 200, 224n.
Bowden, Mrs Kathleen, see MANSFIELD, KATHERINE
Bragdon, Claude, 125, 127–8
Brett, The Hon. Dorothy (Eugenie), 134, 136, 162, 165, 224n.
Brook, Peter (Stephen Paul), xi, 192, 195
Brzeska, Sophie, 70–2
Butkovsky, Anna Ilinishna, 56, 59

'Carco, Francis' (Francesco Carcopino–Tusoli), 14, 45, 72, 75, 133
'Carno, Fred' (a fancier of mumming birds), 165
Chesterton, G. K. (Gilbert Keith), 81–2, 86
Cinnamon, Prince (*Cinnamon and Angelica*), 223

INDEX

Cockbayne, Betty, *see* Murry, Mrs Elizabeth Ada
Connor (a boy struck by lightning), 67
Cook & Son, Thomas ('Koukanssen'), 25
Coote, Howard, 79
Coote, Squire (father), 80–1
'Cosmoi M. M.', *see* Mitrinovic, Dmitri
Croudace, Camilla (educated wolf-bait), 8
'Crowley, Aleister' (Edward Alexander Crowley) (*Frater Perdurabo*), 15, 18n.

Dalai Lama (Thupten Gyatso 13th DL), 25–6
Dalcroze, Emile Jaques- ('Monsieur Jaques'), 100–1
Denikin, General Anton Ivanovitch, 103, 106
Diaghilev, Sergei Pavlovich, 1, 54, 198
Dostoevsky, Fyodor Mikhailovich, 75, 139
Dordjieff, Lama (the Tsanit Khanpo Aghwan), 25, 34n.
Douglas, Major Clifford Hugh, RAF (Reserve) MIMechE, 91–2, 93n., 122–4
Dukes, Sir Paul, 26–7
Dunning, Mrs William J. (an embraceable yogin), 161–2, 165, 167
Dwight, Jessie, *see* Orage, Mrs Jessie

Eliot, T. S. (Thomas Stearns), 79–80, 128, 163, 195, 207, 222
'Elizabeth' (von Arnim, later Countess Russell), 157
Eoung-Ashokh Mardiross (an accurate fortune-teller), 21
Epstein, Sir Jacob, 82

Fabergé, Peter Carl, 29
Finch, Professor Henry LeRoy, 185, 189

Freud, Professor Sigmund, 123, 185, 189, 197, 207

Gamble, Mary, *see* Murry, Mrs Mary
Gaudier-Brzeska, Henri, 70–1, 75, 77, 123
Georgiades, John (G's father), 19, 21, 33, 221
Gertler, Mark, 74, 121
Gilgamesh (King of Uruk), 21
'Gorki, Maxim' (Aleksei Maximovich Peshkov), 130, 139
Gurdjieff, Dmitri Ivanovitch (brother), 20, 95–6, 101, 224n.
GURDJIEFF, GEORGE IVANOVITCH (pre 1877–29 Oct. 1949)
material:
  birth, 19
  boyhood, 20–2
  burial, 220–1
  business, 23, 26, 100, 148, 191
  cooking, 32, 145, 191, 199, 206, 211
  death, 219
  education, 20–1
  ideas, 27, 29–30, 32, 59–60, 63, 179, 183, 185, 187–8
  marriage, 28
  search, 20–6
  writing, 22–4, 181–3, 185, 187–90
presented as:
  'The Beast', 3–5
  Ushe Narzunoff, 25–6, 221
  Prince Ozay, 26–7, 221
  a certain Hindu, 29, 57
  the Miracle, 59, 63
  Citizen Gurdjieff, 97
  a Teacher of Dancing, 101, 142n., 149, 181, 186, 189–90
  the Grand Lama of Thibet, 34n., 141
  Beelzebub, 184, 190–1
  Monsieur Bon-bon, 186
  an incarnation of Lucifer, 210
mise en scène:
  Alexandropol (pre 1877), 19

INDEX

Kars (1877–1891), 19–21
Wanderjahre (1892–1909), 22–6
Tashkent (1910–1913), 26
Moscow (and Petrograd) (1913–Feb. 1917), 26–32
Alexandropol (Feb. 1917–June 1917), 32, 62
Essentuki (Uch Dere and Tuapse) (July 1917–Aug. 1918), 32–3, 62, 94–6
Sochi (Oct. 1918–Jan. 1919), 98–9
Tiflis (Jan. 1919–June 1920), 99–103, 110
Constantinople (Istanbul) (June 1920–summer 1921), 125–7
Berlin and Hellerau (summer 1921–July 1922), 131–2
London (visits Feb. and March 1922), 132
Paris (July 1922–Oct. 1949), 135, 190–1
Fontainebleau (Oct. 1922–1933), 135–6, 140, 143–60, 179
New York (visits 1924, 1931 and 1948), 19, 200, 204–6
Meetings with:
Ostrowska (c. 1914), 28
OUSPENSKY (April 1915), 58
Hartmann (Dec. 1916), 30
'Olgivanna' (spring 1919), 101
Pinder (spring 1919), 101
Salzmann (spring 1919), 100
Bechhofer (Nov. 1919), 106
Bennett (Aug. 1920), 126
ORAGE (Feb. 1922), 132–3
MANSFIELD (Oct. 1922), 144
LM (Oct. 1922), 144
MURRY (Jan. 1923), 159
Anderson (spring 1924), 201
Watson (Jan. 1931), 204–5
Wright (June 1931), 206

Haigh, Emily Alice, *see* 'Beatrice Hastings'
Hardie, (James) Keir, 80
Hardy, Thomas, 120–1

Harris, Frank, 68–9
Hartmann, Mme Olga Arcadievna de, 30, 98, 101–2, 135, 138, 180, 183, 224n.
Hartmann, Thomas ('Foma') de, 30, 94–5, 101, 111n., 149, 152, 154, 209, 219–20, 224n.
'Hastings Beatrice' (Emily Alice Haigh) (1879–1943)
as lover and women's liber, 84–5, 87–91, 213–14
as writer, 87–8, 213–14
sorts out:
MANSFIELD, 88, 91, 114, 198
Modigliani, 90
ORAGE, 87, 89, 213
death, 214
Heap, Jane, 195, 199–200
Heppenstall, (John) Rayner, 170, 172–4, 222
Hinton, Charles Howard, 55
Huxley, Aldous (Leonard), 196, 207

Ivanov, Dr (expert in scientific tautology), 21

Jackson, Holbrook, 82–3, 85
Jingles (a very steady horse), 197, 216
'Johnson, Lydia' (a dancer), 100
Joyce, James, 1, 192

Kafian, Adèle, 146, 156, 159
Kant, Immanuel, 55
Karsavina, Tamara, 30, 206
Keats, John, 119, 170–1, 177
Kenney, Rowland, 124, 128–9, 152
'Kingsmill, Hugh' (Hugh Lunn), 69
Kneipp, Pfarrer Sebastian (world authority on Kneippism), 10, 130
Knopf, Alfred A., 125, 190
Koteliansky, Samuel Solomonovich ('Kot'), 130, 136, 139
'Koukanssen', *see* Cook & Son, Thomas
Kschessinka, Mathilde (*prima ballerina assoluta*), 54

255

INDEX

Labori, Mme (a professional widow), 135, 138
Lawrence, D. H. (David Herbert) (1885–1930)
sorts out:
  Frieda, 76
  GURDJIEFF, 3, 200, 203–4, 210
  MANSFIELD, 15, 73, 112, 118, 203–4
  MURRY, 75, 118
  OUSPENSKY, 197
death, 210
use in concrete preparation, 210–11
Lawrence, Mrs Frieda (Emma Maria Frieda Johanna von Richthofen), 73, 75–6, 159, 164–5, 168, 197, 210–11
Lawrence, T. E. (Thomas Edward) ('Lawrence of Arabia'), 195, 208n.
Lea, Frank Alfred, xi, xii
'Lenin' (Vladimir Ilyich Ulianov), 28, 32, 188
Lewis, Sinclair, 198
'LM' (IDA CONSTANCE BAKER) (19 Jan. 1888–4 July 1978)
birth, 35
death, 223
interim roles as:
  astronomer, 223
  bodyguard, 40
  bottle-washer, 13, 46
  cat-minder, *see* Wingley
  cook, 46
  doormat, 36–7, 41–2, 44
  financier, 12, 38, 41–3
  friend, 36, 44–6, 134, 164
  'good conduct girl', 8, 36, 40, 42
  hair-dresser, 42
  mourner, 43, 159
  nurse, 45–6
  pupil, 35
  tea room proprietor, 133–4
  tool setter, 44, 46

Luhan, Mrs Mabel (Evans Dodge Sterne), 196–7, 199–201, 203, 211
Luhan, Tony (Antonio), 201

Mahupuka, Maata ('Martha Grace'), 37
Maintenon, Mme de (Françoise d'Aubigne, Marquise de), 135
Mairet, 'Philip' (Philippe), 93n., 128
Maistre, Violet le, *see* Murry, Mrs Violet
Manoukhin, Dr Ivan, 130–1, 133–4, 137, 139, 141, 155
MANSFIELD, KATHERINE (14 Oct. 1888–9 Jan. 1923)
material:
  birth, 7
  inner search, 15–16, 114–15, 117, 134, 137
  death, 158
mise en scène:
  Wellington NZ (Oct. 1888–Jan. 1903), 7–8
  Queen's College (April 1903–Oct. 1906), 8–9. 35–7
  New Zealand (Dec. 1906–July 1908), 9–10, 37–8
  Beauchamp Lodge (and Carlton Hill) (Sept. 1908–Feb. 1909), 38
  Glasgow (March 1909), 39
  Wörishofen (June–Dec. 1909), 10, 39
  Rottingdean (April–Aug. 1910), 11, 40
  Abingdon Mansions (July 1910), 11, 17n.
  Cheyne Walk (Aug.–Dec. 1910), 11–12, 40
  Clovelly Mansions (Jan. 1911–Aug. 1912), 13, 41
  Runcton (Sept.–Nov. 1912), 70–1
  Baron's Court (July–Dec. 1913), 42
  rue de Tournon (Dec. 1913–Feb. 1914), 42, 72
  Gray (Feb. 1915), 14

INDEX

Quai aux Fleurs (March 1915), 90–1
Villa Pauline (Jan.–April 1916), 75
Tregerthen (April–May 1916), 75–6
Old Church Street (Feb.–Dec. 1917), 44
Hôtel Beau Rivage (Jan.–March 1918), 16, 45
Select Hôtel, Paris (March–April 1918), 17, 46
The Elephant (Aug. 1918–Sept. 1919), 46
Ospedaletti (Oct. 1919–Jan. 1920), 47
Villa Isola Bella (Sept. 1920–April 1921), 113–20
Chalet des Sapins (July 1921–Jan. 1922), 120, 129, 131
Victoria Palace Hotel (Feb.–May 1922), 131, 133
Randogne/Sierre (June–Aug. 1922), 134–5
Warwick Gardens (and Gwendwr Road) (Aug.–Sept. 1922), 137–9
Select Hôtel, Paris (Oct. 1922), 140–1
Prieuré (Oct. 1922–Jan. 1923), 143–158
meetings with
LM (April 1903 aged 14), 8, 35–6
Col. Baker (24 Aug. 1908 aged 19), 38
Trowel, G. (autumn 1908 aged 19), 10
Bowden (winter 1908–1909 aged 20), 10, 38
ORAGE (Feb. 1910 aged 21), 10–11, 87
Hastings (March 1910 aged 21), 11, 87
MURRY (Dec. 1911 aged 23), 12, 41
Harris (June 1912 aged 23), 69
Gaudier (June 1912 aged 23), 70

Carco (Dec. 1913 aged 25), 72; (Feb. 1915 aged 26), 14
Lawrence (March 1914 aged 25), 73; (April 1916 aged 27), 75
Manoukhin (31 Jan. 1922 aged 33), 131
ORAGE (30 Aug. 1922 aged 33), 136
OUSPENSKY (14 Sept. 1922 aged 33), 137–8; (30 Sept. 1922 aged 33), 139
Pinder (?12 Oct. 1922 aged 33), 140
Young (14 Oct. 1922 aged 34), 141
GURDJIEFF (17 Oct. 1922), 144
Olgivanna (19 Oct. 1922), 146
OUSPENSKY (Nov. 1922), 152
Ostrowska (Nov. 1922), 154
MURRY (9 Jan. 1923), 157
Margueritte (an innocent), 65, 67, 167
Mashka (a donkey), 95, 97–8
Mendeleev, Dmitri Ivanovich, 192
Merkouroff (a well connected sculptor), 57
Merston, Ethel, 148, 151
Mevlevi, 64n.
Mitrinovic, Dmitri ('M. M. Cosmoi'), 91–2, 93n., 122–4, 128
Modigliani, Amedeo, 90, 213
Morell, Lady Ottoline (Violet Anne), 16, 196
Morris, William, 81, 84
Mosley, Sir Oswald (Ernald), 170
Muir, Edwin, 123, 128, 132
Mukransky, Prince, *see* GURDJIEFF, GEORGE IVANOVITCH
MURRY, JOHN MIDDLETON (6 Aug. 1889–13 March 1957)
birth, 66
education, 66–7
examination (1912–1923), *see under*

examination – *Continued*
  MANSFIELD, KATHERINE
  weddings:
    (KATHERINE MANSFIELD, 3 May 1918), 46, 77
    (Violet le Maistre, 24 April 1924), 165
    (Betty Cockbayne, 23 May 1931), 169
    (Mary Gamble, 10 March 1954), 178
  editorships:
    Rhythm, 12–13, 67–9, 71–2, 86, 88
    Blue Review, 72, 86
    Athenaeum, 116
    Adelphi, 164–5
  tender scenes (1923–1957):
    Ditchling (and Mrs Dunning), 161–2
    Pond Street (and Brett), 162
    the Old Farm, Twyford (and Mimi), 162–3
    Freiburg (and Frieda), 165
    the Old Coastguard Station (and Violet), 165–7
    the Old Rectory, Larling (and Betty), 169–73, 176
    the Oaks, Langham (Adelphi Centre) (and Helen), 172–4
    Lodge Farm, Thelnetham (and Mary), 176–7
  death, 221–2
  burial, 222–3
Murry, Mrs Kathleen Mansfield, *see* MANSFIELD, KATHERINE (1st wife, 1918–1923)
Murry, Mrs Violet (Violet le Maistre) (2nd wife, 1924–1931), 165–8
Murry, Miss Katherine ('Weg') (daughter by Violet), 166, 221
Murry, John Middleton Jr ('Colin', 'Col') (son by Violet), 166, 170, 173, 175–7
Murry, Mrs Elizabeth Ada (Betty Cockbayne) (3rd wife, 1931–1954), 168–71, 173–8, 221

Murry, Mrs Mary (Mary Gamble) (4th wife, 1954–1957), 176, 221

Narzunoff, Ushe, 25–6, 34n., 221
Nasser Eddin, Mullah, 188
Neill, A. S. (Alexander Sutherland), 132
Nietzsche, Friedrich Wilhelm, 82, 84, 87, 187, 189
Nicholas II, Tsar, 25, 28–30, 32, 54, 61
Nicoll, Dr Henry Maurice Dunlop (Maurice Nicoll), 123–4, 128, 134, 138, 152, 197
Nijeradze, Prince (cf. 'Nizheradze'), 24
Nott, Mrs Rose Mary, xii, 160n.

'Olgivanna' (Mrs Olga Iovonovna Lazovich Milanoff Wright), 101, 146–7, 149–51, 153, 155, 158–9, 160n., 206
Orage, Sarah Ann (mother), 79–80
Orage, William (father), 79
ORAGE, 'ALFRED RICHARD' (JAMES ALFRED) (22 Jan. 1873–5 Nov. 1934)
  birth, 79
  education, 79–80
  editorships:
    New Age, 11–12, 85–7, 123
    New English Weekly, 211–12
  transactions with:
    Bechhofer, 90
    Coote, 79–81
    Douglas, 91–2, 122–3
    GURDJIEFF, 132, 150, 153
    Hastings, 84–5, 87, 89
    Jackson, 82, 85
    MANSFIELD, 10–11, 87–8, 136–7, 150
    Mitrinovic, 91–2, 93n., 122
    Muir, 124
    MURRY, 12, 88, 130, 158, 164
    OUSPENSKY, 56, 89–90, 104, 109
    Shaw, 82, 85–6
    Toomer, 201

INDEX

Walker, Jean, 80–1, 84
Wallace, 84–5, 138
death, 171, 212
burial, 212
Orage, Mrs Jean (Jean Walker) (1st wife), 80–1, 83–4
Orage, Mrs Jessie (Jessie Dwight) (2nd wife), 211
Osokin, Ivan (*Strange Life of Ivan Isokin*), 52, 64n.
Ostrowska, Countess J. (wife of G.), 6n., 28, 94, 127, 142n., 150, 154, 181, 209
OUSPENSKY, PIOTR DEMIANOVICH (5 March 1878–2 Oct. 1947)
material:
  birth, 48–9
  burial, 217
  death, 216
  eternal recurrence, 49–50, 52, 60, 64n.
  family, 49–50, 52–3
  In Search of the Miraculous, 217, 224n.
  Tertium Organum, 55, 59
mise en scène:
  Second Moscow Gymnasium (1889–1893), 49–50
  Wanderjahre (1896–1900), 50
  Moscow (1901–1908), 51–3
  Constantinople (Istanbul)/Cairo (1908), 53–4
  The Errant Dog, St Petersburg (1909–summer 1913), 54–6
  London (transit autumn 1913), 56
  Egypt/Ceylon/India (winter 1913–Aug. 1914), 57
  Petrograd (and Moscow) (Nov. 1914–May 1917), 48, 57–62
  Alexandropol (June 1917), 62
  Essentuki (Uch Dere and Tuapse) (July 1917–May 1919), 62–4, 95, 104
  Ekaterinodar (July–Nov. 1919), 104–5
  Rostov-on-Don (Dec. 1919), 107–9
  Novorossiysk (Jan. 1920), 109
  Constantinople (and Prinkipo) (Feb. 1920–Aug. 1921), 109, 125–6
  Warwick Gardens (and Gwendwr Road), London (Aug. 1921–Oct. 1922), 132, 137–9
  Prieuré (visit Nov.–Dec. 1922), 152
  Mendham, USA (Feb. 1941–Dec. 1946), 214
  Lyne Place (and Colet Gardens) (Jan.–Oct. 1947), 215–16
meetings with:
  Sherbakov (c. 1907 aged 29), 53
  Volinsky (1909 aged 31), 54
  Tolstoi (1909 aged 31), 54
  Butkovsky (spring 1913 aged 34), 56
  ORAGE (autumn 1913 aged 35), 56, 89–90
  GURDJIEFF (April 1915 aged 37), 58
  Pinder (July 1919 aged 41), 104
  Bechhofer (Dec. 1919 aged 41), 106
  GURDJIEFF (July 1920 aged 42), 126
  Lady Rothermere (Aug. 1921 aged 43), 128
  ORAGE *et al.* (Aug. 1921 aged 43), 128
  Eliot (Sept. 1921 aged 43), 196
  MANSFIELD (Sept. 1922 aged 44), 137–9
  Walker (Oct. 1923 aged 45), 129
Ouspensky, Mme Sophie Grigorevna (wife), 61, 103, 152
'Ozay, Prince', 26–7, 221

Philos (a sagacious dog), 148
Picasso (Pablo Ruiz y), 1, 198

INDEX

Pinder, Major Frank S., 101, 109–10, 140–1
Plato, 81–2
Plowman, 'Max' (Mark), 168–9, 172
Pogossky, Mme A. L., 90
Pound, Ezra (Loomis), 1, 86, 92, 93n., 195, 198–9, 207
Priestley, J. B. (John Boynton), 207
Prjevalsky, Nikolai Mikhailovich, 22
Pushkin, Alexander Sergeivich, 182

Rabelais, François, 188
Radiguet, Raymond, 213
Rasputin, Grigory Efimovitch, 28, 30, 54
Raven, Canon (a subscriber to the 39 Articles), 174
Rees, Sir Richard (Lodowick Edward Montagu), 170, 184
Rinsberry, Rebecca (your hair scientifically brushed), 42
Roberts, Carl E. Bechhöfer, see Bechhofer-Roberts, Carl E.
Rothermere, Lady Mary Lilian, Viscountess (née Share), 124, 127–8, 134, 147, 152

Sabaheddin, Prince, 126
Salzmann, Alexandre de, 100, 102, 111n., 132, 142n., 153–4
Salzmann, Mme Jeanne de, 64n., 100–1, 111n., 132, 154, 160n., 219
Saurat, Professor Denis, 180
Savitsky, 'Lonya' (Leonidas), 103, 156
Schlumberger, Mme von (a feminist), 145
Seabrook, William, 205
Shakespeare, William, 182, 221
Shaw, (George) Bernard, 81–2, 85–6, 132
Sheldon, Dr William Herbert, 192
Sherbakov (a mystery), 53, 56–7
Shiemash, Ashiata (*Beelzebub's Tales to his Grandson*), 188–93
Sisson, Aaron (*Aaron's Rod*), 75, 207

Smith, Joseph (£60 of immortality), 84
Socrates, 87
Spahlinger, Dr Henry, 120
'Stalin' (Joseph Vissarionovich Djugashvili alias 'Nizheradze'), 24, 34n.
Stein, Gertrude, 1, 192, 195, 198
Stjoernval, Dr Leonid, 30, 48, 94, 102
'Swift, Stephen' (Charles Hoskin alias 'Godwin' alias 'Charles Granville' alias 'Henry Charos James'), 72

Tchekov, Anton Pavlovich, 11, 119, 139, 166
Thumb, General Tom (not especially large), 7, 14
Tolstoi, Count Alexei Nikolaievich, 54
Tolstoi, Count Leo Nikolaievich, 54, 110, 165, 182
Toomer, Jean, 195, 201–2
'Trotsky' (Lev Davidovich Bronstein), 27–8, 188
Trowell, Arnold ('Caesar'), 9, 37–8
Trowell, Garnett, 10, 38–9

Ukhtomsky, Prince Esper Esperovich (*cf.* Prince Lubovedsky), 25

Vitvitskaia, Mme, 22, 28
'Volinsky, A. L.' (Akim Lvovic Flekser), 54–5

Wallace, Dr Lewis Alexander Richard ('M. B. Oxon.'), 84–7, 123, 130
Walker, Jean, see Orage, Mrs Jean
Walker, Dr Kenneth (Macfarlane), 129, 134, 215
Walter, Charlie (an all-purpose disposable boy), 40
Watson, Dr John B. (Broadus), 192, 204–5
Weekley, Professor Ernest, 73, 78n.

INDEX

Welch, Dr William J., 218–19
Wells, H. G. (Herbert George), 82, 210
Whorf, Benjamin Lee, 189
Wilde, Oscar (Fingal O'Flahertie Wills), 9, 10, 114
Wilson, Colin (Henry), 129, 185, 187
Wingley (an itinerant cat), 119, 129, 131, 133
Woolf, (Adeline) Virginia, 183, 194
Wooster, Bertie, 68
Wright, Frank Lloyd, 205, 207–8

Wright, Mrs Olga (wife), *see* 'Olgivanna'

Yeats, William Butler ('*Frater Demon est Deus Inversus*'), 82, 198

Young, Dr James Carruthers, 93n., 123–4, 138, 141, 143, 146, 152, 154, 158, 166, 169–70, 175, 197, 199, 224n.

Young, Helen (wife) ('Nehale'), 170, 172–3

Zaharoff, Andrei A., 30, 48, 99, 107–9